Taxonomy for the Technology Domain

Lawrence A. Tomei
Robert Morris University, USA

 Information Science Publishing

Hershey • London • Melbourne • Singapore

Acquisition Editor:	Mehdi Khosrow-Pour
Senior Managing Editor:	Jan Travers
Managing Editor:	Amanda Appicello
Development Editor:	Michele Rossi
Copy Editor:	Bernard Kieklak
Typesetter:	Jennifer Wetzel Neidig
Cover Design:	Lisa Tosheff
Printed at:	Yurchak Printing Inc.

Published in the United States of America by
    Information Science Publishing (an imprint of Idea Group Inc.)
    701 E. Chocolate Avenue, Suite 200
    Hershey PA 17033
    Tel: 717-533-8845
    Fax: 717-533-8661
    E-mail: cust@idea-group.com
    Web site: http://www.idea-group.com

and in the United Kingdom by
    Information Science Publishing (an imprint of Idea Group Inc.)
    3 Henrietta Street
    Covent Garden
    London WC2E 8LU
    Tel: 44 20 7240 0856
    Fax: 44 20 7379 3313
    Web site: http://www.eurospan.co.uk

Library of Congress Cataloging-in-Publication Data

Taxonomy for the technology domain / Lawrence A. Tomei, editor.
    p. cm.
  Summary: "This book suggests a new classification system for classroom teaching that includes literacy, collaboration, decision-making, infusion, integration, and technology. As with most taxonomies, each step offers a progressively more sophisticated level of complexity by constructing increasingly multifaceted objectives addressing increasingly complex student learning outcomes. "-- Provided by publisher.
  Includes bibliographical references and index.
  ISBN 1-59140-524-6 (hard) -- ISBN 1-59140-525-4 (softcover) -- ISBN 1-59140-526-2 (ebook)
 1. Educational technology. 2. Teaching. 3. Learning. 4. Classification of sciences. I. Tomei, Lawrence A.
  LB1028.3.T36 2005
  371.33--dc22
                                2004023607

British Cataloguing in Publication Data
A Cataloguing in Publication record for this book is available from the British Library.

All work contributed to this book is new, previously-unpublished material. The views expressed in this book are those of the authors, but not necessarily of the publisher.

Taxonomy for the Technology Domain

Table of Contents

Preface

Introduction

In 1956, a research team of renowned educators would re-define the essence of teaching in the context of three domains. Earlier, educational psychology established itself as a branch of psychology focusing on the development of effective teaching techniques and the assessment of learning outcomes and progress.

How educators perceive their role influences the nature and character of their interaction with technology. In our book, *Professional Portfolios for Teachers: A Guide for Learners, Experts, and Scholars* (Wilcox & Tomei, 1999), we viewed the lifelong career of an educator as divided into roles and responsibilities best depicted as: teacher-as-learner, teacher-as-expert, and teacher-as-scholar. This same classification is helpful to distinguish who should read this book and why.

Target Audience: Who Should Read This Book

Teacher-as-Learner

The relationship between theory and practice in the knowledge base of teaching and in the professional preparation of teachers is a topic of long-standing debate in teacher education. This distinction has never been more controversial than in the preparation of teachers to use technology in the classroom. Often posed as a dichotomy between technology as a content area and technology as a tool for learning, the best in pre-service teacher preparation programs are obligated to provide both technology knowledge and practice.

At the knowledge level, technology includes an understanding of basic operations and concepts, use of technology to enhance their own productivity and professional preparation, and an understanding of the social, ethical, legal, and human issues surrounding the use of technology in schools.

At the practice level, technology involves designing and developing effective learning environments and experiences supported by technology, implementing a technology-based curriculum to maximize student learning, and evaluating technology resources to facilitate a variety of instructional strategies (ISTE, 2003).

The Taxonomy for the Technology Domain offers the Teacher-as-Learner a host of practical examples of how to incorporate technology literacy, collaboration, and decision-making into future lessons while, at the same time, accumulating the necessary skills and competencies to use technology effectively for their own lifelong learning.

Teacher-as-Expert

The Teacher-as-Expert is the teacher in the classroom. While the typical undergraduate pre-service program lasts four years, this particular phase of an educator's career may last four decades. From the first day at the podium to the final class session, technology promises to be a constant companion in this journey towards professional development and personal growth.

Classrooms are most alive when teachers are learning with their students. Nowhere is that more obvious than with technology. Many teachers rely on their students to provide the technical skills necessary to effectively use technology in the classroom. Professional development is most powerful when teachers form learning communities that support and sustain their collective growth, even if that learning support comes from their own charges (Bizar, 2003).

Teachers who are learning in their own classrooms are very often working at the edge of their comfort zones in areas where they have not gone before. These teachers are modeling for students that learning never ends, that even teachers have room to grow, and that students have knowledge that can be shared and valued.

Classrooms and schools that are most successful use "best practice" strategies for teaching and learning, including technology. Teachers who serve not only as dispensers of knowledge (the proverbial "sage on the stage") but also as facilitators alongside their students (the "guide by the side") form true learning communities best supported by the technology-based resources that become part and parcel of their curriculum.

The Taxonomy for the Technology Domain provides the Teacher-as-Expert with the theoretical foundations and practical applications to infuse and integrate technology into the scope and sequence of their everyday instruction.

Teacher-as-Scholar

Quality teaching requires significant knowledge of subject matter and teaching strategies, and the tools to acquire that knowledge. Professional teachers continuously pursue the depth and breadth of pedagogy and content through such activities as professional reading and writing, professional interactions with peers and others, professional study, and active participation in professional organizations to ensure that their teaching is engaging, dynamic, imaginative, contemporary, functional, and of useful substance to students (University of Oklahoma, 2003).

Quality teaching requires the technical skill to investigate sources of and solutions to classroom problems. Professional teachers are expected to possess the research skills to diagnose student learning performance, reinforce what supports and remediate what impedes movement toward successful educational outcomes for their students.

The Taxonomy for the Technology Domain offers the Teacher-as-Scholar the requisite research support at each proposed classification level. Research Implications are made available in the key expository chapters while a more comprehensive investigation of the taxonomy is considered in the final chapter.

The Taxonomy for the Technology Domain is provided here for consideration by all educators according to their focus throughout their educational careers, either as a Teacher-as-Learner, Teacher-as-Expert, or Teacher-as-Scholar.

Foundations and the Taxonomy for the Technology Domain

The foundations of education provide the critical underpinnings for the new Taxonomy for the Technology Domain. The first four chapters are particularly important for the Teacher-as-Learner as well as those who need a refresher in the domains of teaching and the psychologies of learning.

The popular schemata for organizing classroom objectives are presented in Chapter 1 and include an examination of the cognitive, affective, and psychomotor domains. Learning objectives in the cognitive domain encompass the "recall or recognition of knowledge and the development of intellectual abilities and skills." The affective domain takes in individual "changes in interest, attitudes, and values, and the development of appreciations and adequate adjustment." The psychomotor domain embraces physical skills and the performance of actions involved in learning described as "the manipulative or motor-skill area" (Bloom, 1956).

Chapter 2 explores behavioral psychology and how human activities change as a result of extrinsic motivators such as incentives, rewards, and punishments. Behaviorists advocate influencing behavior through the systematic adjustments of stimulus-response reinforcements. Cognitive psychology holds that information is more likely to be acquired, retained, and retrieved for future use if it is learner-constructed, relevant, and built upon prior knowledge. Humanist psychology focuses on individual growth and development and stems from the theory that learning occurs primarily through reflection on personal experience, and as a result of intrinsic motivation.

Taxonomies and their effectiveness as teaching strategies are explored in Chapter 3. Simply put, a taxonomy is a classification system. Benjamin Bloom created what is arguably the most famous classification for educators when he presented the Taxonomy of Educational Objectives. In his landmark exposition, Bloom developed a series of six progressive steps of cognitive development. In that single manuscript, he offers educators a rubric for developing instructional objectives at increasingly advanced levels of higher order thinking. Following in his footsteps, Krathwohl and Kibler completed the then-known domains of education with their affective and psychomotor taxonomies.

As a teaching strategy, the taxonomy uses the behavioral learning objective, constructed to embody the characteristics of an observable task, measurable learning condition, and established standard of performance. A properly constructed learning objective involves a *task* that the student must perform to demonstrate mastery of a particular goal. There must be little doubt as to the *conditions* (i.e., specific activities) under which the learning is to occur. Lastly, learning objectives must stipulate what constitutes successful learning; *standards* are used to authenticate successful learning.

Chapter 4 connects the critical relationships between technology and the foundations of education described in previous chapters. The domains, psychologies, and taxonomies of education provide the essentials upon which the Taxonomy for the Technology Domain is built and uncovered in subsequent chapters. It provides a foothold for further exploration in order to reveal the true impact and effect of this newest classification system for teaching and learning.

Applications and the Taxonomy
for the Technology Domain

With the foundations of education firmly established, the Taxonomy for the Technology Domain is introduced and the text expands upon the six levels of the new classification scheme from the perspectives of the teacher, learner, and administrator and sets forth successful applications of technology for teaching and learning.

Chapter 5 establishes the latest taxonomy for teaching and learning — the Taxonomy for the Technology Domain — and is the "heart" of the book. Each of the six levels that comprise technology is introduced, as well as its impact on education and historical evolution. Literacy, collaboration, decision-making, infusion, integration, and tech-ology incorporate a new set of skills and competencies into a curriculum that better reflect the demands of everyday learning in today's classroom and corporate training environment.

The central chapters in the text (Chapters 6 through 11) are divided into three key elements. Please note the "headline" that precedes these sections both below and throughout the text. The banner graphic provides a visual cue for the theoretical foundations, practical applications, and research implications for the Taxonomy for the Technology Domain.

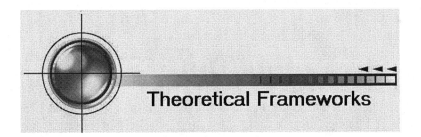

Theoretical Frameworks

Chapters 6 through 11 begin with the theoretical foundations of technology and education by providing a concise definition and historical framework, pertinent standards, and an examination of the domains and psychologies of teaching and learning at each level of the new taxonomy. The Theoretical Foundations of the Taxonomy for the Technology Domain are:

- **Definition and Historical Origins.** The textbook definition establishes each level of the taxonomy followed by a brief perspective of how the level came to fit into the overall classification of technology.

- **Standards.** Successfully integrating technology is realized only by adopting a common set of standards, lesson plans, and learning environments based on knowledge, application, problem solving, and the ethical use of technology. In the chapters that follow, each stage of the new taxonomy is connected with the technology skills and competencies established by international, national, state and professional organizations and local technology programs.

Research has found that standards for technology often embrace universal issues surrounding its access and use to enhance learning across the curriculum, such as: application of technology to enhance teaching, planning, assessing, reporting, and personal professional development; use of appropriate technology to enhance planning, communication, financial management, and the flow of information within an organization; formulating and implementing a strategic plan for technology; and, the effective assimilation of technology change (ISTE, 2003). Achieving each of these goals is essential to technological competency.

- **International and National Levels.** In a unique partnership with teachers and teacher educators, curriculum and education associations, government, businesses, and private foundations, ISTE developed a comprehensive set of educational technology standards as part of a National Educational Technology Standards (NETS) Project. At the international and national levels, ISTE has published standards addressing teachers National Educational Technology Standards for Teachers (NETS*T) and students (NETS*S), and administrators. And, the Collaborative for Technology Standards for School Administrators provided the technology tasks appropriate for administrators (Collaborative for TSSA, 2003).

- **State Level.** At last count, some 45 states have adopted, adapted, or referenced ISTE NETS standards in their in state-wide technology plans, teacher certification, administrative licensure, curriculum and student learning assessment plans, or other official state documents pertaining to the integration of technology for teaching and learning.

- **Professional Organizations.** ISTE provides the implementing standards for teachers and students for this examination. The Collaborative for Technology Standards for School Administrators (TSSA) developed a national consensus of what K-12 administrators should know and be able to do with respect to the effective use of technology. These standards are indicators of effective leadership for technology and schools and are used in the development of the taxonomy.

- **Local Level.** SUCCESS is a comprehensive, integrated, education-focused program for the infusion of technology into the curriculum and teaching strategies of a school (Tomei, 2003). In Year One of the SUCCESS program, participants create their own technology-based instructional lessons and use them in their classrooms under the observation of the school principal. In Year Two, participating schools integrate technology into their K-12 curriculums. Each participating school receives a set of technology skills depicting the competencies desired from students beginning in kindergarten and progressing through secondary school. In Year Three, networking adds the principles and concepts of teaching at a distance to their growing bank of technology-based instructional teaching strategies.

Together, the international, national, state and professional organizations, and local standards form the foundation for the Taxonomy for the Technology Domain. How they are eventually applied for teaching and learning is the purview of domains, psychologies, and lesson design.

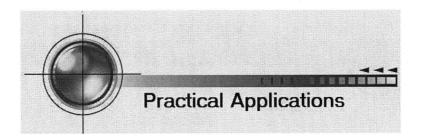

Practical Applications

Practical Applications

Foundations are followed by an historical development of learning objectives from the perspective of three major domains: cognitive, affective, and psychomotor. Next, a host of new action verbs and ample illustrative learning objectives comprising the practical applications of the taxonomy for classroom teachers and instructional technologists.

- **The Domains of Teaching.** As the text continues to unfold into the six levels of the taxonomy, the new classification system fine-tunes itself to take full advantage of the various strengths of each domain. In simplest terms, the cognitive domain concerns itself with mental activities and the process of understanding information. The affective domain concentrates on attitudes, values, and beliefs. And, the psychomotor domain involves aspects of physical skills and motor processes.

- **The Psychologies of Learning.** In a similar manner, behaviorism, cognitivism, and humanism provide insight into how teachers teach and learners learn. Behaviorism relies on objective behavior as evidence of understanding stemming from a response to an observable motivation. Cognitivism prefers to understand learning by examining mental constructs – how knowledge is represented and committed to memory. Humanism emphasizes the self-perception and the meaning attached to personal experiences. Likewise, the Taxonomy for the Technology Domain finds varying degrees of each psychology, so important to the uses of technology for teaching and learning, in its six classification levels.

- **Appropriate Technologies and Action Statements.** To help students, teachers, and administrators develop their host of skills and competencies, each of the six chapters compiles an inventory of appropriate technologies and recommended action statements used in creating technology-based learning objectives. Each chapter presents selected lesson plans demonstrating how these technologies operate at that level with respect to actual classroom learning.

The technologies identified offer an inventory of resources appropriate for addressing teaching and learning at each level of the taxonomy. The recommended action verbs assist in designing and developing learning objectives lessons (or units of instruction with technology integrated into the curriculum) to ensure effective learning.

Research Implications

Research Implications

The results of an initial inquiry into the use of the new taxonomy for preparing technology-based classroom applications is shared to establish quantitative support for the use of the taxonomy in real-world learning environments. A significant number of actual lesson plans were uncovered and their learning objectives categorized according to grade level (i.e., early childhood, elementary, middle school, and secondary) and by core academic content areas (i.e., mathematics, science, social studies, language arts, and other). The results of the research are presented as each level of the taxonomy unfolds.

Investigations into the Taxonomy for the Technology Domain

Since the advent of the mainframe computer in the 1950s, a technological revolution in education has been underway, providing a growing inventory of tools with the potential to facilitate students' thinking, problem solving, and learning strategies (Rowe, n.d.). By 1956, taxonomies developed by Benjamin Bloom and his colleagues had become a major influence in the analysis, design, development, implementation, and evaluation of technology-based lessons. Their classification systems for learning in the cognitive, affective, and psychomotor domains have impacted the way teachers teach and students learn.

In 2001, the case for a new taxonomy for the technology domain was introduced and a new course set for teaching and learning in the 21st century (Tomei, 2001). Research confirms that lessons consciously prepared in the cognitive, affective, and psychomotor domains using a taxonomy for encouraging higher-order thinking produce a higher occurrence of successful student learning outcomes. Taxonomies simply do a more thorough job of matching teaching strategies with student learning (Whitton, 1996).

Chapter 12 expands upon the preliminary data-gathering research (provided as Research Implications under each of the six levels of the Taxonomy for the Technology Domain). This subsequent investigation was to determine *relationships* between the levels of the Taxonomy for the Technology Domain most commonly addressed in technology-based lesson plans and the grade levels and academic content areas they represented. In sum, the investigation sought to establish the viability of the taxonomy as a classification scheme and the legitimacy of technology as its own domain for learning.

The research used an analysis of variance to determine if grade levels or academic content areas exhibit a correlation to the levels of the Taxonomy for the Technology Domain. In other words, the study examined the relationship between the levels of the taxonomy and grade level, looking to find whether objectives created for the lower levels of the taxonomy were predominant at lower grade levels. It also scrutinized whether a correlation exists between certain taxonomy levels and particular academic content areas.

In general, the investigation found evidence of correlation between the taxonomy *within* the grade levels represented by the data. It did not, however, find a link between the levels of the taxonomy *among* grade levels. Most instances of technology-based objectives were found at the lower levels of the taxonomy across grade levels. Even at the secondary level, the predominance of objectives were at the Literacy Level 1.0 of the taxonomy.

The study found a relationship between the taxonomy and *certain* subject areas, although the connections varied considerably in intensity. Specifically, the correlation was strongest in the core academic subject areas of science, math, language arts, and social studies.

Transition

The initial chapters of this text provide the underlying theories and principles that set the stage for the Taxonomy for the Technology Domain. Examinations of the cognitive, affective, and psychomotor domains establish a foundation in the principles of teaching that apply directly to teaching with technology. The review of the traditional psychologies of behaviorism, cognitivism, and humanism laid the necessary groundwork for technology as its own learning style. Together, the domains of teaching and the psychologies of learning form the pillars necessary to couch instructional technology as a teaching strategy and learning style in its own right. It comprises a theory worthy of further investigation.

It is the intent that the Taxonomy for the Technology Domain serve as a desktop reference guide during the analysis, design, development, implementation, and evaluation of new technology-based instructional materials. Too much teaching of technology has already occurred at the lower ends of the taxonomy. While several reasons can be offered, the most serious is probably the lack of teacher understanding of technology as both a content area in and of itself as well as a tool for learning. The Taxonomy for the Technology Domain addresses these shortcomings by exploring how technology should be applied considering both grade level and content area. Teachers would do well to consider the taxonomy whenever creating new learning objectives that incorporate technology in order to take better advantage of their own teaching strategy as well as the various learning styles of diverse student populations.

It is hoped that the Taxonomy for the Technology Domain will advance the disciplines for teaching and learning and provide further foundation upon which to evolve the technology domain.

References

Bizar, M. (2003). *Teacher-as-learner.* National-Louis University, North Central Regional Educational Laboratory. Retrieved from the World Wide Web: *http://www.ncrel.org/mands/docs/9-1.htm*

Bloom, B.S., Englehart, M.B., Furst, E.J., Hill, W.H., & Krathwohl, D.L. (1956). *Taxonomy of educational objectives. The classifications of educational goals. Handbook I.*

Collaborative for Technology Standards for School Administrators. (2003). *Technology standards for school administrators, TSSA Draft* (version 4.0). Retrieved from the World Wide Web: *cnets.iste.org/tssa/view_standards.html*

International Society for Technology in Education (ISTE). (2003). *Educational technology standards and performance indicators for all teachers.* National Educational Technology Standards for Teachers. Retrieved from the World Wide Web: *cnets.iste.org/teachers/t_stands.html*

International Society for Technology in Education (ISTE). (2003). *Technology foundation standards for all students.* National Educational Technology Standards for Students. Retrieved from the World Wide Web: *cnets.iste.org/students/s_stands.html*

Roblyer, M.D. (1981). Instructional design verses authoring of courseware: Some crucial differences. *AEDS Journal.*

Rowe, H. (n.d.). *Personal computing: A source of powerful cognitive tools.* Retrieved from the World Wide Web: *www.educationau.eduau/archives/CP/REFS/rowe_cogtools.htm*

Tomei, L.A. (2001). *Teaching digitally: A guide for integrating technology into the classroom.* Norwood, MA: Christopher-Gordon Publishers.

Tomei, M. (2003). *The SUCCESS program.* Unpublished Manuscript. Duquesne University.

University of Oklahoma, College of Education. (2003). *Teacher education: Professionalism, leadership, understanding, and scholarship.* Conceptual Framework. Retrieved from the World Wide Web: *http://www.ou.edu/education/concept.htm*

Whitton, D. (1996). *Beyond Bloom.* Retrieved from the World Wide Web: *www.nexus.edu.au/teachstud/gat/whitton.htm*

Wilcox, B., & Tomei, L.A. (1999). *Professional portfolios for teachers: A guide for learners, experts, and scholars.* Norwood, MA: Christopher-Gordon Publishers.

Chapter 1

Domains of Teaching

Introduction

This chapter establishes the domains of teaching as one of two "pillars of instructional technology" and offers the necessary grounding in the history and evolution of cognitive, affective, and psychomotor teaching.

The cognitive domain encompasses intellectual objectives that deal with "the recall or recognition of knowledge and the development of intellectual abilities and skills." The affective domain takes in individual "changes in interest, attitudes, and values, and the development of appreciations and adequate adjustment." Finally, the psychomotor domain embraces physical skills and the performance of actions involved in learning described as "the manipulative or motor-skill area" (Bloom, 1956).

Cognitive Domain

Definition

Cognition refers to mental activities, an approach to teaching that focuses on the very process of delivering information and imparting new concepts. To understand the connections between concepts, information is parsed and rebuilt with logical connections. As a result, the retention and recall of that material increases.

Concepts

Cognition involves the mental processes of knowing, perception, reasoning, attention, learning, memory, thought, concept formation, language, problem solving, judgment, and the development of behavior in children. Research has opted to understand cognition from, among others, the perspective of teaching. For example, one aspect of the cognitive domain is remembering previously learned material. The skill involves recall of a wide range of instructional material, from specific facts to complete theories. But any recall of information requires the same basic brain functions shared by all learners. Another perspective of cognition is the ability to grasp meaning of instruction evidenced by translating new information from one form to another, by interpreting material, or by estimating future trends or effects.

The ability to teach in new and concrete situations includes the application of rules, methods, concepts, principles, laws, and theories while a further aspect of cognition concerns the ability to break down material into its component parts so that it mat be better identified, analyzed, and understood. Further refinement of this technique requires the teacher to assemble the component parts to form a new whole. Defining cognition culminates in ability to value instruction based on definite criteria and a network of internal and external standards of success.

At its pinnacle, meta-cognition has been recognized as an essential skill for teaching to learn. Cognitive strategies are employed to help an individual achieve a particular goal (e.g., understanding a text) while meta-cognitive strategies ensure that a particular goal has been reached. Knowledge is considered to be meta-cognitive if it is actively used to achieve an overarching instructional goal. Knowing how one learns is a critical strength in the cognitive domain.

Theorists and Their Theories

Robert Gagne is recognized for turning the art of instruction into a science and heralding the advent of cognitive teaching. His unique contributions were developed during World War II when he was asked to formalize the process for instructing farmers and housewives in the art of airplane manufacturing. Given America's delay in entering the war, Gagne was pressed into teaching these skills in 30 days instead of the normal two-year apprenticeship program. Gagne's instructional design models recognized schemata, scaffolding, and knowledge construction as the key building blocks that would ultimately define the cognitive domain. A recognized leader in the field, Gagne's efforts as an instructional researcher and learning theorist influenced instructional design for the next 30 years (Gagne, 1987).

On the heals of Gagne's discovery, Benjamin Bloom led a group of educational psychologists in a collaborative effort to develop a classification system that would reflect the then-known accepted levels encompassing the process of learning. By 1956, his system of classification was known as "Bloom's Taxonomy of Cognitive Outcomes." Although Bloom was one of the first instructional theorists to distinguish the cognitive, psychomotor, and affective domains of human learning, his taxonomy of the cognitive domain is widely acknowledged as the most prominent of three domains used by teachers and trainers in many of today's classrooms (Driscoll, 1991).

Howard Gardner and his theory of multiple intelligences suggest that there are distinct manifestations of intelligence possessed by diverse individuals in varying degrees. According to Gardner, the existence of multiple intelligences calls for teaching that takes advantage of the particular intelligences of each person. Individuals with strong interpersonal or verbal/linguistic intelligences should be encouraged to pursue these strengths both in the classroom and in the real world. Gardner asserts that multiple intelligences represent not only different content domains but also different learning modalities. Individuals may possess a higher degree of intelligence in one subject matter area while demonstrating a distinctly different strength in another. Gardner contends that all humans have some degree of each intelligence. Others are more gifted in a particular area or combination of areas.

Applications for Teaching

Teaching strategies must allow for and accommodate individual differences or, better phrased, individual strengths. Applications for teaching further this discussion of effective teaching strategies.

According to Robert Gagne, there are nine events that trigger the sequence of events he believes are appropriate for all lessons. They include: gaining the attention of the learner; informing the learner of the target objectives; stimulating recall of prior knowledge; presenting the instructional content; guiding the teaching; eliciting repeated performance (practice); providing critical feedback; assessing performance; and, enhancing retention and transfer. Determining whether or not the skills learned are ever applied to future situations is often impossible for teachers. As a substitute, the repetition of learned concepts is a tried and true means of reinforcing retention. Technology will come to play a key role in encouraging both retention and transfer.

The *Taxonomy of Cognitive Outcomes* is the banner for teacher preparation across K-12, post-secondary, military and corporate training (Anderson, & Krathwohl, 2001; Phillips, 1997). Although not a pedagogical tool from its earliest inception, Bloom went on to differentiate six levels of cognitive development. Knowledge, comprehension, application, analysis, synthesis, and evaluation are hierarchical in their design, sequential in their application, and pedagogical in their impact on technology.

The theory of multiple intelligences has many implications for teachers in terms of classroom instruction. The theory offers seven intelligences needed to productively function in society. Teachers must consider these intelligences as equally important when designing and delivering instruction, recognizing a broad range of talents and skills. In contrast to traditional education systems, the cognitive domain, according to Gardner, places equally strong emphasis on the development of kinesthetic, musical, and interpersonal skills as is placed on the more traditional concentration on verbal and mathematical intelligences. Specifically, the seven multiple intelligences include: logical-mathematical intelligence; linguistic intelligence; spatial intelligence; musical intelligence; body-kinesthetic intelligence; interpersonal and intra-personal intelligences; and naturalist intelligence. As we shall see, technology offers the best hope for incorporating as much intelligence as possible into a potential unit of instruction.

Affective Domain

Definition

The word "affect" comprises a variety of constructs; specifically, educators describe attitudes, beliefs, tastes, appreciations, and preferences. Krathwohl, Bloom, and Masia outline the best-known use of the term in this even broader sense in the handbook: *Taxonomy of Educational Objectives: The Affective Domain* (1964). They consider "affective" to be a generic term describing such phenomena as emotions, attitudes, beliefs, moods, and conation.

Concepts

As Piaget noted, "at no level, at no state, even in the adult, can we find a behavior that is purely cognitive without affect nor a purely affective state without a cognitive element involved" (Rosenburg and Carl, 1960). In its simplest terms, the affective domain is quite simple: thinking is cognitive, feelings and emotions are affective. Most attempts to define the affective domain introduce related elements such as environmental cause and effect, social behavior and personal achievement, and simple to complex explanations of behavior. Most research accepts certain characteristics of the affective domain in an attempt to describe its impact on teaching. An emotion is just such a characteristic, ranging from positive to negative. Grief, joy, fear, and anger are all emotions. Feelings refer to sensations that are part of the affective experience. Sweaty palms, constricted breathing, dry mouth, and other symptoms describe the body's reaction to an affective, emotional experience. Attitudes are defined as "mental or neural states of readiness, organized through experience, exerting a directive or dynamic influence upon the individual's response to objects and situations with which it is related" (Allport, 1935). Attitudes are psychological conditions acquired as a result of experiences and impact the way we teach and learn.

The final concept associated with the affective domain is beliefs and belief systems. Beliefs are defined as inferences made by an observer about underlying states of expectancy and a belief system as having represented within it some organized psychological but not necessarily logical form, each and every one of a person's countless beliefs about physical and social reality (Rokeach, 1986).

Theorists and Their Theories

Krathwohl, Bloom, and Masia (1964) are arguably the most renowned contributors to an understanding of the affective domain and how an understanding of personal interests, attitudes, and values allow individuals to adjust successfully to an ever-changing environment. Krathwohl (1964) further explored affective classroom behaviors along a continuum from individual awareness of a phenomenon to a pervasive outlook on life that influences one's actions. In a cooperative exploration, these theorists provided the most commonly accepted classification of the affective domain: receiving, responding, valuing, organization, and characterization.

In *Assessing Affective Characteristics in the Schools*, Anderson (2000) proposed that the affective dimension of students could be categorized by the characteristics of values, academic self-esteem, anxiety, interests, locus of control, attitude, and preferences. He suggested that these affective characteristics must include essential features of feelings and emotions, be typical of the thoughts or behaviors of the person, involve an intensity or strength of feelings, integrate positive or negative direction or orientation of feelings, and recognize a target towards which the feeling is directed.

Walberg (1984) suggested that certain factors accounted for the bulk of school learning and that many of those factors were part of the affective domain. The factors were grouped into student aptitude, classroom instruction, and the environment. According to Walberg, native intelligence explained a full half of the differences in individual learning. Personal motivation accounted for another ten percent, and self-concept accounted for only three percent. Reinforcement, cues and feedback, and cooperative learning were revealed as the three top instructional effects concerning affective domain.

Martin (1989) stated, "The affective domain is a complex and often nebulous area in which to design instruction. In addition, there is a great deal of confusion about which constructs should be included in the domain and which should be omitted." Martin argued that issues of teaching style and instructional design should be resolved before developing classroom curricula.

In current literature, defining the affective domain has taken a back seat to cognitive research. What little research has been directed toward the affective domain has done so primarily by comparing an individual's emotions and feelings with the more accepted cognitive thinking skills. While this may have been an acceptable starting point for yesterday's classroom environment, it represents a much too narrow view of the importance of this domain and its components of feelings and emotions when determining successful student learning outcomes. Together, emotions, feelings, attitudes, and beliefs comprise the dimensions of the affective domain and play an immeasurable role in the successful application of technology.

Applications for Teaching

Krathwohl's affective domain taxonomy is the best known of the affective applications for teaching. His contributions are based on the degree of internalization; that is, the degree to which an attitude, emotion, value, or interest is incorporated into the learner's personality. *Receiving* refers to the learner's willingness to attend to a particular classroom activity. Teaching is concerned with getting, holding, and directing student attention and learning involves outcomes of simple awareness, representing the lowest level of the affective domain. *Responding* refers to a higher level of participation on the part of the learner. Receiving is accompanied by a particular reaction. *Valuing* is concerned with the worth or value attached by the learner to a particular object, phenomenon, or behavior and implies a degree of acceptance and commitment. Learning outcomes are sufficiently consistent and stable to make the value clearly identifiable. *Organization* brings together different values, resolving conflicts, and building internally consistent value systems. The emphasis is on comparing, relating, and synthesizing learning outcomes and requires significant interpersonal interaction. At the highest level of the affective domain, characterization by a value or value complex, the learner's value system controls behavior for a sufficiently long time to develop a lifestyle. Learning at this level covers a broad range of activities, social as well as individual.

Relational teaching is a group of ideas, techniques, and practices that promotes active listening and coaching with the presentation of content material in the classroom. This interweaving promotes character growth, builds community in the classroom and gets results with all learners, including "difficult," "at-risk" and divergent learners. In addition, it diffuses potential school violence by replacing the isolation and alienation often felt by these learners with inclusion and engagement. The principles of relational teaching include establishing safety through strong boundaries and consequences, giving unconditional positive regard, teaching with loving warmth, modeling authenticity and listening skills, personalizing the classroom and curriculum whenever possible, connecting pleasure with learning, and assisting the learner student to identify and take action toward individual goals (Bosniak, 1998).

Psychomotor Domain

Definition

The psychomotor domain is concerned with the development of physical skills ranging from simple physical competencies to those that demand complicated muscle coordination. Musical and athletic performance, writing in cursive, and oral reading are typical classroom examples of psychomotor skills. In the early stages of psychomotor development, the learner mirrors the teacher, repeating demonstrated physical activity and utilizing trial and error until an appropriate response is achieved. The learner continues to practice a particular skill or sequence until it can be performed with proficiency but may still lack complete confidence in the task. Confidence is indicated by a quick, smooth, accurate performance, requiring a minimum of energy so that the response is performed without hesitation. At even more advanced levels of development, the skills are so well ingrained that the individual modifies movement patterns to fit special requirements or to meet an unfamiliar problem situation. Until finally, the psychomotor response is totally automatic and the learner begins to experiment, creating new motor-based ways to manipulate materials, abilities, and skills.

Concepts

In education, the psychomotor domain includes behaviors that span a continuum from fine motor skills, such as the mastery of musical instruments or precision tools, to actions which evidence gross motor skills, such as dance or athletic accomplishment. For the educator, psychomotor skills are defined as the ability to perform kinesthetic classroom activities requiring development of the senses, precision, and timing. Teachers develop the main qualities of psychomotor skills ystematic practice, breadth of experience, attention to quality of performance, and repetition of complex tasks. Educators tend to slight the psychomotor domain when designing and developing course materials, preferring to concentrate instead on the more "exciting" cognitive and affective domains. It will become apparent throughout this text how technology is brought to bear to overcome psychomotor shortfalls.

Theorists and Their Theories

Several theorists surface as prominent proponents of teaching and learning in the psychomotor domain. Benjamin Bloom's research group did not develop in-depth categories of this domain, claiming lack of experience in teaching these skills. However, Simpson, Harrow, and Dave developed their own presumptions about psychomotor development.

The psychomotor domain measures skill performance involving the manipulation of objects, tools, supplies, or equipment. Appropriate criteria for outcomes in the psychomotor domain involve accuracy within a certain tolerance limit, speed, degree of excellence, or reference to other material outlining the criteria for judgment. A research team, led by Bloom himself to study the domains separately, was not able to uncover psychomotor objectives in the literature and, as a result, they did not write a third handbook specifically addressing the psychomotor domain.

Elizabeth Simpson, as well, explored the psychomotor domain, specifically, the sequencing of motor skills. Lower-level objectives are inherently less complex than objectives at the higher levels and, in general, are easier to exhibit. Teaching psychomotor skills build on competencies arranged hierarchically from simple to complex.

Anita Harrow created yet another taxonomy for the psychomotor domain, organized according to the degree of coordination from involuntary responses to learned capabilities. Simple reflexes represent the lowest level of the taxonomy while complex neuromuscular coordination make up the highest levels. Reflex movements encompass actions elicited in response to some stimuli. No learning is associated at this level. Basic fundamental movements are inherent patterns that form by combining basic reflex movements with complex skilled movements. The perceptual stage of the taxonomy refers to reactions to stimuli that produce adjustments to the environment such as visual, auditory, kinesthetic, or tactile discrimination. The fourth stage targets physical activities that require endurance, strength, vigor, and agility. The fifth stage involves more skilled movements that result in efficiency when performing a complex task. The highest stage of Harrow's classification of psychomotor skills is non-discursive communication via bodily movements ranging from facial expressions through sophisticated body postures, gestures, and facial expressions such as complex dance movements. While Harrow focused on the physical aspects of coordination for her classification, R. H. Dave based his taxonomy on demonstrated skill performance.

R. H. Dave (1967) introduced the levels of imitation, manipulation, precision, articulation, and naturalization. At the lowest level, imitation is evidenced by the ability to perform a demonstrated skill or skill set, in other words, the ability to copy what is modeled by the teacher. Manipulation is the ability to perform according to instruction rather than observation and to follow oral or written directions. Precision is the ability to perform the desired skills with accuracy and completeness without need of a model or set of directions. Articulation is demonstrated as an ability to perform the same skill within a reasonable time frame while naturalization is the ability to perform that skill automatically and efficiently as an internalized practice. All classification schemes, it seems, are intrinsically both hierarchical and sequential.

Applications for Teaching

For Simpson, teaching psychomotor skills involves mastery of physical abilities, including: coordination, dexterity, manipulation, grace, strength, speed; actions which demonstrate the fine motor skills such as use of precision instruments or tools; or, actions which evidence gross motor skills such as the use of the body in dance or athletic performance. Psychomotor learning is characterized by perception, the ability to use sensory cues to guide physical activity and provides the learner with the necessary skills to distinguish, identify, and select. Learning also encompasses a set: a readiness to act that requires the learner to demonstrate an awareness or knowledge of the behaviors needed to carry out the skill. Guided response includes imitation and demands of the learner a hands-on involvement in the skills demonstrated by the teacher. Mechanism is the ability to perform more complex motor skills and occurs at the intermediate stage of learning. Complex overt response, adaptation, and origination complete Simpson's domain as the learner matures his or her psychomotor abilities to perform ever more complex psychomotor skills to fit existing conditions, new circumstances, and original situations (Simpson, 1972).

Harrow's view of the domain varies from Simpson in its emphasis on psycho-motor movement. Reflex movements at the lowest level give way to basic loco-motor movements and manipulative movements, followed by a focus on perceptual and physical abilities, and finally, skilled and expressive/interpretive movement (Harrow, 1972).

Finally, Dave's insight into the psychomotor domain involves skills and skill sets. His theory takes the learner from merely observing a skill and attempting to repeat it, to independently performing and modifying the skill, to internalizing or making the skill automatic (Dave, 1967).

Technology Domain

Definition

The newest domain for teaching addresses technology first and foremost as its own viable content area. Computers were first introduced into the curriculum as content to be learned similar to science, mathematics, and literature. Therefore, the initial applications of technology as a teaching strategy centered on computer literacy skills to be mastered.

As computer hardware and software matured, so did technology's ability to augment the teaching process. Since computers were first introduced into the classrooms of the 1980s, teachers have sought to integrate the newest technologies on a regular basis. Classroom technologies began with radio, television, and film prior to the advent of computers. Since then, teaching with technology has included everything from computer-assisted instruction to multimedia technology, from programming languages to digital video, from grade book software to videoconferencing.

As teachers matured in their uses of technology for instruction, students themselves have evolved as users of technology for learning. Many would say that, indeed, students have been the impetus for this evolution. Teaching tools have advanced from word processing and spreadsheets to electronic commu-nications, advanced graphics representation, and online virtual Internet tours. Each innovation merits its own discussion of impact and importance in teaching with technology.

Concepts

Instructional technology embraces a host of issues including pedagogical theory, hardware or software, methods and uses, and evaluation of effectiveness. In many cases, these debates leave unexamined some fundamental assumptions about what constitutes instructional technology or how we think about such innovative applications. Experts often avoid addressing these disagreements directly, so it is no surprise that published research in the field appears disjointed and inconclusive.

Theorists and Their Theories

In his *Critical Theory of Technology*, Feenberg (1991) suggests that people usually adopt one of two theories of technology. The instrumental theory focuses on the uses of technology rather than on the technology itself. Technology is not inherently bad or good, rather, the failed or successful use of technology determines its effectiveness. The substantive theory places the emphasis on technology design. Unsuccessful applications of technology would fault the designer (i.e., the teacher) rather than the learner. After considerable research, Feenberg goes on to define a third approach, a critical theory of technology, combining elements of both previous approaches. Feenberg agrees with the substantive theory that technologies inevitably change practices. At the same time, he agrees with the instrumental theory by noting that it is the teacher who decides the practices to be adopted during the all-important design phase.

Applications for Teaching

Many states have adopted technology content standards describing desirable student knowledge, skills, and abilities. Most provide a profile of student achievement at several performance levels, for example, advanced, proficient, intermediate, and novice. The Montana Standards for Technology (2002), for example, offer several competencies (and accompanying rationale) for consideration as shown in Table 1.

Specifically, technology content includes, as a minimum, an understanding of the basic operations of instructional technologies such as desktop computers,

Table 1. Montana Standards for Technology Content (2002)

Standard	Rationale	Example Content
Understanding the basic operations of technologies.	Students need to construct a base of technical skills in order to be competent and confident users of technology. These basics will assure safe and efficient operation as students apply technology.	Computer science Computer hardware • Mainframes • Minicomputers • Microcomputers
Technologies to enhance logical reasoning.	Students must strengthen their reasoning skills using the elements of logic provided by computer programming languages.	Computer software • Programming languages
Technologies for communication.	Today and tomorrow's citizens need to communicate effectively using appropriate technologies. Citizens need to use appropriate communication technologies to collaborate and to exchange ideas and information.	Communications • Networks • Protocols
Responsible use of technology and understanding its impact on individuals and society.	Students need to understand that today's technology is an extremely powerful tool impacting all aspects of human life. In using this technology students should demonstrate both sound judgment and respect.	Technology-impacted: • Standards • Policies • Laws
Skills, knowledge and abilities to apply a variety of technologies to conduct research, manage information and solve problems.	Current and emerging technology tools will provide increased and alternative methods for problem solving and thinking. Students must be able to assess the credibility of information sources, use sophisticated search technologies to support research, problem solving and decision-making.	Information science • Library science • Management information systems • Decision-making systems

computer programming and office productivity software, networking, and the responsible use of technology and its impact on individuals and society. In today's classroom, a major issue with technology as both a content area and tool for learning is the fact that the substance of the technology curriculum changes so rapidly.

Ever since its recognition as an academically rich content area, the evolution of technology has undergone several iterations. The bar is raised every year as more and more students enter the classroom having grown up with technology in the home.

A high-quality curriculum views technology as a valued content area to be learned and mastered alongside science, mathematics, and literature. Effective teachers understand technological systems and how they work together. They develop an appreciation of concepts and attitudes while using technology-based tools, equipment, materials and processes, safely and effectively in and around the classroom. Good teachers explore creative talents in their students through integrated technology-based experiences. They employ a systematic approach toward the resolution of simple and complex tasks utilizing creative problem-solving techniques derived from information system theory and practice and realize the benefits of technology education as it relates to the application of knowledge, skills, and innovations.

Teachers teach better when they employ an instructional strategy that is most closely linked to their own particular teaching style — and that includes the integration of *Technology as Teaching Tool*. Most teachers balance the use of technology to plan, design, and implement learning environments with the need to use technology to enhance their own classroom productivity and promote professional development.

Additionally, research has found that students learn better when an instructional strategy (whether that strategy is technology-based or not) is linked to their own particular learning style (Woodward, Markman, & Fitzsimmons, 1994). For example, concrete learners often find success in a text-based environment while abstract learners thrive in a more visual-based environment with tools such as projected visuals, graphics applications, and multimedia. Technology ultimately impacts both perspectives.

Computer-assisted instruction (CAI) has been used successfully for teaching elementary students and adult learners, particularly with respect to remedial and enrichment instruction. For example, drill and practice instruction is very effective as a patient tutor for slower learners, where more concentrated coverage of material is needed to ensure individual mastery. Tutorial and problem-solving instruction is a practical means of ensuring class-wide competency in prerequisites such as computer literacy skills. Likewise, discovery and simulation software is a potent venue for motivating learners to master basic lesson objectives.

Assessment and its impact on education have taken on added importance in recent years. Technology for teaching has kept pace by introducing innovative tools for teaching that include test building software, electronic portfolios for authentic evaluation, and grade book software to address the practical aspects of grade keeping. To be sure, the quantity of video, audio, and multimedia resources for teaching the ethical, legal, and human issues surrounding technology and its proliferation in our society have also increased. Table 2 offers a recap of the major categories of technologies used for teaching.

Table 2. Technology Standards for Teaching with Technology

Technology Standard	General Teacher Skills	Specific Level of Teacher Competency	Example Technologies
Technology operations and concepts	Teachers possess a sound knowledge and understanding of technology operations and concepts.	• Demonstrate introductory knowledge, skills, and understanding of concepts related to technology • Demonstrate continual growth in technology knowledge and skills to stay abreast of current and emerging technologies.	Multimedia computer operation Troubleshooting
Planning and designing learning environments and experiences	Teachers plan and design effective learning environments and experiences supported by technology.	• Design developmentally appropriate learning opportunities that apply technology-enhanced instructional strategies to support the diverse needs of learners. • Apply current research on teaching and learning with technology when planning learning environments and experiences. • Identify and locate technology resources and evaluate them for accuracy and suitability. • Plan for the management of technology resources within the context of learning activities. • Plan strategies to manage student learning in a technology-enhanced environment.	Graphics design Presentation software Authoring software Web page editors
Teaching and the curriculum	Teachers implement curricula that include methods and strategies for applying technology to maximize student learning.	• Facilitate technology-enhanced experiences that address content standards and student technology standards. • Use technology to support learner-centered strategies that address the diverse needs of students. • Apply technology to develop students' higher order skills and creativity. • Manage student-learning activities in a technology-enhanced environment.	Computer-assisted and Computer-managed instruction: • Drill and practice • Tutorial • Gaming • Simulation • Discovery • Problem-solving

Table 2. Technology Standards for Teaching with Technology (continued)

Technology Standard	General Teacher Skills	Specific Level of Teacher Competency	Example Technologies
Assessment and evaluation	Teachers apply technology to facilitate a variety of effective assessment and evaluation strategies.	• Apply technology in assessing student learning of subject matter using a variety of assessment techniques. • Use technology resources to collect and analyze data, interpret results, and communicate findings to improve instructional practice and maximize student learning. • Apply multiple methods of evaluation to determine students' appropriate use of technology resources for learning, communication, and productivity.	Test building software Electronic portfolios Gradebook software Self-testing instruments
Productivity and professional practice	Teachers use technology to enhance their productivity and professional practice.	• Use technology resources to engage in ongoing professional development and lifelong learning. • Continually evaluate and reflect on professional practice to make informed decisions regarding the use of technology in support of student learning. • Apply technology to increase productivity. • Use technology to communicate and collaborate with peers, parents, and the larger community in order to nurture student learning.	Online professional development courses Computer-based self-study programs
Social, ethical, legal, and human issues	Teachers understand the social, ethical, legal, and human issues surrounding the use of technology in schools and apply those principles in practice.	• Model and teach legal and ethical practice related to technology use. • Apply technology resources to enable and empower learners with diverse backgrounds, characteristics, and abilities. • Identify and use technology resources that affirm diversity • Promote safe and healthy use of technology resources. • Facilitate equitable access to technology resources for all students.	Video • Films and slides • DVD and digital video clips Audio • Tape recordings • Digital sound bytes Conferencing • Interactive video • Teleconferencing • Computer conferencing

Technology as a teaching tool demands consideration in each of the following areas of student development: (1) working individually and collectively to maintain a common goal; (2) developing self-esteem and an appreciation for quality work through personal accomplishments; (3) developing leadership abilities while understanding the importance of others in the social arena; (4) gaining an understanding on how technology impacts the environment, societal technological, and biological systems; (5) improving technological literacy as a wiser consumer through integrated activity-based technology educational experiences; (6) making informed occupational and vocational decisions pertaining to a lifelong career; and, (7) integrating general education with the content areas of technology education. All teachers are expected to meet these minimum competencies for teaching with technology.

Aside from understanding technology as a content area, acquisition of certain technology-based skills and competencies is becoming an essential characteristic of teaching in the 21st century. As a tool for teaching, Tomei (2001) offers three popular tools.

Text-based materials provide hard copy resources that make very effective teaching and assessment tools for the classroom. Student handouts, remedial content material, and personalized enrichment activities are created using common word processing software. More complex study guides, worksheets, and workbooks are built with desktop publishing tools. For many teachers, the bottom line (i.e., successful learning outcomes) is simple: no matter how much "high-tech" resources are available, sometimes text-based material is still the best way for a student to learn a lesson objective.

Visual-based materials support both abstract and concrete learning with a variety of technology tools. Multimedia and hypermedia join an array of visual hardware and software that began with the graphics-based Apple II personal computer in 1978. There are arguably more visual-based resources for the classroom than any other medium.

However, the Internet and *Web-based materials* are quickly overtaking visual media as the most prolific teaching environment for the classroom. Web-based materials such as virtual tours, lesson home pages, search engines, and portals provide the latest in state-of-the-art opportunities for teaching. Table 3 presents some of the most popular implementing technologies available for primary (teacher-initiated) and secondary (student-initiated) classroom applications.

Table 3. Technology Competencies to Support Student Learning

Technology Competencies	Target Technologies	Implementing Technology (P)rimary/(S)econdary Media
• Understand the ethical, cultural, and societal issues related to technology.	Electronic forums: • E-mail • Online chat rooms • Threaded discussions	Text-based materials
• Demonstrate responsible use of technology systems, information, and software.	Graphics	Visual-based materials
• Use technology tools to construct and share new concrete information.	Database Spreadsheet	(P) Text-based materials (S) Visual-based materials
• Use technology tools to construct and share new abstract knowledge and produce creative works.	Graphics	Visual-based materials
• Use technology tools to enhance learning, increase productivity, and promote personal creativity.	Word processing Desktop publishing	Text-based materials
• Use telecommunications to interact with peers, experts, and other audiences.	Electronic mail Online chat rooms Listservs File transfer and Telnet Internet	Web-based materials
• Evaluate and select new information resources based on expected learning outcomes.	Virtual tours Interactive lessons Hypertext	(P)Web-based materials (P)Visual-based materials (P)Text-based materials
• Use technology to locate, evaluate, and collect information from a variety of sources.	Internet Electronic Media • E-zines • CDROM journals • Microfiche	(P)Web-based materials (P)Visual-based materials (S)Text-based materials
• Use technology resources for solving problems, making informed decisions, and sharing the learning with peers.	Spreadsheet Database Graphics	(P)Text-based materials (S)Visual-based materials

Conclusion

Compared with the cognitive, affective, and psychomotor domains of learning, the technology domain is just as important and just as deserving of our attention in support of successful teaching. The next chapter changes focus 180 degrees to examine the compact of technology on the traditional psychologies of learning.

References

Allport, G.W. (1935). Attitudes. In C.A. Murchison (Ed.), *A handbook of social psychology* (Volume 2) (2 volumes). New York: Russell.

Anderson, L.W. (2000). *Assessing affective characteristics in the schools*. Lawrence Erlbaum.

Anderson, L.W., & Krathwohl, D.R. (eds.). (2001). *A taxonomy for learning, teaching, and assessing: A revision of Bloom's Taxonomy of educational objectives*. New York: Longman.

Bosniak, M. (1998, April). Relational teaching for teachers 2000. *The Education Digest, 83*(8).

Dave, R. (1967). *Psychomotor domain*. Berlin: International Conference of Educational Testing.

Driscoll, M.P. (1991). *Psychology of learning for instruction*. Boston: Allyn & Bacon.

Feenberg, A. (1991). *Critical theory of technology*. Oxford Publishing.

Gagne, R. (1987). *Instructional technology foundations*. Hillsdale, NJ: Lawrence Erlbaum.

Harrow, A. (1972). *A taxonomy of the psychomotor domain: A guide for developing behavioral objectives*. New York: McKay.

Krathwohl, D.R., Bloom, B.S., & Masia, B.B. (1964). *Taxonomy of educational objectives. Handbook II: Affective domain*. New York: David McKay.

Martin, B.L. (1989, August). *A checklist for designing instruction in the affective domain*. Educational Technology.

Montana Standards for Technology. (n.d.). Retrieved January 4, 2002 from the World Wide Web: *http://www.opi.state.mt.us/ pdf/standards/ ContStds-Tech.pdf*

Phillips, J.J. (1997). *Return on investment in training and performance improvement programs*. Houston: Gulf Publishing.

Rokeach, M. (1986). *Beliefs, attitudes, and values: A theory of organization and change*. San Francisco: Jossey-Bass.

Rosenberg, M.I., & Carl, I. H. (1960). *Cognitive, affective, and behavioral components of attitudes. Attitude organization and change: An analysis of consistency among attitude components*. New Haven, CT: Yale University Press.

Simpson, E. (1972). *The classification of educational objectives in the psychomotor domain: The psychomotor domain* (Volume 3). Washington, DC: Gryphon House.

Tomei, L.A. (2001). *Teaching digitally: A guide for integrating technology into the classroom*. Norwood, MA: Christopher-Gordon Publishing.

Walberg, H.J. (1984, May). Improving the productivity of America's schools. *Educational Leadership*.

Woodward, A.L., Markman, E.M., & Fitzsimmons, C.M. (1994). Rapid word learning in 13- and 18-month-olds. *Developmental Psychology*.

Annotated Bibliography

Additional citations for the Domains of Teaching

Bosniak, M. (1997, December / 1998, January). Relational teaching for teacher. *The High School Journal, 81*(2).

Ferdig, R. E., & Weiland, S. (2002). *A deeper psychology of technology: A case study of a girl and her e-mate*. College of Education, University of Florida and College of Education, Michigan State University.

Gagne, R. (1962). Military training and principles of learning. *American Psychologist, 17*, 263-276.

Gagne, R. (1985). *The conditions of learning* (4th edition). New York: Holt, Rinehart & Winston.

Goldfayl, D. (2001). *Affective and cognitive domain learning with multi-media: Two sides of the same coin.* Department of Communication and Language Studies, Victoria University of Technology.

Phillips, J.J. (1991). Measuring the return on HRD. *Employment Relations Today.*

Phillips, J.J. (1994, Autumn). *In action: Measuring return on investment.* American Society for Training and Development, Alexandria.

Chapter 2

Psychologies of Learning

Introduction

The primary responsibility of teachers is to promote student learning. This chapter explores the schools of educational psychology and how human activities change as a result of extrinsic motivators such as incentives, rewards, and punishments. Behaviorists advocate influencing behavior through the systematic adjustments of stimulus-response reinforcements. Cognitive psychology holds that information is more likely to be acquired, retained, and retrieved for future use if it is learner-constructed, relevant, and built upon prior knowledge. Humanist psychology focuses on individual growth and development. It stems from the theory that learning occurs primarily through reflection on personal experience, and as a result of intrinsic motivation.

Simply put, a taxonomy is a classification system. Benjamin Bloom created what is arguably the most famous classification for educators when he presented the Taxonomy of Educational Objectives. In his landmark exposition, Bloom developed a series of six progressive steps of cognitive development. In that single manuscript, he offers educators a rubric for developing instructional objectives at increasingly advanced levels of higher order thinking. Following in his footsteps, Krathwohl and Kibler completed the then-known domains of education with their affective and psychomotor taxonomies.

Figure 1. Teaching-Learning Model (Dembo, 1988)

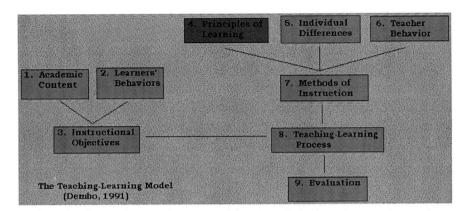

A teacher's selection of educational goals, instructional strategies, and class-room activities are based in part on their belief in the nature of learning. Dembo (1988) demonstrates the impact of teachers on the learning process in his Teaching-Learning Model seen in Figure 1.

Decisions concerning academic content (cell 1) are under the purview of the classroom teacher as are instructional objectives (cell 3), teacher behavior (cell 6), selection of the methods of instruction (cell 7), the teaching-learning process itself (cell 8), and the evaluation of learner behavior (cell 9). In all, the teacher is empowered with responsibility for all but two of the nine components of learning.

Although many factors are responsible for successful learning, the knowledge and application of the Principles of Learning (cell 4) contribute most directly to the fabric of one's teaching strategies.

Traditional Psychologies of Learning

Educational psychology provides insight into the teaching-learning paradigm by defining the many ways in which teachers teach and students learn. Whether the teacher and student are found in primary or secondary schools, colleges or the corporate classroom, the goal of educational psychology has always been to influence the practice and art of teaching.

In the past, behaviorism, cognitivism, and humanism alone have defined the relationships between a teacher's own beliefs and how these beliefs are manifested in actual classroom practice. Knowledge of these learning theories has been covered in numerous textbooks, audiovisual presentations, and supplemental materials. Perhaps the time is ripe to expand these major theories of learning to include technologies as a unique learning style.

Nearly all schools of education offer their charges an introduction to the learning theories purported by the psychologies of behaviorism, cognitivism, and humanism. You are encouraged to examine any personal beliefs about learning from Table 1 below. Check the appropriate boxes to indicate whether you agree or disagree with each statement.

Examine the boxes marked "Agree." Traditionally, statements 4, 6, and 9 are supported most strongly by behavioral educators. Statements 1, 3, and 7 are sustained by the cognitive teachers. Statements 2, 5, and 8 are evidenced in the classroom of the humanistic teacher.

Responses will fall into a particular pattern. Consider yourself a predominant advocate of that particular educational psychology. Force yourself to identify the strongest bent – no one is an eclectic at this point in our exploration of psychology. Most teachers agree with other statements as well, but nearly everyone shows a tendency in one area. For now, remember this dominant school of psychology. Later, after examining more deeply the theories and theorists of these important schools of educational psychology, the exercise will be repeated (with some modifications) to determine if there has been a change in your thinking.

The remainder of this chapter highlights the most important concepts of each psychology and introduces its most reknowned theorists and classroom applications. The chapter provides a refresher to more detailed discussions of learning theories as they apply in the classroom and some liberties have been taken to simplify the tenets of each psychology.

Table 1. Personal Beliefs about Teaching and Learning

Agree	Disagree	I Believe that...
❑	❑	1. The best learning occurs when the teacher has considered prior student knowledge and teaches new material in light of this previous learning.
❑	❑	2. The school experience should address basic student needs first including food, safety, and positive peer relationships.
❑	❑	3. The teacher should help students monitor their own classroom behavior as well as help them understand how they learn.
❑	❑	4. Curriculum should be organized along subject matter lines that are carefully scoped and sequenced.
❑	❑	5. Students should establish their own individual standards for learning and be entrusted with the evaluation of their own learning outcomes.
❑	❑	6. Students should be graded according to a uniform set of standards of achievement that the teacher sets for the entire class.
❑	❑	7. Teachers should ask students to demonstrate their work so that they can understand what students are thinking when solving problems.
❑	❑	8. Learners can be trusted to determine their own learning goals and should contribute to the process of choosing what they learn.
❑	❑	9. Learners need grades and gold stars (for children) or pay increases and promotions (for adults) and other extrinsic incentives as motivation to learn and to successfully meet established learning objectives.

Modified from Applying Educational Psychology in the Classroom (Dembo, 1988)

Psychology of Behaviorism

Definition

Behaviorism offers a theory of animal and human learning focusing on objective, observable behaviors while discounting, for all intents and purposes, mental activities. Behavioral theorists define learning strictly in terms of acquiring new behaviors. It originated in the field of psychology and grew to embrace an even wider perspective.

Concepts

Behaviorism, as a school of educational psychology, focuses on the observable effects of the environment on learning rather than on mental or cognitive processes. According to the behaviorist, it is the environment that provides stimulation and learner response to stimulation equates to learning. To the behaviorist, learning must be both observable and measurable and the possibility for repeating successful learning is contained in the principle of reinforcement. Modifying the learning environment changes student behavior and, therefore, affects successful student learning outcomes. The behaviorist view offers numerous solutions for classroom management, curriculum design, and content presentation.

Theorists and Their Theories

In years past, teachers believed that the best way to learn was through repetition. Behaviorism dominated educational thinking since the time of *Ivan Pavlov* and his experiments with animals. In early classrooms, students would spend their time copying spelling words, reciting historical dates, and rehashing mathematical formulas until they "learned" the information from rote memory.

Many classroom activities are learned through this process, known as classical conditioning. For example, students learn to attribute negative feelings to mathematics because they recall the unpleasant experience of going to the blackboard to demonstrate the (often incorrect) results of their homework. Difficult questions elicit anxiety from students who are conditioned to fear math and often generalize that fear to other subjects, such as foreign languages or science. Changing the pattern of the unconditioned stimulus and unconditioned response often results in changes in the behavior (and therefore the attitude) of the learner toward school in general.

One of the first behaviorists to put theory into practice was *E. L. Thorndike*. His theory of connectionism dominated educational practice in the United States during the first part of the twentieth century. Connectionism views learning as a process of "stamping in" or forming "connections" between the stimulus and its response. Thorndike's most important contributions, however, were the linked Laws of Effect and Exercise. The former law states that any connection between a situation and a response, accompanied or followed by a satisfying state of affairs, strengthens that connection and increases its chances of recurring. Likewise, when an annoying state of affairs is combined with or follows a connection, the strength of that connection is weakened and its chances of recurring reduced.

The Law of Exercise offers the classroom teacher validation for memorizing important concepts. The more a connection is practiced, the stronger the bond becomes, while the less a connection is exercised, the weaker it becomes. Thorndike's theories applied to the classroom have led to a number of widely accepted educational practices, such as flash cards, multiplication tables, and even gold stars.

An ardent student of his past mentors, *B.F. Skinner* added a new wrinkle to behaviorism by instilling the psychology into everyday educational practice. In his research, Skinner concluded that behaviors were not simply elicited responses, but rather the consequence of reinforcement from the environment. Operant conditioning added reinforcement to the equation and produced a new formula for learning: stimulus → response → reinforcement.

Teachers who accept Skinner's perspective acknowledge that the behavior of their students is learned — a response to past and present classroom environment. For example, classroom troublemakers "learn" to be disruptive because they seek attention (reinforcement) from their teachers and peers. Withdrawn students, on the other hand, learn that their environment does not reinforce their need for social interaction so they become reserved and silent. Student behavior, then, is best understood in terms of the learner's reinforcement history.

Consequently, the teacher must become aware of the behavioral processes required to change undesirable behavior in their students. Teacher responsibility, according to the behaviorist, is to construct an environment in which the probability of reinforcing proper student behavior is maximized. Learning is fostered by careful presentation of information in an organized sequence. Per Skinner (1978), there were two types of reinforcement. The first, called positive reinforcement, is defined as the presentation of a stimulus that increases the probability of a response. A student is hot and thirsty (stimulus). She locates the nearest soda machine and deposits several quarters (response). The can of soda that appears in the tray becomes an example of positive reinforcement. As a result, the chances of the student repeating the behavior increase.

Negative reinforcement occurs when an unpleasant stimulus is removed in an attempt to increase the behavior. Motivation by threats is an example of negative reinforcement. For example, as the teacher distributes the examination (stimulus), the child becomes ill (response). The student is permitted to go to the nurse's station. The response of becoming ill has been followed by discontinuance of the test (negative reinforcement). The teacher might well expect the "sickness" behavior to increase in frequency in similar future test situations.

While the goal of reinforcement (either positive or negative) is to increase certain behavior, the purpose of punishment is to decrease its recurrence. By nature, a behavior followed by punishment is less likely to be repeated.

Punishment also takes two forms. The first occurs when the consequences of a behavior decreases the behavior itself, such as demerits followed by detention, extra homework, or additional laps around the gym. The second type is often called removal punishment because it involves removing the stimulus. When parents take away privileges for inappropriate behavior, they apply this form of punishment with the effect of decreasing the behavior that initially led to the punishment. Negative reinforcement and punishment are often confused. It may help to remember that negative reinforcement is always associated with increases in behavior, while punishment always involves decreasing or eliminating behavior.

Applications for Learning

Much of how behaviorism has been applied in the classroom implicates technology. For example, one of the first universally recognized applications of behavioristic principles in action was *programmed instruction*. Although there has been considerable controversy regarding the merits of programmed instruction as the sole method of teaching, many educators agree that this particular application contributes to more efficient classroom procedure and successfully supplements conventional teaching methods. Programmed instruction enables students to work individually while demanding active participation on the part of the learner. As computer technology became more ingrained into the culture of teaching and learning, computer-assisted instruction emerged as a behavioral application.

Computer-Assisted Instruction, or CAI, implies several types of learning activities involving computers. In addition to CAI, related terminology includes computer-based education, computer-based instruction, computer-enriched instruction, computer-managed instruction, and the like. For purposes of the

Taxonomy for the Technology Domain, cataloging these classroom applications as behavioral in nature is important.

Mastery Learning implies a grasp of specific learning objectives and uses corrective instruction to achieve a minimum level of competency in every learner. It assumes that virtually all students can learn what is taught in school if their instruction is approached systematically, if they receive the attention required when and where difficulty is encountered, if they are given sufficient time to achieve mastery, and if there is some clear criterion of what constitutes mastery. Benjamin Bloom proposed a model of learning based on the belief that if each student was allowed the time needed to learn the material, and the time was appropriately spent, the student would achieve the specified learning objectives. If the learner was unsuccessful with one particular teaching strategy, an alternative strategy was in order. Bloom noted that in traditional methods, students who failed to master the material in the first unit were likely to experience difficulty in following lessons. What was needed, he believed, was feedback and corrective action to diagnose individual learning difficulties and prescribe specific remediation procedures that would help students learn.

Psychology of Cognitivism

Definition

In cognitive theory, knowledge is viewed as a symbolic mental construct in the learner's mind. Learning is the means by which these symbolic representations are committed to memory. As opposed to behaviorism, knowledge is measured by what learners know and not necessarily by what they do. The ability to distinguish between knowledge of concepts and knowledge of procedural steps involved in the concepts is critical. Learning takes place when information is received into the mind and processed to make some sense of it. Learning new information is possible by connecting existing information and storing it for later retrieval.

The role of the teacher is to present new information in a way that helps the learner attend to, encode, and retrieve data. The successful cognitive teacher organizes information and helps students link it to existing information.

Concepts

Cognitive psychologists view the student as an active contributor to the teaching-learning process. Those who adhere to this psychology of learning believe that teachers are more effective if they know the prior knowledge that the student already possesses before beginning a lesson. Cognitive teachers introduce strategies that help the learner acquire knowledge more effectively and teach them how to learn, remember, think, and recall.

Cognitive-developmental psychologists emphasize stages in learning development. They promote an understanding of the nature of thinking in planning instruction. They correlate cognitive development to human growth and learning to the iterative process of assimilation and accommodation.

Cognitive-constructivist psychologists, on the other hand, view human learning as constructed knowledge formed by the individual following various encounters with new information and concepts. To them, knowledge is a series of building blocks placed one on top of the other by the successful teacher to help construct student understanding.

Theorists and Their Theories

One of the most prominent characteristics of cognitive psychology is the age-stage developmental perspective. *Jean Piaget* is arguably the most widely read and adopted proponent of this perspective. His theory identifies stages of intellectual, or cognitive, development. The child's stage of development sets limits on learning and influences the type of learning that should occur. Intellectual growth is not a quantitative process, but rather a qualitative operation in which significant differences between the thinking of children and adolescents as well as between preschool and primary school students are accepted.

According to Piaget (1966), people are born with the ability to organize their thinking processes. His concept of "schemes" as the basic building blocks of learning is organized systems of actions or thought that allow mental representation of world events. Organization, assimilation, and accommodation are the key elements of a complex balancing act. The search for that balance is known as equilibration. In actual practice, it is the state of disequilibrium that motivates the learner to seek solutions to new problems.

Table 2. Piaget's Stages of Cognitive Development (1966)

Stage	Approximate Age	Characteristics
Sensorimotor	0 - 2 Years	Begins to make use of imitation, memory, and thought. Begins to recognize that objects do not cease to exist when they are hidden. Moves from reflex actions to goal-directed activity.
Preoperational	2 - 7 Years	Gradually develops use of language and ability to think in symbolic form. Able to think operations through logically in one direction. Has difficulties seeing another person's point of view.
Concrete Operational	7 - 11 Years	Able to solve concrete (hands-on) problems in logical fashion. Understands laws of conservation and is able to classify and sequence objects.
Formal Operations	11- Adult Years	Able to solve abstract problems in logical fashion. Becomes more scientific in thinking. Develops concerns about social issues, identity.

Piaget believed that learners advance through the same four stages (see Table 2) in exactly the same order. Stages are linked to age but serve only as general guidelines for individual development. According to his research, some children take longer to pass between stages while others may remain in one stage of development.

While Piaget believes that development precedes learning, *Lev Vygotsky* believed that learning comes before development. He believes that developmental processes lag behind the learning processes pointing out that children often complete tasks with the help of others that they could not accomplish working independently. Abilities that children exhibit when assisted by teachers are critical to his concept called the *zone of proximal development,* the difference between an individual's current and potential level of development.

Age-stage theorists abound in the school of cognitive psychology. *Erik Erikson* departs from Piaget's look at how children develop mentally and focuses instead on a learner's needs to understand the society in which they live. After studying child-rearing practices in several cultures, he concluded that all humans have the same basic needs and that each society must provide for those needs, albeit differently. A true cognitivist, Erikson views development as a series of stages each with its particular goals, concerns, accomplishments, and dangers. The stages are inter-dependent with accomplishments at later stages contingent on how conflicts are resolved in earlier years. For him, each stage involves a conflict between two opposing values — both of which must be mastered before progression to the next higher level is possible (Erikson, 1950).

Applications for Learning

In *Discovery Learning*, students are questioned by the teacher and expected to discern the particular principle hidden within a lesson objective. The purpose is to develop thinking skills. The teacher carefully plans the sequence of questions to be asked to help the learner uncover the abstractions taught, order the examples in the lesson, and use the reference materials and resources provided. Otherwise, valuable classroom time is wasted.

For *David Ausubel*, the key to the acquisition of knowledge is primarily through reception rather than discovery. *Reception Learning* classrooms present concepts, principles, and ideas that must be understood, not discovered. The more organized and focused the presentation, the more thoroughly the individual learns. Ausubel's most famous contribution to cognitive educational psychology was the advanced organizer. In this approach to learning, teacher materials are carefully organized and sequenced. Students receive the most usable materials using the most efficient delivery media. In many cases, that means technology. Learning progresses deductively from general to specific and not inductively as with discovery learning.

Finally, *Information Processing* views memory from the perspective of a computer model. Like the computer, the human mind takes in information, operates on that information, changes its form and content, stores the information, retrieves it when recalled, and generates appropriate responses. Some proponents suggest that learning is best approached through the study of memory and that the operation of the human brain actually resembles a large bank of computers all operating at the same time (in parallel).

Psychology of Humanism

Definition

Humanistic psychology emphasizes the study of the whole person. Human behavior is viewed through the eyes of the learner rather than the teacher. Humanistic educators believe that an individual's behavior is inextricably connected to inner feelings and self-image and is not solely the product of environment. Humanists study meaning, understanding, and the personalized experiences involved in learning. They emphasize characteristics that are shared by all humans such as love, grief, caring, and self-worth. Learning, as a result, is influenced by self-perceptions and the meanings attached to personal experiences.

Concepts

Proponents of humanism describe student actions not from the viewpoint of the teacher, as do behaviorists, but rather from the vantage point of the learner. Teachers are concerned with self-actualization, that is, the potential of a person to achieve individual satisfaction. The humanistic teacher creates an educational environment that fosters self-development, cooperation, positive communications, and personalization of information.

Theorists and Their Theories

Abraham Maslow has long been recognized as one of the leading humanistic proponents. Both the education and business communities have adopted his work wholeheartedly.

An important aspect of his theory is based on the premise that within each individual is two forces: one that seeks growth while, at the same time, another that actively resists it. Maslow's Hierarchy of Human Needs includes five autonomous levels (see Table 3).

Maslow's hierarchy has important implications for the teacher in the classroom. The national school breakfast program is an excellent example of how the federal government recognized the impact of this theory on learning. Children

Table 3. Hierarchy of Human Needs (Maslow, 1970)

Stage	Needs	Description
1	Physiological/ Biological	First-level needs are the most demanding. Only after hunger, thirst, and the need for shelter have been satisfied, do the needs at the next higher level emerge.
2	Safety	Needs include security, protection from physical and emotional harm, and the desire for good health.
3	Belonging and Love	Such needs in the individual seek family and friends and the feeling of acceptance and friendship in relations with others.
4	Esteem	Esteem moves individuals to their first internal demand for self-respect, autonomy, achievement along with status, recognition, and attention.
5	Self-Actualization	Assumes that lower needs have been satisfied; personal motivation is re-directed towards developing one's potential to "become" what you are capable of achieving in life.

who come to school without breakfast are not interested in becoming self-actualized. Research agrees that classroom learning rarely begins until the first three stages of the hierarchy have been satisfied.

Carl Rogers, on the other hand, believes that humans have a natural desire to learn. He supports this position with documented observations of a child's natural curiosity as they explore the environment. They are eager to learn and they discover for themselves while attempting to make meaning of their surroundings — even if that meaning is sometimes wrong. So, what happens to these children after years of formal schooling? What causes the loss of such innate excitement about learning by the time some student reach secondary school? These are good questions, says Rogers, and one that teachers must resolve when delivering their own classroom lessons (Rogers, 1961).

Teachers are primarily facilitators of learning. In contrast to the traditional teacher who assumes full responsibility for the learning process, the humanistic teacher shares that responsibility with the student. The teacher serves as guide and model, providing the resources needed to learn. Genuineness defines the relationship between teacher and student and empathetic understanding — the ability to view the world through students' eyes — is a necessary characteristic of the humanistic teacher.

Applications for Learning

Cooperative learning in the traditional classroom invokes a multiplicity of images. Some educators believe assigning individual projects and allowing students to interact satisfies the criteria for cooperative learning. Others envision students sitting together as they do their homework, asking questions and offering responses to others' inquiries as sufficient. Unfortunately, neither of these examples adequately defines the cooperative learning experience. For a lesson to be considered cooperative learning, it must exhibit several basic elements.

Students must perceive that they "cooperate and graduate" together. Positive interdependence demands that students share common goals, divide the tasks, share resources and information, assume responsibility for different roles, and, most importantly, receive their rewards based on group performance.

Learners must share the nature of the task, decide the best approach to the assignment, and dialog with one another to solve the problem. Face-to-face interaction is stressed while each student develops a sense of personal responsibility to the group. Oftentimes, individual accountability is the most violated principle in a cooperative learning situation.

Placing students in groups and telling them to work "cooperatively" is a formula for failure unless they are taught the collaborative skills necessary for social interaction. The teacher must first establish working relationships as a requisite skill before cooperative learning can bear results. Finally, cooperative learning occurs when groups discuss, process, and evaluate their own efforts while maintaining an effective working relationship among all members of the group.

In the late 1960s, a study advocating the development of the *Open Classroom* as a model for elementary education was introduced into the body of research. The concept of an open classroom quickly spread to schools throughout the United States. Its advocates acclaimed it both a philosophy of education and a proper application of humanistic and cognitive psychology. Prominent educators evolved a list of "themes" commonly attributed to *Open Education,* including such characteristics as humaneness, respect, and warmth; individualized instruction and evaluation (with no text books or workbooks); and, a warm and accepting learning environment.

Psychology of Technology

Definition

Technology is defined as the application of knowledge to solve problems and extend human potential (*Webster's Seventh New Collegiate Dictionary*, 2002). But unlike the traditional psychologies of education, technology encompasses several interrelated areas each of which expands our understanding of the multiple concepts attributed to this newest psychology of learning.

Concepts

Suitably applied technology focuses on integrated, experience-based instruction designed to challenge learners to discover their world and create new realities, solve problems and construct new solutions, and understand the social and cultural implications of technologies in the global community. Learners are introduced to a variety of tools, machines, computer systems, communications, presentation media and materials, processes and technological systems in order for them to become knowledgeable about all aspects of applied science, its evolution, potential, and utilization. Given such a broad range of challenges, it is no wonder technology has taken on so many different facets.

Technology, first and foremost, is a literacy. The U.S. Department of Education (1996) defines technology as, "computer skills and the ability to use computers and other technology to improve learning, productivity, and performance." Another definition describes technology as a "process of preparing learners to apply computer skills in the investigation of reading, writing, math, and science through practical hands-on lab experiences that results in the increased knowledge of how to solve problems and make life better for mankind" (Dictionary.com, 2003). Technology, then, is a language, a vernacular for dealing with the world, learning its secrets, and addressing the myriad of challenges it puts forward.

Technology is also a learning tool—actually, many learning tools. Specifically, educational technology includes computers, media, decision-making, and collaborative technologies that promote learning. The Association for Educational Communications and Technology defines educational technology (AECT, 1977, Parts 1-3) as a "complex, integrated process involving people, procedures, ideas, devices, and organization, for analyzing problems and devising, implementing, evaluating, and managing solutions to those problems, involved in all aspects of human learning." So then, technology represents the set of skills and competencies necessary to solve real-world problems.

Lastly, students, teachers, and practicing professionals consider technology an academic content area in its own right, worthy of examination and exploration. The terms used to describe this brand of technology is information technology and computer science technology, reflecting a concern for all aspects of managing and processing information and its broad impact on the individual, large organizations and companies, and society as a whole. To prepare students for positions in industry, programs in information technology, sometimes called information systems or management information service, are offered at all levels of formal education.

Defining technology, then, is appropriate only in the broadest of concepts. Technology takes on many different definitions depending on the word or words that immediately precede it. Keep this in mind as we explore the emblematic theorists that have laid the groundwork for the Taxonomy for the Technology Domain.

Theorists and Their Theories

There are many proponents for recognizing technology as its own psychology for learning. However, the discipline, literature, and research base is still so (relatively) new that few leaders have yet to surface. As a result, this section of the chapter introduces only a few advocates whose works have contributed to the body of knowledge specifically supporting the use of technology for learning. The classification schemata used to discuss technology concepts once again serves to organize the discussion, namely, technology as a literacy, technology for learning, technology for teaching, and technology as a discipline. The references cited at the end of each chapter form their own bibliographic review of pertinent literature.

The "information age" that began quietly enough in the 20th century has exploded in the new millennium. Denise E. Murray is the director of the National Centre for English Language Teaching and Research, Macquarie University, Sydney, Australia. She provides an outstanding history of technology. According to Murray, much of the established literature on technology as a literacy is drawn from parallels between the advent of the printing press in 15ᵗʰ century Europe and the introduction of the computer (Murray, 2000).

The similarities between how early proponents must have viewed the potential of mass-produced textbooks and innovators who purchased the first Apple IIs for the classroom are uncanny. Prior to the mechanization of the printed word, oral literacy reigned supreme as professors delivered their diatribes in the confine of a classroom. When the first mass-produced texts entered the academic scene, it must have seemed that the learned educator standing before the receptive student body would quickly fade into extinction. Why would students pay so dearly in terms of time and money for an undersized seat in an overcrowded classroom when for considerably less time and expense they could receive the same instructional material by reading reknowned authors who happened to be lucky enough to mass-produce their own discourse? The answer, of course, was literacy.

At the outset of the printing press, most members of the mass target audience could not read. It is hard to say whether the printing press increased literacy or literacy increased the demand for books. Most likely, it was a combination of both.

Technology, in the form of desktop computers, arrived on the scene in the late 1970 courtesy of two pioneers, Steve Jobs and Steve Wozniak, who had visions of selling personal computers with little red apples affixed to their covers. Within a decade, literally millions of personal computers were manufactured, thousands finding their way into the classrooms of the most innovative schools. Yet, similar to the printed word, instructional technology grew very little during the ensuing decades as humans fought to garner a (technology) literacy that would serve to make these machines the newest educational learning tools.

In another article from the *Language Learning & Technology Journal*, Godwin-Jones provides technology literacies for our consideration cataloged under the more generic literacies of reading, writing, and electronic resources. Under reading, the author places such technological skills as word processing, digital text books, the Internet, CD-ROM-based publications, and online libraries as channels for accessing journals, travel reports, newspaper articles, reviews, family histories, government reports, recipes, etc. (Godwin-Jones, 2000). Writing literacies include such technology as electronic mail, bulletin boards, instant messaging and online chat rooms plus electronic devices such as Palm organizers and cellular phones equipped with small screens. At numerous colleges and universities, students are expected to master such state-of-the-art electronic literacies as e-mail, word processing, spreadsheets, and the Internet. Other skills include digital sound and video, graphics design and presentation, computer-assisted instruction, computer-managed learning, drill and practice software, and other high-tech learning management systems.

Bertram and Levin offered perhaps the first classification system for technologies used for learning. In their article, *Technology as Media: The Learner Centered Perspective* (2001), Bruce and Levin explain that the balance between learning and doing is impacted by new technologies. Their taxonomy of technology focused on a learner-centered framework for systematically developing powerful learning environments based on the natural impulses of a child proposed by John Dewey: inquiry, communication, construction, and expression. In this innovative taxonomy, the diversity in uses of technologies for learning is captured by four different media for learning, based on the goals of the learner.

At the outset of the classification, media for inquiry represents technologies used for learning through inquiry and they cite innovative learning approaches in science, mathematics, and engineering as evidence of the successful application of such technologies. Media for communication offers a suite of technologies for learning through an electronic exchange of ideas. Many innovative uses of technologies for learning are represented at this level, including online learning management systems such as WebCT, Blackboard, and FirstClass, in addition to the more popular electronic communications such as electronic mail, bulletin boards, and chat rooms.

From here, the authors depart from the more traditional concepts of technology by examining media for construction, technologies used for learning through the construction of new knowledge. Problem-based and project-based learning approaches are cited as key examples. Finally, media for expression is depicted as technologies used for learning through expression, particularly in the language arts.

The learner-based taxonomy of technology posited by Bruce and Levin encompasses learning combined with emerging technologies to provide a basis for systematically designing more powerful contexts for learning and thereby characterizes a leading concept in the psychology of technology.

Few proponents of technology have offered as much insight into technology as a learning strategy as Reeves and Jonassen, two noted authors with considerable testimony to the power and potential of technology in the classroom.

In his article, *Evaluating What Really Matters in Computer-Based Education*, Reeves introduces 14 dimensions that establish the pedagogical underpinnings for assessing the strength of technology to initiate powerful instructional interactions, monitor learner progress, empower effective teachers, accommodate individual differences, and promote cooperative learning (Reeves, 1998). Within each dimension, the author defines a continuum for all aspects of the psychology of technology for teaching, including (and we will only mention five of the 14 here): epistemology (objectivism to constructivism), psychology (behavioral to cognitive), experiential validity (abstract to concrete), teacher role (didactic to facilitative), and motivation (extrinsic to intrinsic). His investigation into the value of these pedagogical dimensions provides a necessary framework for viewing technology as a tool for teaching.

Jonassen (1996) describes, "Mindtools as a way of using a computer application program to engage learners in constructive, higher-order, critical thinking about the subjects they are studying." With technology, the learner enters an intellectual partnership and begins to access and interpret information, and organize personal knowledge in new ways. The author explores many (if not all) of the psychologies of education as they pertain to technology: the pedagogy of higher order thinking; critical, creative, and complex thinking abilities; and, collaborative skills.

Together, Reeves and Jonassen encourage a constructivist learning environment, an atmosphere in which teachers create their own technology-based cognitive tools, and the use of technology in realistic, meaningful situations for target learners.

The U.S. Department of Education (1996) defined technology as, "computer skills and the ability to use computers and other technology to improve learning, productivity, and performance." It lists four related goals that ensure all students and teachers have equitable access to and effective use of technology. It is wise for those considering the integration of technology into the school curriculum to consider that the federal government expects its teachers to use computers and the information superhighway, access modern multimedia computers, connected to the information superhighway, in their classrooms, and utilize effective software and online learning resources.

Jonassen and Reeves also collaborate to examine technology as a discipline. In their 1996 treatise, certain technology-based cognitive tools are recommended to engage the learner. They include computer programming, hypermedia/ multimedia authoring systems, semantic networks, expert (intelligent) systems, databases, and spreadsheets.

Finally, we must acknowledge the International Society for Technology in Education (ISTE) for defining technology as a viable content area. At the state level, 48 of the 50 states have adopted, adapted, aligned with, or otherwise referenced at least one set of ISTE standards in their state technology or curriculum plans (2003). According to ISTE (2003), technology as a discipline encompasses: basic operations and concepts; social, ethical, and human issues; productivity tools; communications tools; research tools; and, problem-solving and decision-making tools.

Applications for Learning

At its roots, technology as a literacy demands a minimum level of competency on the part of every learner. From the research, a skill set provides K-12 schools with a scope and sequence embracing the parts of a computer including: input, output, and peripheral devices; office productivity tools such as word processing, spreadsheets, databases, and paint-and-draw utilities; communications tools including electronic mail, synchronous, and asynchronous software; Web-based capabilities including navigation browsers, online research, and HTML editors; and, digital imagery with presentation software, cameras, and scanners.

At higher levels, applications for learning include all manner of educational technologies that broaden the range of tools to include an understanding of the various hardware and software aspects of technology. Table 4 reveals some of the most common technologies found in the classroom for teaching and learning.

The applications of instructional technologies focus on a broader range of capabilities with the inclusion of specific applications that enhance the learning experience. Effective instructional technology is the application of educational technologies by a well-prepared teacher using validated principles of instructional design and development to produce effective technology-based instruction. Some common examples of appropriate instructional technologies are shown in Table 5.

Information technology and computer science technology programs include a wide range of subject matter content areas, including: more traditional com-

Table 4. Handy Reference Guide to the Most Common Educational Technologies

Calculators/ Graphing Calculators	List Servers
Computer Assisted Instruction	MIDI Interfaces
Databases	Multimedia Computers
Desktop Publishing	Music Synthesizers
Drill-and-Practice Instructional Media	Newsgroups
Electronic Mail	Office Productivity
Digitized Encyclopedias	Problem Solving Instructional Media
Games Instructional Media	Simulation Instructional Media
Groupware	Spreadsheet
Graphic Presentation	Tutorial Instructional Media
Hypertext/Hypermedia/Hyperlinks	Video (Film, Videotape, Laserdisc, DVD)
Internet	World Wide Web
	Word Processing

Table 5. Common Instructional Technologies

Appropriate Instructional Technologies	Example Classroom Applications	Specific Applications	Notes
Web authoring tools	Publish syllabus or other classroom resources	• Netscape Composer • Macromedia Dreamweaver • Microsoft FrontPage • HTML Code	By publishing online materials, learners access these resources from any Internet-capable system with connectivity. Learners are able to prepare for class and/or review lesson information, or enhance their understanding at their own discretion.
Scanners, digital cameras, harvesting the Internet for photos, sound, and video.	Supplement traditional lecture with digital imagery	• Adobe Photoshop • PowerPoint • Paint and Draw Utilities	Creating teacher-made digital imagery provides learners with photos, sound, and video materials that enhance the teaching and learning experience by focusing learner attention on specific lesson objectives.
E-reserve library services, E-books CD-journals	Provide links to required or supplemental online reading materials	• CD-ROM-based journals and periodicals • HTML links to online resources	Online materials are an effective supplement to text-based course texts and handouts. These materials are accessible from any Internet-ready computer from school, office, or home.

Table 5. Common Instructional Technologies (continued)

Learning Management Environments	Provide synchronous and asynchronous collaboration	• WebCT • First Class • Blackboard • Horizon Live • Cyber Grad	LMEs provide online bulletin boards, threaded discussion forums, chat rooms, and interactive teacher-learner collaborative tools for online communications.
Online Learner Assessment Tools	Provide graded and non-graded practice reviews, quizzes, and examinations	• WebCT Exam Tool • Blackboard Quiz Tool	Online assessment tools are effective media for student self-evaluation, providing individual reviews at the student's own pace. Immediate feedback is required and the quality of that feedback is critical to this instructional strategy.
Video and Audio Classroom Presentations	Audio and video-based classroom discussion via distance learning	• Videoconferencing • Audio-conferencing	The tele-classroom offers reliable video and/or audio interaction between teachers and students geographically separated in different venues.
Group Brainstorming Sessions	Facilitate brainstorming either in the classroom or at a distance	• E-mail • Chat Rooms • Instant Messaging • Inspiration (c) Brainstorming Software	Collaborative tools allow students to share ideas via real-time, give-and-take conversational writing. Many of these tools provide a convenient archiving function so teachers (as well as missing students) can view successful sessions via digital logs offline.

puter hardware; programming languages and operating systems; management information systems; software engineering; and, information system security. In this new millennium, information technology takes on more pioneering endeavors such as: communication and networking; machine and computational learning; electronic commerce; the impact of information on society, and, the Internet with all its related applications.

Conclusion

Instructional learning theory and the application of technology in the classroom are firmly grounded in the major schools of educational psychology. From such beginnings have evolved modern thinking about how learning occurs and ultimately how technology affects that learning. Behaviorism brings to the table an historical foundation for learning at its most rudimentary base. Classical and operant conditioning first attempted to explain the nature of learning and continue today to explain the value of competency-based programs such as mastery learning.

Cognitivism and its concept of schemata have their roots in the decades of the 1950s and 1960s as they continue to impact learning. The most recent educational persuasion, humanism, is a child of the 1970s and its commitment to the personalization of learning.

With the advent of technology as an educational psychology, our beliefs about learning are changing. Take a look at the *Personal Beliefs About Teaching and Learning* (Table 6) again. This time, beliefs reflecting the psychology of technology have been added.

Remember that statements 4, 6, and 9 portray the behavioral educator who views learning as a reaction to stimulus → response → reinforcement. Statements 1, 3, and 7 are cognitive descriptors for educators who see learning as a series of stages, ages, and schemata. Statements 2, 5, and 8 typify the humanistic educator and the perspective that all learning is self-imposed.

To this initial account, statements 10, 11, and 12 have been added to reflect the characteristics and demeanor of the technologist — the educator who recognizes another instructional strategy that encompasses text-, visual-, and Web-based materials with applications in the classroom in support of a wider range of learning styles.

Your personal characterization may have changed since the beginning of this chapter. You have most likely altered your traditional view of educational psychology as behavioral, cognitive, or humanistic. Did you also take on characteristics of the technologist?

Can you defend (at least to yourself) why you view yourself as you do?

Do you feel as though you are more of an eclectic, someone who believes that a combination of all four psychologies, in some particular proportion, best serves your learners in the classroom?

To satisfactorily employ the Taxonomy for the Technology Domain that follows, you must have a working knowledge of all four psychologies of education.

Table 6. Personal Beliefs about Teaching and Learning

Agree	Disagree	I Believe that...
❏	❏	1. The best learning occurs when the teacher has considered prior student knowledge and teaches new material in light of this previous learning.
❏	❏	2. The school experience should address basic student needs first including food, safety, and the positive peer relationships.
❏	❏	3. The teacher should help students monitor their own classroom behavior as well as help them understand how they learn.
❏	❏	4. Curriculum should be organized along subject matter lines that are carefully scope and sequenced.
❏	❏	5. Students should establish their own individual standards for learning and entrusted with the evaluation of their own learning outcomes.
❏	❏	6. Students should be graded according to a uniform set of standards of achievement that the teacher sets for the entire class.
❏	❏	7. Teachers should ask students to demonstrate their work so that they can understand what students are thinking when solving problems.
❏	❏	8. Learners can be trusted to determine their own learning goals and should contribute to the process of choosing what they learn.
❏	❏	9. Learners need grades and gold stars (for children) or pay increases and promotions (for adults) and other extrinsic incentives as motivation to learn and to meet established learning objectives.
❏	❏	10. Teachers should provide text-, visual-, and Web-based instructional materials to support as many individual student-learning styles as possible when presenting a lesson.
❏	❏	11. Teachers should remain abreast of the latest instructional technologies and model the application of technology for teaching and learning in the classroom.
❏	❏	12. Effective teachers know their own personal instructional preferences and how to integrate instructional materials that support other learning styles.

Modified with Technology as an Educational Psychology

References

Association for Educational Communications and Technology (AECT). (1977). *The definition of educational technology: A summary.* Washington, DC.

Bertram, C.B., & Levin, J.A. (2001). *Technology as media: The learner centered perspective.* University of Illinois, Urbana-Champaign. Paper presented at the 2001 AERA Meeting, Seattle, Washington Symposium. What Teachers Should Know about Technology: Perspectives and Practices, March 2001.

Bruner, J.S. (1960). *Intuitive and analytic thinking.* Cambridge, MA: Harvard University Press.

Dembo, M.H. (1988). *Applying educational psychology in the classroom* (3rd edition). New York: Longman Publishers.

Dictionary.com (2003). Lexico Publishing Group, LLC. Retrieved from the World Wide Web: *http://dictionary.com*

Erikson, E.H. (1950). *Childhood and society.* New York: Norton Publishing.

Godwin-Jones, R. (2000, September). Emerging technologies literacies and technology tools/trends. *Language Learning & Technology, 4*(2), 11-18.

International Society for Technology in Education (ISTE). (2003). National Educational Technology Standards (NETS) for students, teachers, and administrators. Retrieved from the World Wide Web: *http://cnets.iste.org*

Jonassen, D.H. (1996). *Computers in the classroom: Mindtools for critical thinking.* New York: Prentice-Hall.

Jonassen, D.H., & Reeves, T.C. (1996). Learning with technology: Using computers as cognitive tools. In D.H. Jonassen (Ed.), *Handbook of research on educational communications and technology.* New York: Macmillan.

Maslow, A. (1970). *Motivation and personality* (2nd edition). New York: Harper & Row.

Murray, D.E. (2000, September). Changing technologies, changing literacy communities*? Language Learning & Technology, 4*(2).

Piaget, J., & Inhelder, B. (1966). *The psychology of the child.* Perseus Books.

Reeves, T.C. (1998). *The impact of media and technology in schools.* Research report prepared for the Bertelsmann Foundation. The University of Georgia.

Rogers, C. R. (1961). *On becoming a person.* Boston: Houghton Mifflin.

Skinner, B. F. (1978). *Reflections on behaviorism and society.* Englewood Cliffs, NJ: Prentice-Hall.

U.S. Department of Education. (1996). *Getting America's students ready for the 21st century: Meeting the technology literacy challenge.*

Chapter 3

Taxonomies of Education

Introduction

This chapter explores the key to taxonomies and their effectiveness as a teaching strategy. The explanation lies in their use of learning objectives constructed to embody three primary characteristics: an observable task, particular learning conditions, and established standards of performance. A properly constructed learning objective involves an *observable task* that the student must perform to demonstrate that the goal has been mastered. There must be little doubt as to the *conditions* under which the learning will occur, namely, the actions students are expected to demonstrate. Finally, learning objectives must stipulate what constitutes successful learning. *Standards* authenticate successful learning.

Taxonomies for the Cognitive Domain

Following the 1948 convention of the American Psychological Association, Benjamin S. Bloom took the lead in formulating a classification of "the goals of the educational process." Three "domains" of educational activities were identified. The first of these, the cognitive domain, involves the concept of knowledge and the development of intellectual attitudes and skills. Eventually, Bloom (1956, 1974) and his co-workers established a hierarchy of educational objectives generally referred to as Bloom's Taxonomy that characterizes objectives from the simplest behavior to the most complex. Cognitive objectives concern themselves with the development of knowledge and the structure of learning. Knowledge, comprehension, application, analysis, synthesis, and evaluation are among the most practical aspects of teaching and learning.

Levels of the Cognitive Taxonomy

Knowledge is defined as remembering previously learned material and may involve the recall of a wide range of material from specific facts to complete theories. Knowledge represents the lowest level of learning outcomes in the cognitive domain and often the minimal level of learning required for student success. Rote memory and the simple recall of facts, rules, definitions, and procedures are essential.

Comprehension is the ability to grasp the meaning of material. Evidence of this skill is demonstrated by translating material from one form to another (words to numbers), by interpreting material (explaining or summarizing), and by estimating future trends (predicting consequences or effects). Such learning outcomes go beyond simple memorization of content material. They involve abstractions demonstrated by restating problems, offering examples, and suggesting future actions.

Application refers to the ability to use learned material in new and concrete situations and includes the application of rules, methods, concepts, principles, laws, and theories. Learning outcomes in this area require an even higher level of understanding than those in previous levels and involve the fairly straightforward process of linking principles and concepts to situations not previously experienced.

Analysis is the fourth level of complexity and requires the student to break down concepts into component parts, from general to specific, so that its organizational structure may be more readily understood. Analysis includes identifying parts, understanding the relationship between those parts, and applying organizational principles that make them interact as a whole. Learning outcomes at this level require an understanding of both content and structural form.

Synthesis refers to the ability to construct the parts (analyzed in the previous level) to form a new whole. Synthesis involves communication, planning, research, and an understanding of abstract relations along with schemata for classifying information. Learning objectives created in this area stress innovative behavior with an emphasis on forming new patterns, integrating previously divergent concepts into new knowledge, and moving from specifics back to the general.

The most complex level of cognitive understanding is that of *evaluation,* involving both judgment and decision-making. This level of the cognitive taxonomy is concerned with the ability to judge the value of material based on definite criteria. Measures of student learning focus on both internal (i.e., student-generated and student-oriented) and external (i.e., teacher-generated and teacher-oriented) outcomes. Learning outcomes presuppose mastery of all previous levels while incorporating human judgment absent in the lower classifications.

Action Verbs

The most appealing aspect of Bloom's taxonomy is the subsequent list of action verbs commonly found in all cognitive learning objectives. Created by educators, they represent intellectual activity at each of the respective levels. The very best verbs embrace observable, measurable actions and target a specific level of thinking. Table 1 presents a list of these verbs for the cognitive domain.

Table 1. Cognitive Domain

Taxonomy Classification	Action Verbs that represent intellectual activity on this level
Knowledge	Arrange, define, duplicate, label, list, memorize, name, order, recognize, relate, recall, repeat, reproduce, state
Comprehension	Classify, describe, discuss, explain, express, identify, indicate, locate, recognize, report, restate, review, select, translate
Application	Apply, choose, demonstrate, dramatize, employ, illustrate, interpret, operate, practice, schedule, sketch, solve, use, write
Analysis	Analyze, appraise, calculate, categorize, compare, contrast, criticize, differentiate, discriminate, distinguish, examine, experiment, question, test
Synthesis	Arrange, assemble, collect, compose, construct, create, design, develop, formulate, manage, organize, plan, prepare, propose, set up, write
Evaluation	Appraise, argue, assess, attach, choose compare, defend estimate, judge, predict, rate, core, select, support, value, evaluate

Learning Objectives

When designing technology-based instructional materials, teachers should be concerned with developing clear descriptions of desired student outcomes that describe in general what learners will know or be able to do following the lesson. Outcomes are based on the needs of the learner and an understanding of what the learner should know about a particular subject.

Well-written learning objectives are carefully worded and include characteristics that describe: (a) the specific conditions under which the learning will occur, (b) the behavior that will evidence the learning, and (c) the criteria for a

Table 2. Example Learning Objectives in the Cognitive Domain

Example Learning Objective	Abstract or Concrete	Taxonomy Level	Condition	Behavior(s)	Criteria
Given a map of United States, students will be able to correctly match 40 of the 50 states with their capital cities.	Concrete Matching 40 of 50 states is observable and measurable	Knowledge	Given a map of United States…	…students will be able to correctly match states with their capital cities.	…40 of the 50 states…
Students will describe how the linear polarize method affects corrosion rates and discuss when they are best used to treat metals.	Abstract How will teachers assess "describe"?	Application	Unclear	Students will describe and discuss…	Unclear
In a one-page essay, students will summarize President Kennedy's Inaugural Address underlining at least 3 of 5 points discussed in class.	Concrete/Abstract Underlining 3 of 5 key points is observable; summarizing is not.	Analysis	In a one-page essay…	…students will summarize (abstract) and underline (more concrete)…	…at least 3 of 5 points discussed in class.
Components of GNP are consumption, investment, exports, and government expenditures. Then, prepare a 10-minute argument that outlines 3 ways that GNP could be used to both increase taxes and personal savings.	Abstract/Concrete "Preparing an argument" is mostly an abstract concept. Using a 10-minute limit and requiring 3 methods makes it more concrete.	Evaluation	Components of GNP are consumption, investment, exports, and government expenditures.	Prepare an argument that outlines ways that GNP could be used to both increase taxes and personal savings.	….ten-minute argument… …outline 3 ways…

successful learning experience. Table 2 offers some example learning objectives using action verbs in the cognitive domain.

Taxonomies for the Affective Domain

David Krathwohl (1964), in collaboration with Bloom and Mascia, took the lead to produce a parallel taxonomy to the cognitive domain that would explain the development of human attitudes, principles, codes, and values.

Since teachers first entered the classroom filled with wide-eyed students, they have understood the need to view their charges as both thinking and feeling individuals. When designing contemporary instructional programs, the distinction between cognition and emotion is often overlooked. Yet, this distinction frequently means the difference between a successful learning experience and a classroom failure. During the mid-twentieth century, psychology turned its attention away from its formerly exclusive cognitive perspective towards a more affective bent.

Initially, humans were thought to be at the mercy of their innate drives and passions. As behaviorism became dominant, the affective nature was discounted. Indeed, the excitement surrounding behavioral successes in both the job market and the classroom resulted in a movement to preclude the affective from scientific journals altogether (Brown & Farber, 1951). The issue was even more exacerbated with the 1960's view of human learning as a metaphor for the computer. The affective sphere of human development was often characterized as "a regrettable flaw in an otherwise perfect cognitive machine" (Scherer, 1984).

Figure 1. Misunderstood Affective Terms

Affective Term	Clinical Definition
Affect	A feeling or emotion as distinguished from cognition, thought, or action
Emotion	An intense feeling; a complex and usually strong subjective response, as love or fear; a state of agitation or disturbance
Feeling	A sensation perceived by the sense of touch; an indefinite state of mind; an affective state of consciousness, such as that resulting from emotions, sentiments, or desires; an emotional state or disposition; nonintellectual or subjective human response

Dictionary definitions associated with the affective domain demonstrate how difficult it is to clearly articulate its breadth. For example, affect, emotion, and feelings, oftentimes used interchangeably by the uninitiated, spark considerably different meanings when precisely defined by an affective psychologist (Figure 1). The term "feeling" itself possesses four different connotations for its advocates.

Levels of the Affective Taxonomy

Five progressive stages constitute personal growth in the affective domain. These levels include receiving, responding, valuing, organizing, and characterizing.

- **Receiving** (or attending) represents the lowest level of development and is evidenced in learning objectives that stress awareness, a willingness to actively accept the new information, and the ability to selectively respond to a stimulus. From the teacher's standpoint, receiving is concerned with getting, holding, and directing the student's attention.

- **Responding** demands an increased level of acceptance, willingness, and appreciation. It refers to active learning on the part of students who must be motivated not to just receive information from the previous level, but to take overt action to learn. Responding suggests the desire for students to become sufficiently involved in or committed to a learning objective so as to explicitly seek successful outcomes and personal satisfaction.

- **Valuing** moves the student to the judgment level of the affective domain and emphasizes acceptance, preference, and commitment. Valuing is motivated not by the desire to comply or obey but by the learner's commitment to the inherent value of the behavior. Learning objectives written for this level of the taxonomy are concerned with behavior that is consistent and stable enough to make student judgment possible and predictable.

- **Organizing** is the learner's attempt to assimilate new values, making them consistent and compatible with previous learning. Organizing brings together previously unassociated values, attitudes, and emotions in an effort to build an internally consistent value system.

- **Characterizing** internalizes values further and places them in the learner's hierarchy of principles and personally adopted standards. These values must have permanent control of behavior for a sufficiently long period of time to become pervasive, consistent, and predictable.

Action Verbs

Action verbs in the affective domain are typically more abstract than their cognitive counterparts. The terminology used to represent intellectual activity on the five affective levels is often more vague, involving covert consequences and imprecise learning outcomes. The cause of all of this nondescript goal-setting lies in the internalization of affective behaviors within the learner and less reliance on concrete evidence to substantiate classroom learning. Table 3 offers action verbs found in many affective learning objectives in this important domain.

Table 3. Affective Domain

Taxonomy Classification	Action Verbs that represent intellectual activity on this level
Receiving	Differentiate, set apart, separate, accumulate, select, combine, listen, control, acknowledge, ask, attend, be aware, listen, receive, reply, select, show alertness, tolerate, use, view, watch
Responding	Comply, follow, commend, volunteer, discuss, practice, acclaim, augment, agree (to), answer, ask, assist, communicate, comply, consent, conform, contribute, cooperate, discuss, follow-up, greet, help, indicate, inquire, label, obey, participate, pursue, question, react, read, reply, report, request, respond, seek, select, visit, volunteer, write
Valuing	Relinquish, specify, subsidize, help, support, protest, debate, argue, accept, adopt, approve, complete, choose, commit, describe, desire, differentiate, display, endorse, exhibit, explain, express, form, initiate, invite, join, justify, prefer, propose, read, report, sanction, select, share, study, work
Organizing	Theorize, abstract, compare, balance, define, formulate, organize, adapt, adhere, alter, arrange, categorize, classify, combine, compare, complete, defend, explain, establish, formulate, generalize, group, identify, integrate, modify, order, organize, prepare, rank, rate, relate, synthesize, systemize
Characterizing	Revise, change, complete, rate, manage, resolve, act, advocate, behave, characterize, conform, continue, defend, devote, disclose, discriminate, display, encourage, endure, exemplify, function, incorporate, influence, justify, listen, maintain, modify, pattern, practice, preserve, perform, question, revise, retain, support, uphold, use

Learning Objectives

Learning objectives that amplify feelings, emotions, or degrees of acceptance or rejection fall within the affective domain. To design an affective learning objective, teachers must grasp the concepts of internal versus external motivation.

Table 4. Example Learning Objectives in the Affective Domain

Example Learning Objective	Value/ Personal/ Esthetic/ Development	Taxonomy Level	Condition	Behavior(s)	Criteria
During the first 10 minutes of the new course, students will listen for and recall the name of newly introduced people and reintroduce two other students without error.	Value Development / Significance of others	Receiving and Responding	During the first 10 minutes of the new course …	… students will listen for and recall the name of newly introduced people…	… reintroduce two other students without error.
Students will evidence their knowledge of social responsibility by designing a plan for improving corporate fiscal responsibility and following through by writing a 5-page letter of support to their congressman.	Value Development / Significance of institutions	Valuing	Students will evidence their knowledge of social responsibility …	… designing a plan for improving corporate fiscal responsibility and… writing their congressman	… writing a 5-page letter of support
During Monday first homeroom period, students will prepare weekly calendars of assignments and prioritize time to meet the needs of the school, family, self.	Personal Development / Self-management	Organization	During Monday first homeroom period…	… students will prepare weekly calendars of assignments and prioritize time …	… to meet the needs of the school, family, self.
After reviewing the lesson on anti-war demonstrations of the 1970s, students will prepare their own 5-minute demonstration that exemplifies two opposite positions on the impact of war in today's society.	Esthetic development / Cultural Appreciation	Characterization	After reviewing the lesson on anti-war demonstrations of the 1970s…	…students will prepare their own demonstration on the impact of war in today's society.	own five-minute demonstration … exemplifies two opposite positions…

For many educators, the use of affective objectives is downplayed because the criterion for success is so often not a simple pass/fail situation. Rather, achievement may lie somewhere on a continuum since it encompasses individual learner change. Krathwohl and his colleagues discovered that the levels of complexity within the affective domain were as predictable and progressive as they were within the cognitive domain.

Value development, personal development, and esthetic development represent three key processes targeting learning objectives in the affective domain. Value development includes appreciating the significance of self, others, and institutions. Personal development encompasses self-management, emotional management, and social management. Esthetic development gauges self-expression and cultural appreciation. Together, the five levels of the affective domain and the key processes join forces to create crucial learning objectives for the classroom. Table 4 offers some examples of objectives using common action verbs attributed to the affective domain.

Taxonomies for the Psychomotor Domain

Following the footsteps of Bloom and Krathwohl, Kibler et al. (1970) attempted to define the domain concerned with the physical dimensions of learning, from gross to fine movements and nonverbal to verbal activities. Psychomotor learning is demonstrated by physical skills, including, but not limited to: physical coordination and dexterity; simple and advanced object manipulation; refined movements involving grace, strength, and speed; actions which demonstrate the fine motor skills such as use of precision instruments or tools; and, actions which evidence gross motor skills such as the use of the body in dance or athletic performance.

Levels of the Psychomotor Taxonomy

Unlike the cognitive or affective domains that precede it, the psychomotor domain is characterized by its more tangible focus on the physical dimension of its sphere of influence. The various physical dimensions of the psychomotor domain are illustrated in Figure 2.

Figure 2. Various Foci of the Psychomotor Domain

Skill Development in the Psychomotor Domain (Kibler and Bloom, 1970)	Physical Development of Human Movement in the Psychomotor Domain (Little, 2002)	Kinesthetic Development in the Psychomotor Domain (Casey, 2001)
Imitation **Manipulation** **Precision** **Articulation** **Naturalization**	Reflex movements Fundamental movements Perceptual abilities Physical abilities Skilled movements Non-discursive communication	Perception Set Guided Response Mechanism Complex Overt Response Adaptation Origination

Kibler (1970) developed one of the first classification systems with a focus on observable, measurable, physical skill performance. Casey (2001) and Little (2003) added to the knowledge base by concentrating on the physical development of human movement. To further explore this important domain in more detail, Kibler's focus on outcome-based psychomotor skills will be used for the remainder of this chapter.

Imitation occurs at the earliest stages of human learning, often taking the form of a reflexive response. This first stage of the psychomotor domain characterizes initial mastery of complex skills. Learning begins with a readiness to tackle a particular activity or skill. Imitation entails repeating an act that has been demonstrated until the anticipated response is achieved.

As learners continue to practice specific skills or assimilate a successful sequence of activities, psychomotor development becomes routine and actions are performed with confidence and proficiency. *Manipulation* is more complex than imitation, but the learner still cannot be considered "skillful." The ability to perform the target kinesthetic activity in an easy, precise, harmonious way with constantly changing circumstances lies beyond this level of psychomotor development.

Precision encompasses the first level of the psychomotor domain in which a specific skill is mastered to the point that it can be considered an automatic response. Characterized by a quick, smooth, accurate performance requiring a minimum of energy, precision is performed without hesitation.

Articulation involves a higher level of performance. Here, the skill set of the learner is so well developed that the individual adapts and accommodates movements to fit new situations and demands in response to unique, never-before-encountered problem situations.

At the summit of the psychomotor domain, *naturalization* integrates learned responses into instinctive and effortless performance. The learner experiments with physical movement, creating new motor accomplishments to manipulate the environment as a direct result of understanding, ability, and skill. At this step of the taxonomy, the learner responds instinctively, more or less without thinking.

Action Verbs

The psychomotor domain runs the gamut from simple to highly complex motor skills. A skill is defined as the "ability to perform kinesthetic activity in an easy, precise, harmonious way with the constant changing circumstances," involving the senses, application of precision and accuracy, and timing (Hussain, 2003). Some common action verbs for the psychomotor domain are proposed in Table 5. In the particular case of the psychomotor domain, more action verbs are used interchangeably among levels than with any of the previous taxonomies.

Learning Objectives

Learning objectives in the psychomotor domain characteristically involve issues such as time of training, systematic practice, experience, quality of performance, repetition, and complex tasks (e.g., mastering the art of a musical

Table 5. Psychomotor Domain

Taxonomy Classification	Action Verbs that represent intellectual activity on this level
Imitation	Begin, assemble, attempt, carry out, copy, calibrate, construct, dissect, Duplicate, follow, mimic, move, practice, proceed, repeat, reproduce, respond, organize, sketch, start, try, volunteer, throw, run, swim, walk
Manipulation	Acquire, assemble, complete, conduct, do, execute, improve, maintain, make, manipulate, operate, pace, perform, produce, progress, use, type, tune an instrument, use workshop tools, drive a car
Precision	Achieve, accomplish, advance, automate, exceed, excel, master, reach, refine, succeed, surpass, transcend, use sign language, mime, use body language
Articulation	Adapt, alter, change, excel, rearrange, reorganize, revise, surpass, transcend, produce vowel sounds, recite a poem, speak comprehensively, transmit a verbal message
Naturalization	Arrange, combine, compose, construct, create, design, refine, originate, transcend

instrument). Physical-based objectives center their attention on motor skills coordination, participation in moderate to vigorous physical activities, basic non-locomotor movements (e.g., bend, twist, push, swing, shake) and locomotor movements (e.g., run, leap, hop, slide, skip), and the physical relationship between practice and the improvement of skills. The kinesthetic student learns better by taking notes; using their sense of touch to examine, explain, and explore; being exposed to new ideas via classroom demonstrations; personally practicing and acting out contemporary concepts; and, constructing and exhibiting learning in a tactile-based environment.

Table 6. Example Learning Objectives in the Psychomotor Domain

Example Learning Objective	Skill/ Physical/ Kinesthetic / Development	Taxonomy Level	Condition	Behavior(s)	Criteria
Students will complete a 12-minute walk/run test on a 40-meter track within prescribed times for their age group.	Physical	Imitation	…on a 40 meter track …	Students will complete a 12-minute walk/run test …	… within prescribed maximum times for their age group.
Students will achieve above the 70th percentile in four events: long jump, javelin throw, 100 meter dash, and hurdles based on set performance standards for their grade level.	Skill	Manipulation	… based on set performance standards for their grade level.	… in four events: long jump, javelin throw, 100-meter dash, and hurdles…	Students will be able to achieve above the 70th percentile…
Using word processing and multimedia software, students will create five expressive gestures expressing their favorite slang terms.	Physical	Articulation	Using word processing and multimedia software…	… create (five) expressive gestures expressing their favorite slang terms….	…five expressive gestures…
With selected background music, the student will perform a 2-minute dance routine that demonstrates the key elements of each style of dance.	Skill	Precision	With selected background music…	…the student will perform a 2-minute dance routine…	… that demonstrates (all) the key elements of each style of dance.

Objectives written for the psychomotor domain play on a student's desire to remain physically involved in the learning tasks at hand. They prefer to move when they think, role-play, or act out ideas. Such objectives also refer to natural, autonomic responses or reflexes.

Physical activities are not necessarily exclusive to the psychomotor domain. For example, objectives involving physical activity may remain in the affective or cognitive domain. An example of a physical task that supports cognitive development would be looking through a microscope and identifying and drawing cells. The instructional intent of this activity is not to develop proficiency in microscope viewing or in illustrating cell structure. Instead, the physical actions merely support thinking and recognition skills, both exclusive to the cognitive domain. The learner uses the psychomotor activity to achieve cognitive objectives, namely, to identify, recognize, and differentiate varied types of cells. If the physical activity supports cognitive or affective development, teachers should label the objective as such and avoid the term psychomotor (Harrow, 1972). Table 6 presents examples of learning objectives written for this domain.

Taxonomies for the Technology Domain

Prior to the end of the 20th century (or at least since the 1960s), teachers relied on taxonomies for the cognitive, affective, and psychomotor domains for constructing classroom-learning objectives. Technology has rapidly expanded its influence as a content area and as a tool for teaching and learning since its introduction into the classroom. Still, there has been no advancement toward establishing a separate classification system for technology-based instruction. However, in the 1997 issue of the Journal of Educational Computing Research, Bruce and Levin described a new way of classifying uses of educational technologies, based on a student focus.

It was John Dewey who first considered student learning to be governed by inquiry, communication, construction, and expression (Dewey, 1943). However, Bruce and Levin (1997) found them appropriate for classifying instructional technologies for the classroom as well. The authors' research came upon a stubborn conclusion concerning the future of educational technology. They found that the emergent forms of technology in the classroom could not be satisfactorily accommodated within the prevailing categories of the other domains. As a result, Bruce and Levin proposed their *Taxonomy of Technology as Media* convinced that educators would do well to view the media of technology as their own domain for learning.

Currier and Campbell (2000) introduced the *Scottish Electronic Staff Development Library (SeSDL) Taxonomy*. Although this taxonomy was developed primarily to facilitate the creation of an electronic library, it also drew considerable interest from educational technologists in general and those involved in the use of technology for teaching and learning in particular.

Together, the Technology as Media and the SeSDL taxonomies represent the first thinking into technology as its own domain for learning. The classification levels for designing, developing, and implementing technology-based instructional materials have contributed to the Taxonomy for the Technology Domain introduced here.

Taxonomy of Technology as Media

In 1997, Bruce and Levin stated, "We view the effects of technologies as operating to a large extent through the ways that they alter the environments for thinking, communicating, and acting in the world. Thus, they provide new media for learning…" (Bruce & Levin, 1997).

Technology as a media is not necessarily new. Advocates such as Marshall Mcluhan established the importance of media with his now famous "the media is the message" pronouncement (Mcluhan & Powers, 1989). However, with the advent of classroom technology, previous taxonomies for the cognitive, affective, and psychomotor domain found themselves if not obsolete, then at least deficient when dealing with technology skills and competencies. A new classification system for technology-based instruction was called for and Bruce and Levin are credited as the first educators to propose just such a system.

Levels of the Technology as Media Taxonomy

The authors chose the term "media" to shift the focus of their classification system from hardware and software to the learner. For Bruce and Levin, "media" implies an appreciation of the various functions of technology that link the learner to other learners, teachers, other technologies, ideas, and the real world. Combining a focus on the learner with the view of technology as media, they devised the following levels.

- **Media for Inquiry** characterizes technology as a media for thinking, connecting to the world, extending the senses, and solving real-world problems. Included in this level of the taxonomy is the use of technology for theory building via simulation software; virtual reality environments; models for understanding data, mathematics, and procedures; and, knowledge representation and integration. This level encompasses text, video, and data access by means of the Internet, libraries, and databases. Data collection and analysis is considered by the use of computer-based laboratories and spreadsheet, graphics, and problem-solving software.

- **Media for Communications** views technology as a vehicle for collaboration. Inherent at this level of the taxonomy is text-based word processing and desktop publishing; visual-based presentation graphics; communications-based electronic mail, asynchronous (e.g., bulletin boards) and synchronous (e.g., online chat rooms) conferencing; and Web-based hypertext environments. For Bruce and Levin, media for communications ranked second only to inquiry in the number of successful applications of technology at this level.

- **Media for Construction** serves as the application of technology in practice. Control systems, robotics, and computer-aided design and manufacturing represent technologies on this level of the taxonomy.

- Finally, **Media for Expression** addresses affective knowledge and integrate technologies such as draw and paint software, music composition and editing, interactive video and hypermedia, animation software, and multimedia.

Action Verbs

Unlike the progressive steps of previous taxonomies, technology as media harbors no such hierarchical structure. The Bruce and Levin taxonomy is not sequential, as is its application of technology for teaching and learning. Although

Table 7. Taxonomy for Technology (Media for Inquiry, Communication, Construction, and Expression)

Taxonomy Classification	Action Verbs that represent intellectual activity on this level
Media for Inquiry	Model, simulate, visualize, represent, outline, integrate, access, order, graph, collect, sense, survey, monitor, record, explore, analyze, process, problem solve
Media for Communication	Document, outline, graph, spell, express, publish, present, mail, conference, distribute, collaborate, decide (group), share, teach, tutor, simulate, instruct, drill and practice, mentor
Media for Construction	Control, design, construct, build, manufacture, assemble, collect, invent, fabricate, produce, engineer
Media for Expression	Draw, paint, compose, edit, animate, invent, compile, conceive, revise, amend, alter

matching levels of the taxonomy with appropriate action verbs was never a priority for the authors, an attempt is made here to extract operational terms (Table 7) from the original article (Bruce & Levin, 1997).

Learning Objectives

In order to test their taxonomy, the authors classified various technology-based learning projects according to media. Although many projects were placed in more than one level of the taxonomy due to their complexity, they were able to come to some conclusions about the application of at least three of the four levels. For example, they determined that the categories of inquiry and communication were responsible for most of the projects examined while construction and expression were rarely used. However, they readily admit that the emphasis of the studied projects were on mathematics and science and suggest further research on a comparable set of projects in other curricular areas. Table 8 provides a count of the number of observed projects in each of the four major categories.

An attempt is made here to provide an example learning objective in each of the technology media proposed by Bruce and Levin (Table 9).

Table 8. Number of Entries in Each Taxonomy Category (Bruce and Levin, 1997)

Category	Projects
Inquiry	43
Communication	27
Construction	3
Expression	0

Note: Several projects appear in more than one category and subcategory.

Table 9. Example Learning Objectives in the Technology Domain (Media for Inquiry, Communication, Construction, and Expression)

Example Learning Objective	Taxonomy Level	Condition	Behavior(s)	Criteria
Students will collect 30 days of weather-related statistics using a personal digital assistant outfitted with temperature gathering hardware and correctly graph and interpret the results using an Excel spreadsheet histogram format.	**Media for Inquiry**	… using a personal digital assistant outfitted with temperature gathering hardware …	Students will collect weather-related statistics … using an Excel spreadsheet histogram format	… collect 30 days… and correctly graph and interpret the results…
Students will collaborate on a project to publish and distribute a 30-page tourist pamphlet using desktop publishing software.	**Media for Communication**	… using desktop publishing software.	Students will collaborate on a project to publish and distribute a… tourist pamphlet	… a 30-page tourist pamphlet …
Students will design, construct, and test a simulated volcano eruption that lasts at least 30 seconds using only materials provided in the science lab.	**Media for Construction**	…using only materials provided in the science lab.	Students will design, construct, and test a simulated volcano eruption…	… that lasts at least 30 seconds …
Students will compose a poem in the haiku format and produce a Power Point multimedia presentation with at least 10 slides that exhibit the key features of the work.	**Media for Expression**	… "using" Power Point…	Students will compose a poem… and produce a multi-media presentation …	… with at least 10 slides that exhibit the key features of the work.

SeSDL Taxonomy of Technology

When Currier and Campbell developed the *Scottish Electronic Staff Development Library (SeSDL) Taxonomy,* they were primarily interested in a classification system that could be applied from the perspective of communications and information technology. They were concerned with the process of classifying electronic library resources that pertained to teaching and learning. SeSDL needed a hierarchical structure that reflected the way educational designers develop their instructional materials. Even so, the resulting arrangement of educational technology provides an excellent insight into how it can be effectively used in the classroom.

Levels of the Technology in the SeSDL Taxonomy

The authors propose 16 categories of educational technology. While these distinctions may be necessary for classifying electronic library resources, certain commonalities between levels seem to suggest a more manageable (and certainly less forgettable) accommodation of categories. The authors may not necessarily support such a restructuring of their schemata so it should be understood that the responsibility for this reclassification lies solely with this author.

From the unique perspective of educational technology as an electronic resource, Currier and Campbell devised the SeSDL taxonomy. SeSDL, like the other technology taxonomy examined earlier, is also not hierarchical in design. As such, using technology at the fourth level of the taxonomy does not imply mastery of, or dependence on, previous levels.

- **Computer-Mediated Communication** is the first category of the reordered taxonomy. At this level, learning is enhanced via collaboration and a virtual exchange of ideas using technologies such as asynchronous (electronic mail, bulletin boards, listservs, etc.) and synchronous (online chats, videoconferencing, etc.) communication.

- **Computer-Mediated Learning (CML)** focuses on environments that are an increasingly important part of the strategy for delivering learning. Many colleges (and a growing number of secondary school programs) have CML already in place. Relatively few, however, are using them with large numbers of students and many more are still trying to decide which environments to pursue. Technologies at this level include: virtual learning environments such as the WebCT, First Class, and Blackboard courseware; computer simulation, modeling, and assessment tools; and, educational multimedia such as video, CDROM, and streaming video.

- **Internet Services** deserves its own level of the taxonomy since it encompasses a rich and rapidly expanding inventory of resources. With Internet hosts skyrocketing from a mere one million machines in 1995 to near 110 million in 2001 (Rutkowski, 2001), the corresponding number of innovative services provided via the Web has also increased. In the beginning were electronic mail, telnet, file transfer, newsgroups and gopher. Now, we have the World Wide Web, search engines, digital resource centers, and educational portals. Some of the technologies at this level include Web browsers and search engines; gateways, databases, and Web sites; and, Web authoring tools including editors, Java applets, and Web publishing software.

- **Standards**, likewise, impact the use of educational technologies for teaching and learning to the degree that they merit their own level in this somewhat artificial taxonomy. In the technology domain, standards are engaged on two planes: technology and education. Technologically, norms are a crucial element of any practical application of new technology. The International Committee for Information Technology Standards (INCITS) is the leading proponent for standardization in the field of information and communications technologies (ICT) encompassing storage, processing, transfer, display, management, organization, and retrieval of information. The National Educational Technology Standards Project resulted in an acceptable set of criteria for both teachers and learners surrounding curriculum, administration, communications, and assessment and evaluation.

- **Educational Technology Hardware** represents the fifth classification level. In its original form, the SeSDL taxonomy includes computer networks and associated issues of human-computer interfaces and accessibility, and embedded technology.

- **Educational Technology Software** is the corollary to hardware; together they represent the final level of the taxonomy. They are nearly inseparable in discussions pertaining to the application of educational technology in the classroom. Per the SeSDL designers, software packages for teaching and learning mirror many of the preceding categories, including computer-mediated communications and learning environments, groupware, computer-aided assessment, and Web and multimedia authoring and design applications.

Action Verbs

As with Bruce and Levin's proposed classification system for educational technologies, appropriate action verbs are not historically available to support the application of communications and information technology at each level of the SeSDL taxonomy. As with the Taxonomy of Technology as Media, a similar attempt is made here to offer operational terms (Table 10) to support discussion of the model.

Learning Objectives

Example learning objectives, appropriate for the SeSDL taxonomy, are shown in Table 11 for several levels of classification.

Table 10. SeSDL Taxonomy

Taxonomy Classification	Action Verbs that represent intellectual activity on this level
Computer Mediated Communication	E-mail, word process, share, conference, network, chat, post, videoconference, send, discuss, relay, reply, consult, distribute, interact, exchange (ideas)
Computer Mediated Learning	Teach, learn, design, develop, model, assess, simulate, interact, explore, evaluate, synthesize, analyze, test, represent, prototype, cooperate, study, investigate, survey, imitate, replicate
Internet Services	Surf, search, browse, author, program, code, design, publish, investigate, point and click, link, encode
Standards	Document, comply, store, process, transfer, display, manage, organize, retrieve, practice, demonstrate, charge, measure, judge, copyright, protect
Educational Technology Hardware	Network, interact, access, embed, log on, mouse, point and click, upgrade, keyboard
Educational Technology Software	Load, setup, install program, hyperlink, collaborate, author, simulate, fabricate, build, outline, brainstorm

Table 11. Example Learning Objectives in the SeSDL Technology Domain

Example Learning Objective	Taxonomy Level	Condition	Behavior(s)	Criteria
Given a teacher-made Web page, students will link to four sites pertaining to the Holocaust and answer workbook questions 12 – 25 with 90 percent accuracy.	**Internet Services**	Given a teacher-made Web page… and workbook …	…students will link to four sites pertaining to the Holocaust and answer questions 12 – 25…	… with 90 percent accuracy.
Using the Blackboard learning environment, students will interact with the teacher and their peers via 10-min synchronous communications sessions following the rules for online chats provided.	**Computer Mediated Learning** and **Standards**	Using the Blackboard learning environment… and… rules for online chats provided.	…students will interact with the teacher and their peers via 10-min synchronous communications sessions…	…following the rules for online chats provided.
Using electronic mail and a word processor, French II students will prepare a two-page letter of introduction free of grammar or syntax errors and successfully e-mail the letter to their assigned virtual pen pal.	**Computer Mediated Communication**	Using electronic mail and a word processor…	… French II students will prepare a… letter of introduction… and successfully e-mail the letter to their assigned virtual pen pal.	…prepare a two-page letter free of grammar or syntax errors and successfully e-mail the letter

Summary

Since its introduction into the classroom, little advancement has been made toward establishing a separate classification system for technology-based instruction. Bruce and Levin were first on the scene with their portrayal of technologies from the perspective of media. Their *Taxonomy of Technology as Media* included points of media for communications, construction, and expression. Currier and Campbell continued the expansion of technology with the *Scottish Electronic Staff Development Library (SeSDL) Taxonomy*. Here, technology was viewed from the perspective of communications and information technology and classified as computer-mediated communication, computer-mediated learning, Internet services, standards, educational technology hardware, and educational technology software.

Conclusion

Taxonomies are tools. Learning objectives consciously prepared in the cognitive, affective, and psychomotor domains produce more successful learning outcomes. They simply do a better job of matching teaching strategies with student learning. It is time that instructional technologies join the pedagogical debate that has shaped much of this research base in the past.

Knowledge, comprehension, application, analysis, synthesis, and evaluation represent the cognitive domain and are arguably the most recognized classification levels, thanks in large measure to Benjamin Bloom.

Receiving, responding, valuing, organizing, and characterizing distinguish the affective domain and the teaching of value development, personal growth, and esthetic maturity.

In the psychomotor domain, imitation, manipulation, precision, articulation, and naturalization provide the corresponding levels of maturation of human motor skills.

Technology as Media and the SeSDL taxonomies represent early efforts into technology as the "study of all things technical." As we have seen, each attempt made its mark and advanced the discipline to recognize technology as a domain of teaching and learning in its own right on par with Bloom and his colleagues.

References

Bloom, B.S., Englehart, M.B., Furst, E.J., Hill, W.H., & Krathwohl, D.L. (1956). *Taxonomy of educational objectives. The classifications of educational goals. Handbook I.*

Bloom, B.S., Engelhart, M.D., Furst, E.J., Hill, W.H., & Krathwohl, D.R. (1974). *Taxonomy of educational objectives.* New York: David McKay.

Brown, J., & Farber, I.E. (1951). Emotions conceptualized as intervening variables—with suggestions toward a theory of frustration. *Psychological Bulletin, 48.*

Bruce, B.C., & Levin, J.A. (1997). Educational technology: Media for inquiry, communication, construction, and expression. *Journal of Educational Computing Research, 17*(1).

Casey, H. (2001). University of Louisiana at Monroe. *Developing instructional objectives*. Retrieved July 5, 2001 from the World Wide Web: *http://www.ulm.edu/~rakes/555/objectives/index.htm*

Currier, S., & Campbell, R. (2000, December). SeSDL taxonomy evaluation report. Retrieved from the World Wide Web: *http://www.sesdl.scotcit.ac.uk:8082/ taxon_eval/ SeSDLTaxFinRep.doc*

Dewey, J. (1943). *The child and the curriculum: The school and society.* Chicago: University of Chicago Press.

Harrow, A.J. (1972). *A taxonomy of the psychomotor domain*. New York: David McKay.

Hussain, A.A. (2003). *Psychomotor domain*. Retrieved January 31, 2003 from the World Wide Web: *http://www.geocities.com/eltsqu/ Psycho.htm*

International Society for Technology in Education (ISTE). (2003, December). *National Educational Technology Standards (NETS) for students, teachers, and administrators*. Retrieved from the World Wide Web: *http://cnets.iste.org*

Kibler, R.J., Barker, L.L., & Miles, D.T. (1970). *Behavioral objectives and instruction*. Allyn & Bacon Publishers.

Krathwohl, D.L., Bloom, B.S., & Masia, B.B. (1964). *Taxonomy of educational objectives: The classifications of educational goals. Handbook II.*

Little, J.K. (2003). College of Education, University of Tennessee. *Exploring the world of instructional technologies*. Retrieved February 7, 2003 from the World Wide Web: *http://itc.utk.edu/~jklittle/edsmrt521/*

McLuhan, M., & Powers, B. R. (1989). *The global village, transformations in world, life and nedia in the 21st century*. Oxford University Press.

Rutkowski (2001). *Internet growth charts*. Information Navigators. Retrieved February 7, 2001 from the World Wide Web: *http:// navigators.com/stats.html*

Scherer, K.R. (1984). *On the nature and function of emotion: A component process approach*. Hillsdale, NJ: Erlbaum Publishing.

Annotated Bibliography

Additional citations for the Taxonomies of Education

Gardner, H. (1993). *Frames of mind: The theory of multiple intelligences.* Basic Books.

Gardner, H. (1999). *Intelligence reframed: Multiple intelligences for the 21st century.* Basic Books.

Jonassen, D.H., Hannum, W.H., & Tessmer, M. (1989). Bloom's Taxonomy of educational objectives. In *Handbook of task analysis procedures.* New York: Praeger.

Chapter 4

Technology and Education:
The Implications

Introduction

This chapter establishes the critical relationships between technology and the foundations of education described in previous chapters. The domains, psychologies, and taxonomies of education provide the essentials upon which the Taxonomy for the Technology Domain is built and uncovered in subsequent chapters. It provides a foothold for further exploration in order to reveal the true impact and effect of this newest classification system for teaching and learning.

As an advanced organizer, Table 1 presents a list of some instructional technologies discussed in this and the remaining chapters.

Table 1. Advanced Organizer for Instructional Technologies

Instructional Technologies (Note: technologies are repeated only once but may be implicated in multiple domains, psychologies, or taxonomies)	Implications in ...
• Instructional design systems • Technology-based "cognitive tools" • Computer-based instructional systems • Software engineering • Intelligent performance support systems • Knowledge construction environments	Cognitive Domain
• Internet-based programs and curriculum • Digital technology • Telecommunications	Affective Domain
• "Low-tech" technologies • Implementing technologies • Video and audio technology	Psychomotor Domain
• Programmed instruction • Computer-assisted instruction	Behavioral Psychology
• Computer-based teaching • Computer-delivered instruction • Computer-managed instruction	Cognitive Psychology
• Electronic mail and the Internet • Word processing and desktop publishing software • Graphics presentation software	Humanistic Psychology
• Hyperlinks, Web quests, and online virtual tours • Collaborative communications tools • Graphic organizers	Cognitive Taxonomy
• "Low-tech" technologies • Multimedia-rich technologies • Advanced telecommunications • Virtual learning teams • E-books, digital libraries, and virtual online universities • Wireless laptop computers and computer networks • Emerging technologies (Shockwave, Java, HTML scripting, etc.)	Affective Taxonomy
• Personal assistive technologies • Technology-assisted software • Feedback hardware • Biomechanics technologies	Psychomotor Taxonomy
• Calculators and graphing calculators • Integrated services digital network (ISDN) • Cable access television network (CATV) • Wireless, point-to-point, satellite and cellular (mobile) communications	Technology Taxonomy (Developmental)

Technology and Domains of Teaching

Cognitive Domain

The widespread integration of instructional technology into classrooms has included new developments, with potential impact on instruction, cognition, and student learning. These developments range from innovative research and literature espousing basic theory to practical applications for the classroom to recommended curricula integrating technology-based methodologies and other state-of-the-art techniques.

Technology-Based Implications for Teaching

The application of technology has raised fundamental questions regarding successful learning outcomes. Exploring the impact of instructional technology on the cognitive domain surfaces new questions regarding how various technologies are successfully integrated into a curriculum in ways that make an observable difference in how students learn.

Instructional design systems provide practical applications of cognitive learning theories. The implementation of technology-based instructional classroom materials offers a starting point in understanding the relationships between the design of technological tools, the use of those tools in educational settings, and the implications of that use for cognitive learning.

Technology-based "cognitive tools" examine automated learning systems, simulation and automated performance aids, and tools that enhance and extend the teacher in the classroom (e.g., smart boards, videoconferencing equipment, digital cameras, projection systems, etc.).

Computer-based instructional systems (e.g., software-based tutoring, simulations, hypermedia, multimedia environments, and intelligent tutoring systems) are changing the way students comprehend new knowledge and represent that knowledge in their own schema for learning.

Software engineering has forever altered how a curriculum is designed and how instruction is organized for classroom purposes, which are key aspects of a cognitive learning strategy. "Altered modes of knowledge management, in turn, change our ways of sensing, observing and knowing, with profound consequences for every aspect of human culture" (Kelber, 1995). Software engineering, instructional design systems, and knowledge construction environments evolved from the application of technology in the cognitive domain.

Intelligent performance support systems determine what a learner already knows based on behavior, performance, and other observable activities, and use technology itself to determine a student's level of knowledge.

Finally, technology manifests itself in sophisticated computer-based *knowledge construction environments* playing a key role in understanding the interactions of existing information, the cognitive processes associated with the acquisition of new knowledge and skills, and the ways in which information changes over time as a result of interactions between the learner and the environment.

In short, some aspects of knowledge dissemination are better represented by technology; others are not. Some technologies affect knowledge reception, representation, reconstruction, and recall; others produce little impact. Some implementations of technology test, diagnose, and remediate student learning; others contribute little to observable increases in teaching and learning outcomes. Finally, certain technologies enhance interaction and collaboration between teachers and learners leaving other technologies to augment human decision-making and the time-intensive instructional design process.

Conversely, for each of the technology-enhanced aspects of cognitive learning, examples linger of how technology cannot and should not be employed. Ideally, technology-based applications of cognitive tools are rooted in realistic contexts with results that are personally meaningful for learners. At its base, the impact of the cognitive domain on technology seeks answers to the following questions: How best can a teacher use technologies in the classroom? How will this technology-enriched activity enhance learning for students? How will the teacher know when the use of classroom technology is ineffective? If the application of technology is successful, how can its use be integrated into the curriculum so that all learners benefit?

Affective Domain

Literature that explores the affective use of instructional technology is sparse at best. The trend in educational research is to downplay the affective domain in favor of cognitive study across the board. Statistics indicate an appalling lack of articles related to the affective impact of technology on student learning, a situation that is not expected to change in the foreseeable future.

Technology-Based Implications for Teaching

Where the affective domain is addressed in learning theory literature at all, it tends to occur mostly in regards to emotions (Miller, 1991). Classroom behaviors involving responsibility, self-esteem, sociability, self-management, integrity, and honesty are often the only focus of affective research in technology.

In a recent online search of *"Internet-based programs"* and *"curriculum"* (using the Yahoo search engine), over 52.4 million sites contained science-related keywords while only 829,000 (1.5%) of the sites were ethics-related, 429,000 (0.8%) addressed self-esteem, 589,000 (1.1%) integrity, and 268,000 (0.5) honesty. Ultimately, given the importance of developing technical skills involving the affective domain, a major re-focus is in order to uncover those behaviors vital to the development of student feelings and emotions.

Consider the impact of the affective domain in the creation of technology-based instruction for the classroom. Successful classroom instruction, once the exclusive dominion of the university professor, has evolved from the written textbook (with the advent of the printing press), to audio (with the introduction of the dictaphone), to video (with the popularity of movies and videotape), and finally to digital (with the emergence of the electronic computer). For years, we have watched the effect of popular music on social attitudes. *Digital technology* has furthered this impact with the popularity of CD-ROM players, downloadable Web-based music collections, MP3 players, and music videos.

Without over-dramatizing the current situation, most educators would agree that the social conscience of the world community has been affected (positively or negatively) by global *telecommunications*. E-mail, the Internet, and online chat rooms have added to the electronic forums of previously far-flung societies, coalescing the human race into a global value system unimagined only a few short decades ago. The World Wide Web, instantaneous telecommunications, and multimedia technology has changed forever the expectations of the student in the classroom.

The clear indication is that the design and development of technology-based classroom resources that address only the cognitive domain without attending to other domains neglects a major component of successful teaching. Yet, by and large, this is the current circumstance in which teachers find themselves. It remains an enigma that the field of education has chosen to ignore the proposition that "emotions may influence cognition at least as much as cognition influences emotion" (Meyers & Cohen, 1990). The Taxonomy for the Technology Domain attempts to more fully explore the impact of the affective domain on existing pedagogical and androgogical models of learning and to reduce the overly mechanistic influence of the cognitive domain in the development of technology-based learning materials in support of a more holistic approach to learning and learners.

Psychomotor Domain

To determine the impact of instructional technology on the development of psychomotor skills, teachers must consider several factors and their effects on student learning. First, where does the particular skill falls on a continuum from simple, reflexive competencies to more complex, strategy-based abilities? Skills are also categorized based on whether the learner, the physical object, or both are at rest or in motion. Finally, psychomotor skills are placed in one category if they are characterized with distinct beginning and ending points (e.g., clicking the mouse on a computer) or another category if they involve determining how they relate to the environment (e.g., bowling, running, basketball, hockey).

Technology-Based Implications for Teaching

Most early instruction in psychomotor skills is planned as a variation of a three-stage model: basic minimum knowledge, demonstration of more complex actions, and development of proficiency. Simple tasks with limited background knowledge are demonstrated and explained using a variety of unpretentious instructional technologies, oftentimes called *"low-tech" technologies*. For example, basic computer skills include keyboarding, mouse operations of pointing and clicking, and media preparation (inserting diskettes into floppy, zip, and CD-ROM drives). More complex tasks require new knowledge to be more effectively mastered through observation. Instruction is assisted in this endeavor by *implementing technologies* such as smart boards, simulation software, and overhead and LCD projection systems. Complex tasks, involving a large amount of new knowledge may be learned better through exploratory activities involving the Internet and selected Web sites.

Categories of skills based on motion distinguish among psychomotor learning that occurs when both the learner and the object are at rest, when the learner works with a moving object, when the learner works with a stable object, or when both the learner and the object are in motion. Various technologies come into play at each level. *Video technology* (VCRs and videodiscs) is most suited for teaching psychomotor skills in which the learner is in motion while the object to be manipulated is at rest. Successful instructional materials have been developed that demonstrate the steps required to play an instrument.

The psychomotor domain is inextricably linked to instructional technology at every level of learner development. Some technology, such as *audio and audio-conferencing*, encourages skill acquisition according to verbal cues rather than observation and provides more interaction when both learner and object are otherwise inactive, classroom lecture being a straightforward example.

Technology and Psychologies of Learning

Behaviorism

Behaviorism is a natural extension of the most observable characteristics of technology-enhanced learning. For example, students acquire negative attitudes about school because they associate the experience with unpleasant outcomes such as bad grades or embarrassing confrontations.

Technology-Based Implications for Teaching

Programmed instruction works as a self-paced instructional package to present topics in a carefully planned sequence. It requires the learner to respond to questions or statements by filling in blanks, selecting from a series of answers, or solving problems. Immediate reinforcement occurs after each response as students work in a self-paced mode. The program itself is often incorporated into books, teaching machines, or computers.

Those who do not support programmed instruction in their own classroom acknowledge that it can improve learning, presenting even the most difficult subjects in small steps so that all students succeed. It was Skinner who first proposed the use of teaching machines designed specifically for this purpose. He disclosed the potential benefits of behavior-oriented machines in the classroom. For example, he found that the time between responses and their reinforcement was often too long. For the behaviorist, the immediacy of reinforcement is an important factor in learning. Returning test papers two weeks after an examination poses a serious instructional dilemma. So does the relative infrequency in the consistent use of reinforcement in many classrooms. Finally, there is a lack of organized instructional sequence when teaching complex skills. Skinner believed that teaching machines could successfully address all these concerns.

Computer-Assisted Instruction (CAI) makes firsthand use of technology as its primary instructional media. Deployment of the personal computer in schools created an environment conducive to individualized instruction. CAI uses the computer to present information, provide students with opportunities to practice and re-practice what they learn, and offer additional remedial instruction when required. CAI programs serve three basic functions in schools.

First, the predominant use of CAI is *drill and practice,* those activities found in the basic skills areas to improve speed or accuracy. Drill-and-practice programs provide repeated exercises and individual feedback on designated learning objectives. By working with the computer, it is possible to tailor the type and amount of practice to a student's individual needs.

Simulation programs provide students with opportunities to improve their decision-making or problem-solving skills. They simulate activities that cannot be done in the classroom because they are too expensive, dangerous, or time consuming. A good simulation program focuses on the target phenomenon without extraneous information to distract the student. It also provides a more accurate representation of the phenomenon being studied.

The third category of CAI programs is *tutorials*, which are designed to teach new subject materials. These programs often consist of several screens of textual material followed by an exercise or assessment. Most tutorials adapt instruction by using a student's prior performance to determine what material to present, its level of difficulty, and the rate of the presentation.

Programmed instruction and computer-assisted instruction have a moderately positive effect on student achievement (Rubin, 1996). Drill and practice, simulation, and tutorials, especially, appear to be more successful when supplementing the regular classroom instruction rather than replacing it entirely. The positive synergy of behaviorism and technology is, as might be expected, more significant for elementary and secondary students than college–level, adult learners. Combined with an understanding of teaching and learning provided by the Taxonomy for the Technology Domain, behaviorally-oriented technology overcomes barriers to learning by offering the student an alternative delivery system from basic literacy skills to the study of technology at the highest levels.

Cognitivism

The cognitive school of educational psychology centers on the study of mental functioning, how our minds work, how we think, how we remember, and ultimately, how we learn. Since the time of behaviorism, evidence has been accumulated indicating that people do more than simply respond to reinforcement and punishment. With the growing realization that learning is an active mental process, educational psychologists became interested in how people learn simple and complex concepts and how they approach solutions to problems. As cognitivism matured over the last 40 years, two subordinate schools of thought have emerged: the older views of cognitive psychology emphasize the acquisition of knowledge, while the more contemporary viewpoint sees the construction of knowledge as all-important. These two distinct but related perspectives are evident in the goals of cognitive education that serve to help students process information in meaningful ways so that they can become independent learners (Dembo, 1994).

Technology-Based Implications for Teaching

Instruction for the cognitivist encourages the use of appropriate learning strategies. Reception learning is an instructional strategy that details how learners successfully acquire knowledge, concentrating more on the process of reception than discovery. Rote memory, for example, is not considered meaningful learning. Memorization does not help the learner connect new information with existing knowledge. Expository teaching, on the other hand, encourages meaningful learning when teachers present material in a carefully organized, sequenced, and finished form.

Optimal learning generally occurs when there is a potential match between the learner and the material to be learned. To foster this association, technology supports reception learning and expository teaching via *computer-based teaching* (CBT) and *computer-delivered instruction* (CDI) both of which replicate the steps in cognitive development with respect to the presentation, sequencing, and delivery of new knowledge and its progression deductively from the general to the specific. Lessons begin with an advanced organizer, an introductory statement of a relationship of high-level concepts, broad enough to encompass all the information that will follow (Ausubel, 1963).

Discovery learning embraces the scientific model. Here, learners identify problems, generate hypotheses, test those hypotheses against collected data, and apply conclusions to new situations. The purpose is not so much the acquisition of knowledge as the ability to advanced student thinking skills. In discovery learning, technology in the form of *computer-managed instruction* (CMI) provides resources that address student-developed questions in order to help them grasp a principle or abstraction. Teachers use technology to order the examples in the lesson and ensure that reference materials and equipment are readily available. Discovery learning encourages students to actively use their intuition, imagination, and creativity. Applied in the classroom, technology-supported techniques are evidenced when CMI presents both examples and non-examples of the target concept, helps learners recognize the connections among concepts, poses questions that push students to find their own answers, and, encourages learners to make intuitive guesses and then to test the efficacy of their hypotheses with the real world. Such characteristics define the best in CMI resources.

Cognitivists view knowledge as the outcome of learning and its driving force. In many ways, this school of educational psychology is not only the most widely accepted, but also the most pervasive in its explanation of how learning occurs. The Information Processing Model, a fundamental archetype of the cognitivist perspective, views memory as a computer metaphor. Like the computer, the human mind takes in information, performs operations on it to change its form and content, stores the information, retrieves it when needed, and generates responses to it. Building schemata (reception learning), integrating units of instruction (discovery learning), and modeling teaching and learning after the computer (information processing model) — what better proponents of the Taxonomy for the Technology Domain!

Humanism

From a humanistic perspective, teachers concern themselves with creating a learning environment that is more responsive to the affective needs of their students. Affective needs include those related to a student's emotions, feelings, values, and attitudes. For example: (a) understanding the needs of the learner and creating educational experiences that develop their unique potential; (b) seeking to foster the self-actualization of each learner by personalizing educational decisions and practices; (c) developing a learning climate that is challenging, understanding, supportive, exciting, and free from threat; (d) recognizing the importance of human feelings, values, and perceptions in the educational process; and, (e) developing in learners a genuine concern and respect for the worth of others and skill in resolving conflicts.

Technology-Based Implications for Teaching

In cooperative learning, students work together in small (four to six member) teams that may remain constant for many weeks. Some teachers are of the mistaken notion, however, that simply assigning individual projects and allowing students to interact somehow satisfies the criteria for cooperative learning. Other teachers envision students sitting together as they do their homework, asking each other questions, and offering responses as proof of cooperative learning in action. More contemporary teachers consider broadening the cooperative learning experience using *electronic mail* and the *Internet*, both of which promote learning with a greater degree of technical sophistication.

Open education as a teaching model calls for diversity of manipulative materials. It encourages self-diagnosis where students (or the technology) assess their own work. Individualized instruction shuns textbooks or workbooks. Instead, teachers take notes and assess students one-on-one with formal testing held to an absolute minimum. Finally, professional growth becomes a lifelong learning aspiration as teachers seek assistance from a variety of resources to work with colleagues outside their own classroom. Teachers who adopt open education as a teaching style understand the possibilities of new technologies available to today's classroom teacher.

Text-based materials are prepared with the technological assistance of *word processors* and *desktop publishing software*. Visual-based classroom lessons and interactive student-based instruction are created using *graphics presentation software* such as Power Point, Apple Works, Authorware, and hyper-studio technology. Such teacher-designed instructional materials allow the learner to choose among tasks and activities that contribute to learning. Teachers serve as role models for the learning attitudes, beliefs and habits they wish to foster in their students.

The development of instructional technology is often attributed to the interplay among the various schools as they shape the latest research pertaining to personal learner characteristics, teaching strategies, student learning styles, and the political and social demands placed on schools. As such, the field of instructional technology itself has come to serve as another in a long line of innovative teaching strategies.

Technology and Taxonomies of Education

Taxonomies

The introduction of technologies into the cognitive, affective, and psychomotor domains is a relatively recent phenomenon. Research continues to confirm that instruction consciously prepared in these domains produces a higher occurrence of successful student learning outcomes. Taxonomies simply do a more thorough job of matching teaching strategies with student learning, including technology skills and competencies.

Technology-Based Implications for Teaching

It is not surprising that with the relatively recent adoption of technology as both an academic discipline in its own right and a tool for learning, the predominant taxonomies of Bloom (1956), Krathwohl (1964), Kibler (1970), and Bruce and Levin (1997) have yet to impact the design of technology-based instructional materials to the degree they have other instructional patterns.

Technologies are represented throughout the various levels of the taxonomy for the cognitive domain. The lower levels integrate simple technologies like *graphics presentations* projected on a single computer display, intelligent while boards, or conference room screens. At the moderate levels of the taxonomy, the learner becomes more engaged in the pursuit of information that leads to a better understanding of issues, questions, and concepts. *Hyperlinks, Web quests* (i.e., *online virtual tours*), and *collaborative communications tools* such as electronic mail, bulletin boards, and chat rooms come into play. At the highest levels, individuals analyze materials or ideas by manipulation, organization, and representation in order to make educated assessments and complex judgments. *Graphic organizers* such as Inspiration and Kidspiration promote such brainstorming demands and higher order thinking exercises.

The affective domain embraces many technologies associated with emotions and feelings. Receiving and responding, the two initial levels of the taxonomy, involve traditional *"low-tech" technologies* such as tape recorders, overhead projectors, film projectors, radio and television, and even telephones. Adopting new values (mid-level on the taxonomy) is advanced by *multimedia-rich technologies* such as simulations and role-playing software, discovery learning educational software, and *advanced telecommunications* such as videoconferencing, Web meetings, and distance learning. Scholtz and Wyrley-Birch (2001) found that internalizing new values (the top level of the affective domain) is advanced by integrating technology-based affective experiences into the curriculum using collaborative teaching technologies (*virtual learning teams*), relevant computer hardware and software (*e-books and digital libraries*), computer learning environments (*virtual online universities, wireless laptop computers and computer networks*), and emerging technologies suitable for a student-centered teaching approach (*Shockwave, Java, HTML scripting*, etc.).

The psychomotor domain is often viewed from the strictly physical aspect of learning, an acutely shortsighted interpretation of "learning by doing." This traditional domain has also been referred to as "perceptual-motor skills." Technology has inextricably linked itself to aspects of effective learning in this domain. The lower levels of the psychomotor taxonomy include *personal assistive technologies* (TDD/TTY personal communications devices, input devices and environmental controls, and low-vision products), *technology-assisted software* (text magnifier, screen readers, speech synthesizers, and speech recognition products), and *feedback hardware* (audio and videotape feedback, loco-motor and object manipulation systems, self-referenced replay, and corrective and qualitative information). At higher levels of the taxonomy, more specialized *biomechanics technologies* come into play, including technique/stress equipment, high speed filming and videography, and electronic motion analysis.

The technology taxonomies of Bruce & Levin and the Scottish Electronics Staff Development Library (SESDL) contributed many of the earliest applications of technology for teaching and learning. A myriad of technologies at the lowest levels of these classifications provide capabilities to model, simulate, and otherwise mediate information. Appropriate technologies here include *calculators and graphing calculators*, *databases* and their report-writing features, spreadsheets and their "what-if" scenarios, and the *Internet* with its plethora of modeling and simulation sites.

In an attempt to avoid unnecessary repetition, other communications technologies not previously discussed include a host of capabilities spanning the traditional telephone to *integrated services digital network (ISDN)*, *cable access television network (CATV)*, and *wireless, point-to-point, satellite or cellular (mobile) communications*. At the higher end of the taxonomy, Shetland Islands Council Education Department offered the best descriptors of appropriate technologies in Language Arts: text processing, simulations, adventure games and information handling; in Mathematics: spreadsheets, databases, graph drawing packages, turtle graphics, simulations; in Environmental Studies: control packages, data handling packages to collect, store, analyze and interpret information, simulations; in Fine Arts: graphics, drawing and design packages, music making packages; and, in Religious and Moral Education: text processing and simulations (Shetland Education Authority, 1995).

Conclusion

This chapter establishes the essential and requisite links between technology and the very foundations of education. This chapter brings to a close the preliminary examination of the contributing principles of teaching and learning necessary to set the stage for the introduction of the newest Taxonomy for the Technology Domain. The domains, psychologies, and taxonomies of education presented in Chapter 1, Chapter 2, and Chapter 3, respectively, provide the very foundation upon which the Taxonomy for the Technology Domain was built. You are encouraged not to dismiss this primer out of hand. Doing so places the educator at risk when applying the new taxonomy and its levels of technological relevance to the lesson goals and learning objectives of technology-based units of instruction.

References

Ausubel, D. P. (1963). *Educational psychology: A cognitive view*. New York: Holt, Rinehart and Winston.

Bloom, B.S., Englehart, M.B., Furst, E.J., Hill, W.H., & Krathwohl, D.L. (1956). *Taxonomy of educational objectives: The classifications of educational goals*. New York: Allyn & Bacon/Longman/Pearson Publishers.

Bloom, B.S., Krathwohl, D.L., & Masia, B.B. (1964). *Taxonomy of educational objectives: Affective domain*. New York: Allyn & Bacon/Longman/Pearson Publishers.

Bruce, B.C., & Levin, J.A. (1997). Educational technology: Media for inquiry, communication, construction, and expression. *Journal of Educational Computing Research, 17*(1).

Dembo, M. (1994). *Applying educational psychology in the classroom* (5th edition). New York: Longman.

Kibler, R.J., Barker, L.L., & Miles, D.T. (1970). *Behavioral objectives and instruction*. New York: Allyn & Bacon/Longman/Pearson Publishers.

Rubin, A. (1996, May). *Educational technology: Support for inquiry-based learning model schools partnership*, Research Monograph. Retrieved from the World Wide Web: *http://ra.terc.edu/publications/TERC_pubs/tech-infusion/ed_tech/ed_tech_intro.html*

Scholtz, D., & Wyrley-Birch, B. (2001, March). *Content and language integration: Two experiences*. Conference on Language Integration, Peninsula Technikon, Cape Town South Africa. Retrieved from the World Wide Web: *http://www.pentech.ac.za/pil88/abstract35.htm*

Shetland Education Authority. (1995, April). *Information technology: Understanding and using information technology*. Shetland Islands Council Education Department. Retrieved from the World Wide Web: *http://www.zetnet.co.uk/sea.jnp*

Annotated Bibliography

Additional citations for Technology and Education

Brook, D. (2002, July). *Human education should be humanistic: A progressive philosophy of teaching* (revised). Retrieved from the World Wide Web: *http://www.angelfire.com/or3/tss2/dbteach.html*

Cohen, E.G. (1994). *Designing groupwork* (2nd edition). New York: Teachers College Press.

DeCarvalho, R. (1991). The humanistic paradigm in education. *The Humanistic Psychologist, 19*(1).

Gardner, H. (1993). *Frames of mind: The theory of multiple intelligences.* Boulder, CO: Basic Books.

Gardner, H. (1999). *Intelligence reframed: Multiple intelligences for the 21st century.* Boulder, CO: Basic Books.

Gianconia, R., & Hedges, L. (1982). Identifying features of effective open education. *Review of Educational Research, 52*(4).

Kelber, W. (1995). Modalities of communication, cognition and sense perception: Orality, rhetoric, scribality. *Semeia: An Experimental Journal for Biblical Criticism.*

Krathwohl, D.L., & Bloom, B.S. (1984). *Taxonomy of educational objectives: The classifications of educational goals. Handbook I.* New York: Addison-Wesley/Pearson Publishers.

May, M. (2000, January). Push on to get home computers to poor students. *San Francisco Chronicle.*

Melton, R.F. (1990). The changing face of educational technology. *Educational Technology.*

Meyers, A. W., & Cohen, R. (1990). Cognitive-behavioural approaches to child psychopathology: Present status and future directions. In M. Lewis & S. M. Miller (Eds.), *Handbook of developmental psychopathology.* New York: Plenum Press.

Miller, B.A. (1991). A review of qualitative research on multi-grade instruction. *Journal of Research in Rural Education.*

National Educational Technology Standards for Students: Connecting Curriculum and Technology (ISTE). (2000). Retrieved from the World Wide Web: *http://cnets.iste.org/*

Rogers, C. (1969). *Freedom to learn* (1st edition). New York: Macmillan/Merrill.

Rogers, C., & Freiberg, H. J. (1994). *Freedom to learn* (3rd edition). New York: Macmillan/Merrill.

Tomei, L.A. (2001). *Writing learning objectives using a taxonomy for the technology domain.* Duquesne University, School of Education. Unpublished manuscript.

Chapter 5

Taxonomy for the Technology Domain

Introduction

Many educators accept teaching with technology as perhaps the most important instructional strategy to impact the classroom since the textbook. The Taxonomy for the Technology Domain offers an equivalent view for using technology to enhance student learning. Of course, the very nature of a taxonomy reduces in scope whatever is being categorized because of its tendency to artificially place items into all too convenient "pockets." However, the benefits for teachers who understand the advantages of classifications greatly outweigh the limitations.

Research shows that teachers who use a classification scheme to prepare instructional learning objectives tend to produce successful student learning outcomes (Kibler, Barker, & Miles, 1970; Krathwohl & Bloom, 1984). The complete Taxonomy for the Technology Domain is shown in Figure 1.

Figure 1.

Taxonomy Classification	Defining the Level of the Technology Taxonomy
Literacy Understanding Technology	**Level 1.0** The minimum degree of competency expected of teachers and students with respect to technology, computers, educational programs, office productivity software, the Internet, and their synergistic effectiveness as a learning strategy.
Collaboration Sharing Ideas	**Level 2.0** The ability to employ technology for effective interpersonal interaction.
Decision-Making Solving Problems	**Level 3.0** Ability to use technology in new and concrete situations to analyze, assess, and judge.
Infusion Learning with Technology	**Level 4.0** Identification, harvesting, and application of existing technology to unique learning situations.
Integration Teaching With Technology	**Level 5.0** The creation of new technology-based materials, combining otherwise disparate technologies to teach.
Tech-ology The Study of Technology	**Level 6.0** The ability to judge the universal impact, shared values, and social implications of technology use and its influence on teaching and learning.

Levels of the Taxonomy for the Technology Domain

The classification system proposed for the Technology Domain includes Literacy, Collaboration, Decision-Making, Infusion, Integration, and Tech-ology. As with most taxonomies, each step offers a progressive level of complexity by constructing increasingly multifaceted objectives addressing increasingly complex student learning outcomes

Literacy  Understanding Technology	**Level 1.0** The minimum degree of competency expected of teachers and learners with respect to technology, computers, educational programs, office productivity software, the Internet, and their synergistic effectiveness as a learning strategy.

Definition

Technology for Literacy (Level 1.0) represents the simplest level of technology-based learning. At this level of the taxonomy, literacy is defined as *"the minimum degree of competency expected of teachers and students with respect to technology, computers, educational programs, office productivity software, the Internet, and their synergistic effectiveness as a learning strategy."* The first rung on the technology ladder establishes the most fundamental literacies and basic technology skills necessary for the novice technological learner.

Technological literacy is fundamental to learning, every bit as critical as the traditional skills of reading, writing, and arithmetic. Rapidly changing technologies and increasing international competition characterize today's economy. Society has become complex, diverse, and mobile. Success depends on the ability to acquire technology-based skills and knowledge in order to become a contributing member of a high-technology educated citizenry.

Technological literacy does not require simply knowledge of how to use technology for word processing, spreadsheets, and Internet access. It also entails using these powerful tools for lifelong learning. Recognizing the importance of technological literacy, 80% of Americans feel teaching computer skills is "absolutely essential." More than three-quarters have encouraged a child to use a computer, and 86% believe that a computer is the most beneficial and effective product they could buy to expand their children's opportunities (US DOE, 1996).

Impact of Literacy on Learners

For the learner, literacy demands a level of skill and competency in the use of technology for personal application. At the outset, the list of required abilities appears daunting, including a basic understanding of technology, an appreciation of a growing inventory of technological hardware media, and the operation and application of complex operating systems, office productivity software, and basic software utilities (e.g., paint and draw, virus protection, communications and entertainment).

Literacy presupposes that the learner is able to "talk the talk," that is, to communicate with teachers and peers using developmentally appropriate and technically accurate terminology. The learner should be able to discuss common uses of technology, both inside and outside the classroom, and relate the consequences, both good and bad, of their application in the everyday world. A grasp of environmental responsibilities such as keeping technology safe from food and temperature-related hazards is also reasonable.

Hardware literacy requires the learner to identify basic components of technological media, describe how they function, demonstrate basic care and trouble-shooting, and generalize these capabilities among various hardware platforms. To be considered conversant in technology at this level, the learner must possess certain basic aptitudes related to keyboarding (e.g., use of left and right hand operations, use of spacebar, shift, enter, delete, backspace, etc., and input of alphabetic text at an equivalent rate to handwriting speed), mouse operations (e.g., point and click, wheel procedures, and the use of the right mouse button for triggering pop-down menus), and handling storage media (e.g., diskette and CD-ROM).

Software literacy obliges the learner to navigate within operating systems such as Microsoft Window and Apple O/S, recognizing similarities and differences among commands and functions. Learners must be able to identify and use menus, toolbars, pointers, icons, and pop-down menus, open and close applications, and perform necessary system maintenance operations such as disk repairs, virus protections, software setup and installation and updates. Related troubleshooting skills at this level include the use of editing and undo features, use of manuals and documentation, and familiarity with the various processes for resolving problems. Finally, a literate technology user understands available aids such as tutorials, wizards, templates, and online help manuals.

Impact of Literacy on Teachers

Literacy raises the bar for teachers as well. They must possess the self-same set of skills and competencies of the learner while simultaneously preparing themselves for the application of technology at each of the higher levels of the taxonomy. The teacher must stay abreast of the continual growth in emerging technologies and how these technologies will influence the classroom. A comfort level with the vernacular of technology is presumed. Modeling technology by demonstration and exhibition during instruction is expected. The personal exercise of productivity software and appropriate utilities is a given.

In addition, the teacher must attain a level of proficiency in literacy that encompasses the use of resources sufficient to engage technology in their own ongoing professional development and lifelong learning. Literacy pushes the teacher to "continually evaluate and reflect on professional practice to make informed decisions regarding the use of technology in support of student learning" (ISTE, 2003). Such prescriptions expand the familiarization of technology beyond the learner experience. Involved at this level of the taxonomy are technologies limited not to the desktop computer, but encompassing other high-tech devices such as calculators, personal digital assistants, audio and video devices, as well as other "low-tech" media found in the classroom. More importantly, these technologies must be selected based upon the cognitive, affective, and psychomotor learning strategies.

Collaboration **Sharing Ideas**	**Level 2.0** The ability to employ technology for effective interpersonal interaction.

Definition

Technology for Collaboration (Level 2.0) is defined as *"the ability to employ technology for effective interpersonal interaction."* Effective uses of technology here include appropriate written and oral communication, the professional exchange of information, and interpersonal collaboration.

Collaboration involves the use of telecommunications (electronic interaction) to network with peers, teachers, subject matter experts, and other audiences.

Skills at this level of the taxonomy are evidenced by sharing information in written form (word processing, desktop publishing), by responding to directed personal interchange (electronic mail), and by participating in and interpreting interpersonal dialog (via list servers, chat rooms, and online bulletin boards).

Collaboration is arguably the single most important tool for teaching and learning. It is necessary in order to work cooperatively, gather information, express knowledge, communicate with others in support of direct and independent learning, and pursue personal and professional interests. Once a working literacy is achieved, collaboration moves quickly to the forefront of the list of necessary competencies.

Impact of Collaboration on Learners

For the learner, collaboration is sustained by word processing as the most popular media for presenting and sharing information via written documents, business plans, reports, outlines, and summaries. Competency at this level of the Taxonomy for the Technology Domain dictates use of boilerplate documents with formatting, titles and subtitles, bullets and numbering, and spacing and page layout and design features.

Following closely on the heels of word processing are the skills of electronic mail often referred to as asynchronous collaboration via the Internet. Skills at this level of the taxonomy include the ability to retrieve, read, reply, and forward messages. Advanced capabilities (although expected even at this level of technology) include setup and application of electronic address books to communicate with target groups as well as the ability to send, retrieve, and save various files attached to e-mail messages.

Finally, collaboration is evidenced in the synchronous environment of Internet chat rooms, list servers, and bulletin boards. A new protocol of netiquette has matured from the use of online discussion groups and abbreviated e-mail posts, adding to the historic syntax surrounding the use of correct grammar, mechanics, and spelling. Figure 2 demonstrates some of the most popular considerations of appropriate electronic propriety.

Figure 2. Netiquette Considerations, Abridged (Wilcox & Wojnar, 2000)

Netiquette Considerations

Some General Online Protocols
- Use of CAPITAL LETTERS implies "shouting," and is considered "rude."
- Treat e-mail with the same respect and guidelines that you would use when writing correspondence or hand-written letters.
- Refrain from using abbreviations
- Keep a multicultural perspective when writing online.
- If you are using a word or words that may have several meanings, define the word and clarify the intention of its use.
- Use good judgment in your postings. What you may think is humorous, another person may think is offensive.

Some Chat Session Protocols
- Give the receiver time to process the information and formulate a response.
- Give yourself enough time to trouble shoot technical difficulties, if they should arise, so that you won't be late for class.
- Include the name of the person to whom you are responding, before you type your message.
- Stay focused on the goals and objectives of the chat.
- When working in groups online, assign a role to each person.
- Refrain from entering dialogue until the instructor asks the class if there are any questions.
- If you have a question for your group or for the instructor, please type a question mark (?)
- When you have a lot to say, please type three dots (…), so that the rest of the class knows to hold all other postings until you have completed your thoughts.
- Emoticons (e.g., smiley face) are useful when the words you are typing may be taken two ways.

Impact of Collaboration on Teachers

Perhaps no other level of the taxonomy is as important to successful teaching as collaboration. In order to enhance productivity and professional practice, ISTE calls upon teachers to use "technology to communicate and collaborate with peers, parents, and the larger community in order to nurture student learning" (ISTE, 2003). The technology mandate to communicate emphasizes the importance of this critical tool for sharing information, both from a top-down (administration to teacher to student) and from a bottom-up (student to teacher) perspective. Perhaps it is this directive to connect with the "larger community" that weighs most heavily on teachers to become proficient in the use of technology.

Accepting the role of collaboration, historically, has been more difficult for teachers than the previous level of literacy. While word processing has become an accepted media for sharing ideas both inside and outside the classroom, the issue of accessibility and accountability has perhaps placed obstacles to the benefits of electronic communications. Teachers have been much more reticent to incorporate electronic mail, online chats, and bulletin board posts to their repertoire of collaboration tools.

Asynchronous and synchronous communications seem to open the door to a whole host of unwelcome expectations. Many teachers report that an e-mail sent by a parent comes with an unspoken assumption that a reply is forthcoming straight away. Any delay in this response is viewed as justification for inaction. For example, an unanswered electronic question about tonight's homework assignment excuses an incomplete work paper, often in the minds of both the parent as well as the student. A missed e-mail (whether it was actually sent or not) warrants additional time to complete the assignment (Sometimes called the electronic version of "my dog ate my homework.") An inconsequential posting to a peer's electronic reply ("I concur with your findings.") is offered somehow as proof of student understanding. Finally, irrelevant entries during an online chat session ("I just got back from a weeklong vacation in the Bahamas and the weather was terrific.") frequently are served up as classroom participation by an otherwise inattentive student who has not prepared the assigned readings.

Regardless of its application, collaboration is indispensable as a technology competency. Technology-based communication skills are essential to both the learner and the teacher—justification in part for the placement of collaboration so close to the base of this new classification system. A firm grasp of the competencies displayed at this level of the Taxonomy for the Technology Domain ensures the most productive utilization of these skills for teaching and learning.

Decision-Making Solving Problems	**Level 3.0** Ability to use technology in new and concrete situations to analyze, assess, and judge.

Definition

Technology for Decision-Making (Level 3.0) refers to the *"ability to use technology in new and concrete situations to analyze, assess, and judge."* Included in this definition is the assumed mastery of the concepts and skills from the previous two levels and involves both teacher and student in applied learning situations. Making decisions with the aid of technology requires greater understanding of technology than either of the previous stages. Decision-making technology includes, among others, such important tools as spreadsheets, brainstorming software, statistical analysis packages, and database applications.

The first software application to justify the purchase of personal computers was the electronic spreadsheet in which work and data are stored for manipulation, storage, retrieval, and presentation. Spreadsheets list and analyze data. They format, filter, sort, and edit data. They apply statistical functions, calculate "what if" scenarios, and analyze and visually chart the results.

Brainstorming software provides the learner with a graphical visual organizer during the construction of thematic compositions (e.g., term papers, theses, reports, etc.). Such applications offer structure during the design and development of key concepts inherent in mental tasks, aiding in the numerous judgments inherent in creating position papers, plans, strategies, orientations, and technical reports.

Statistical packages allow the user to perform complex analyses expanding, in many cases, the elementary functions that accompany state-of-the-art spreadsheets. Some of the advanced decision-making functions available in statistical packages include a more thorough set of descriptive statistics, correlation analysis tools, t-test and z-test investigation, rank and percentile analysis, random number generation, regression analysis, and advanced visual presentation tools such as histograms, pie and bar charts, and scatter diagrams. For teachers, these packages often provide calculations of standard deviations and test item analysis in addition to grade book assistance.

A database is a collection of relational information managed hierarchically (from high to low) such as files, records, fields, and data. Files often represent a collection of class rosters, field study data, student explorations, and science experiments outcomes. Files are comprised of individual records that embody meaningful data captured and input for later manipulation. Hierarchically, records contain fields (name, grade, ID number, text scores, etc.) that, in turn, are the stuff of data (characters, numbers, etc.).

Impact of Decision-Making on Learners

Problem-solving skills are advanced with the aid of decision-making technology as students employ strategies for cracking real world problems.

Learners need to become comfortable with entering and editing spreadsheet data in early grades, certainly no later than middle school. File actions to be mastered include open, close, save, and find, edit activities include cut/copy/paste, fill, clear, and delete, undo and repeat. Formulas, formatting, tools, and data manipulation (sorting, filtering, etc.) are also critical skills. Lastly, decision-making skills call for determining appropriate visual charts and graphics for data representation.

Brainstorming software helps learners choose key elements and subordinate concepts during the initial construction of information. For example, a popular method of teaching language arts composition is to begin with "three main points." Brainstorming software visually depicts these fundamental concepts and offers schemata for how subordinate concepts will fall under each important heading. Quickly, learners find themselves using technology to decide when they have constructed a proper thematic arrangement for their paper.

Historically, statistical software is encountered much later in a learner's academic program. With the availability of these powerful mathematical tools, the use of statistical software for decision-making has been pushed down to middle school and, sometimes, even elementary school levels. By middle school, certainly, learners should be introduced to the fundamentals of descriptive statistics (e.g., range, mean, median, mode). They should know how to enter and sort data using technology as well as graphically present original information. By secondary school, the tools of statistical packages add to the technology-based decision-making repertoire of college-bound learners.

Learners should grasp the ability to enter and edit information into a database as part of their mastery of the decision-making level of the Taxonomy for the Technology Domain. Database competencies include tables, queries, forms, and reports. From within a single file, data is maintained in separate storage media called tables that view, add, and update data by offering customized online forms, find and retrieve data via immediate queries, and analyze and print tailored data via specialized report layouts. Class rosters, field study data, student explorations, and science experiments outcomes are a few examples of databases created to assist the decision-making process.

Impact of Decision-Making on Teachers

Assessment of student learning outcomes has achieved remarkable stature in recent years. As a result, effective evaluation strategies are more and more augmented by sophisticated decision-making technologies. Spreadsheets are capable of collecting and analyzing assessment data, interpreting the results, and communicating findings necessary to improve instructional practice and maximize student potential. Statistical software packages afford a greater degree of analysis of both individual performance and inter-evaluation reliability. Database applications, like gradebook software, provide a vehicle for storing important artifacts of student achievement for later retrieval.

In addition to using spreadsheets for more traditional test and measurement purposes, they are also excellent venues for classroom-related decisions related to finances and budgets, schedules, parent-student organization addresses, classroom purchases, and project assignments.

For the more technically sophisticated decision-maker, databases provide a language-oriented environment that encourages high-level manipulation of files, records, and fields within an automated inventory. For example, individual students or small groups may track character traits and compare different characters from different books and compile a database of characters in classical literature. One of the most salient points to consider when evaluating the importance of the creation and use of databases in the classroom is their ability to be revisited throughout the year. They can serve as a yearlong unit at the K-12 level. Creating a database of any kind requires students to think critically; updating and retrieving from a database requires them to re-examine initial decisions while considering the data at progressively higher levels of cognition.

Gradebook technology has matured beyond mere worksheet products. Today's teachers have access to complex grading software that supports the teacher's need for tracking individual student progress in the form of personalized test scores, completion of project and homework assignments, classroom participation, IEP-related (individualized education program) events, anecdotal notes, and performance matching to national, state, and local standards.

Educational researchers and professional education organizations agree on the need to implement multiple evaluation methods to determine the appropriate use of technology resources for learning, communication, and productivity.

Infusion **Learning with Technology**	**Level 4.0** Identification, harvesting, and application of existing technology to unique learning situations.

Definition

Technology for Infusion (Level 4.0) recognizes technology as a powerful strategy for uncovering and exploring academic content. Level 4.0 is concerned with the *"identification, harvesting, and applications of existing technology to unique learning situations."* Here, learning moves from its previous concentration on the external use of technology to solve particular problems to an internal application of technology to learn. It explores the instructional value of otherwise disconnected technology-based materials and selects those appropriate for instruction and individual learning. Infusion is found in printed, audio, visual, multimedia, and Web-based technologies in addition to the more typical categories of educational hardware, software, and networking and incorporates those resources into the classroom.

Learning with technology encompasses the gamut of resources to locate, evaluate, and collect information from a variety of sources. Of course, the Internet has impacted infusion unlike any technology before it. However, infusion was possible even before the network of inter-connected computers.

Learners began to embrace infusion with the partnership between telecommunications and libraries in the 1970s. Initially, telnet software provided connectivity to library collections replacing the card catalog with perhaps the only reliable service provided by the technology of the day. Today, vast electronic inventories of audio, video, CD-ROM-based, and other digitized information provide access to information once thought beyond the reach of the typical learner.

Online catalogs of downloadable educational packages provide freeware, shareware, beta (under development), demonstration, and public domain software and add to the list of infused technology resources. Typical media mandates an understanding of operating systems, memory requirements, file size, and networking. Users must possess the necessary technical skills to launch executable files or prepare compressed files for setup.

Other technology-based materials provide infused materials as well. For example, graphic presentations targeting specific academic content standards and incorporating images, sounds, and video are increasingly available on education Web sites. Similar visual resources along with educational software, electronic worksheets, and Web-based virtual tours provide companion CD-ROMs to newly updated textbooks.

Still, the Internet itself has surfaced as the preeminent source of infused technology. Successful navigation of the millions of available Web sites presupposes a working knowledge of uniform resource locators (URLs and Web addresses), hyperlinks, bookmarks (Favorites), and search engines. The depth of that knowledge depends on whether the Internet is used by learner or teacher.

Impact of Infusion on Learners

The new millennium expects — no, demands — that students become lifelong learners and that they be given the necessary infusion skills to remain learners throughout their lives. Who would have envisioned the impact of the Internet just 15 years ago? Yet, as technology continues to present new opportunities for learning, the identification, harvesting, application, and internalization of technology to unique learning situations (the definition of Infusion) takes on added importance.

What was formerly known as "library skills" is now packaged as "information literacy" as libraries are re-defined by the introduction of new online and CD-ROM-based services. With such expanding resources, learners are better able to use technology to accomplish a variety of tasks including problem-solving, self-directed learning, and extended learning activities. Learners cite electronic resources including information from CD-ROM journals, Internet-based e-zines (electronic magazines), and Web-based audio/video hyperlinks as well as citations from user groups, list servers, and newsgroups.

The availability of educational software, too, has matured into an all-inclusive inventory of infused classroom resources. The Minnesota Education Computing Consortium (MECC) was arguably the first online catalog of K-12 software of any consequence. For the price of a floppy diskette, subscribers could request mathematics, social studies, science, and language arts software often designed by teachers but most often programmed by technologists. Today, freeware and shareware offer learners a substantial online resource in nearly every academic area, hardware platform, and multimedia format. Infusion is also provided by software in the form of applications that permit the user to both view and interact with the software before deciding whether to purchase the full-scale package.

Achieving the status of a lifelong learner implies mastery of the World Wide Web, including basic and advanced search engines (using keywords, indexes, and Boolean logic) as well as Internet "harvesting" skills to capture text, images, sound files, video clips, and even entire Web pages to a desktop computer. The ability to locate, evaluate, and collect information from library resources, CD-ROM publications, online catalogs, and the Internet has greatly advanced infusion as one of the Taxonomy's most important levels.

Impact of Infusion on Teachers

Infusion takes on an even more important role in the teaching-learning process. To be effective, technology must be incorporated into the curriculum and not allowed to serve merely as remedial or enrichment instruction. Infused technologies, offered by a knowledgeable instructor, maximizes student learning options, addresses the diverse needs of individual students, develops their higher order thinking skills, and contributes to stronger academic content throughout the curriculum.

For infusion to be effective, however, teachers must determine when and how technology tools are most useful to address the multiplicity of tasks and problems encountered by the learner. It would be best if teachers were classroom models of infusion, demonstrating their use of technology to research and evaluate the precision and truthfulness of information along with its relevance, suitability, comprehensiveness, and bias with respect to real-world problems.

Lifelong education and professional development shifts the responsibility for learning from the teacher to the student. However, it is the teacher who must ensure that learners are aware of their own learning styles and how infused technology supports their particular professional career path. An excellent example of such possibilities is the proliferation of educational software as infused technology. While every teacher seeks to introduce appropriate educational software (whether demonstration, freeware, or shareware) at suitable points within the curriculum, it is the conscientious teacher who also provides a venue for self-evaluation. The infusion of technology provides abundant opportunities for selecting among a growing inventory of lifelong learning materials.

Tied inexorably to tomorrow's successful infusion of technology are the use of digital broadband, satellite, and cable TV for audio and videoconferencing. Only recently have schools begun to appreciate the power of space-based communication as a resource for teaching subject content unavailable because of cost or distance. In today's classrooms, students and teacher learn together via instruction delivered at a distance. In the future, these services will offer another dimension to learning with technology.

Integration Teaching with Technology	**Level 5.0** The creation of new technology-based materials, combining otherwise disparate technologies to teach.

Definition

Technology for Integration (Level 5.0) is concerned with *"the creation of new technology-based materials, combining otherwise disparate technologies to teach."* The objective of integration is to develop new, previously non-existent, innovative instructional materials to enhance learning. Traditionally, content materials were created by finding a brilliant chapter from a favorite textbook and combining it with a movie or audiotape and perhaps a colorized map from a contemporary atlas to produce a never-before-seen student workbook about the Holocaust. At this particular level of the taxonomy, technologies are identified, harvested, and re-assembled to create new technology-based instructional materials to address individual student learning strengths not previously available.

Throughout the evolution of educational technology since the introduction of computer-assisted instruction in the 1960s, hardware and software have remained within the purview of the technologist. Mainframes with their dumb terminals, minicomputers with intelligent terminals, and even personal computer technology was so primitive in its operation and so technical in its programming that only professionals skilled in computer science, information technology, or computer programming languages could produce successful CAI learning environments.

Thanks to advanced multimedia technology, this is no longer the case. Digital cameras, scanners, CD-ROM burners, digital audio and video media players, and personal computers equipped with state-of-the-art word processing, graphics presentation, and Web editing applications, have made the integration of new instructional materials promising technologies for teaching and learning.

Impact of Integration on Learners

State-of-the-art technology is brought to bear as tools for constructing new instructional materials. Integration occurs as learners strive to compose content-specific resources using word processing to produce text-based instructional materials, graphic presentation software to produce visual-based instructional materials, and Web editing software to produce Web-based materials.

Digital materials (images, sounds, video, and Web sites) harvested from the Internet provide the workings for text-based handouts, worksheets, and study guides. To properly generate such resources, advanced word processing formatting skills are in order including, but not limited to: tables and columns, spelling and grammar checkers, paragraph styles, indentations, forms and frames, borders, and drawing commands.

Visual-based classroom presentations rely on advanced graphics capabilities to combine graphics with text, generate original digital images, audio, and video, integrate charts, graphs, and template designs, transition between and among slides, and animate presentations for more realistic learning.

Web-based lesson home pages also fall within this level of the taxonomy. Thankfully, Web pages are no longer coded in the native hypertext transfer markup language (HTML) programming language. With today's sophisticated Web editors, instructional materials require little more than word processing skills. To create effective lesson Web pages, a familiarity with hyperlinks and some limited experience with inserting images, text, and horizontal lines is sufficient.

Impact of Integration on Teachers

The integration of technology calls for more teacher skills than previous levels. In point of fact, for teachers, integration is the most mature application of technology. Teachers are asked to design, develop, implement, and deliver developmentally appropriate instructional materials to support the diverse needs of their learners. To accomplish this feat, teachers must apply currently accepted research on teaching and learning with technology when planning learning environments and experiences (ISTE, 2003). Planning—a considerable amount of it—plays a key role in successful implementations of integrated technologies as well as advanced skills in creating text, visual, and Web-based instructional materials. Simply put, at this level of the taxonomy, teachers move beyond classroom-centered presentations to prepare student-centered, self-paced, individualized instructional resources.

The Hyperbook is a text-based instructional resource using the advanced capabilities of word processing and desktop publishing software to create practical exercises and activities that guide students through a predominantly cognitive building-block learning experience.

The Interactive Lesson is biased toward behavioral learning using graphics-based visual materials prepared by teachers who control the sequence of the instruction while allowing students to be in charge of the tempo of the lesson.

The Web-based Virtual Tour focuses on the humanistic approach to teaching and employs various teacher-made Internet sites and links to other material important to the learner.

More information about how to prepare each of these integrated technology-based materials is available in *Teaching Digitally: A Guide for Integrating Technology Into the Classroom* (Tomei, 2001).

In addition to producing classroom-appropriate instructional materials, integration includes other applications of technology important to the teaching-learning process. For example, it also involves the application of technology to facilitate a variety of effective assessment and evaluation strategies while determining the appropriate use of resources for learning, communication, and productivity.

Tech-ology The Study of Technology	**Level 6.0** The ability to judge the universal impact, shared values, and social implications of technology use and its influence on teaching and learning.

Definition

Tech-ology (Level 6.0) refers to "*the ability to judge the universal impact, shared values, and social implications of technology use and its influence on teaching and learning.*" Tech-ology is a contraction of "tech" (technology) and "ology" (the study of), therefore, the final stage of the taxonomy addresses the study of technology. Many related issues necessarily come to the fore when considering the effect of technology on the individual learner, the educational institution, the community, and society as a whole.

Impact of Tech-ology on Learners

Learners must come to understand the ethical, cultural, and societal issues related to technology (ISTE, 2003). Only after they realize the importance of technology by stepping through the previous levels of the technology taxonomy can they begin to practice responsible use of technology, the information that it produces, and the power it possesses to impact the human condition.

Tech-ology is impacted by concerns raised by bio-technology (agriculture, cloning, genetics, health, medicine, reproductive technology), convergence (coming together of communication, computers, information, the Internet, and television), creativity (arts, intellectual property, piracy), multi-culturism (including concerns with potential harm to customs, language, religion, social interaction), e-conomics (and the changes in business and e-commerce), matters of equity (including the "digital divide" and global technology parity), government and politics (with online campaigns, fund-raising, and advocacy), innovations (artificial intelligence, cryo-technology, and robotics), and national security fears (cyber-warfare, information security abuses, and chemical and biological terrorism).

How are students to develop positive attitudes toward technology in a society that seems to wield such capacity to threaten its global citizens? How can teachers encourage technology-based lifelong learning, collaboration, personal pursuits, and productivity when technology can inflict global chaos and such personal infringements to basic civil liberties?

Impact of Tech-ology on Teachers

Teachers must come to appreciate the social, ethical, legal, and human issues surrounding the use of technology in schools and how those issues impact the real world experiences of their charges. In addition, the ISTE encourages teachers to model as well as teach legal and ethical practice related to technology use, apply technology resources to enable and empower learners with diverse backgrounds, characteristics, and abilities, identify and use technology resources that affirm diversity, promote safe and healthy use of technology resources, and facilitate equitable access to technology resources for all students (ISTE, 2003). However, these encouragements fall short of a call for changing curricula to integrate technology into the academic areas in which these issues surface.

The impact of technology must also be considered in peripheral areas of concern to teachers, such as career development, teaching as a profession, and the future of education as a discipline. Participants in a recent study by the Rand Corporation (Harvey & Purnell, 1995) were found to be enthusiastic about the opportunities technology provides including the use of multimedia resources technologies to model real world situations, the use of technology in support of just-in-time professional development opportunities, and the integration of telecommunications (telephones, fax machines, voice mail, networks, etc.) to overcome isolation so often found in a school/training environment, encouraging instead collegial conversation, discussion, exchange of information, and access to information otherwise difficult to attain.

Conclusion

Literacy, Collaboration, Decision-Making, Infusion, Integration, and Technology offer a new perspective for integrating technology into the classroom. The sooner this taxonomy is adopted, the sooner teachers and learners can use a common vocabulary of definitions, activities, and technology-based learning objectives and the sooner instructional technology will mature into a successful teaching and learning strategy in its own right.

References

Harvey, J., & Purnell, S. (Eds.) (1995). *Technology and teacher professional development* (Workshops on Critical Issues). Rand Corporation.

International Society for Technology in Education (ISTE). (2003, December). *National Educational Technology Standards (NETS) for students, teachers, and administrators.* Retrieved from the World Wide Web: *http://cnets.iste.org*

Kibler, R.J., Barker, L.L., & Miles, D.T. (1970). *Behavioral objectives and instruction.* Allyn & Bacon Publishers.

Krathwohl, D.L., & Bloom, B. S. (1984). *Taxonomy of educational objectives: The classifications of educational goals. Handbook I.* New York: Addison-Wesley/Pearson Publishers.

Tomei, L.A. (2001). *Teaching digitally: A guide for integrating technology into the classroom.* Norwood MA: Christopher-Gordon Publishers.

U.S. Department Of Education. (1996). *Getting America's students ready for the 21st century: Meeting the technology literacy challenge.*

Wilcox, B.L., & Wojnar, L.C. (2000, August). *Best practice goes online.* Reading online. Retrieved from the World Wide Web: *http://www.readingonline.org/articles/art_index.asp?HREF=/articles/wilcox/index.html*

Chapter 6

Technology Literacy (Level 1.0)

 Literacy **Understanding Technology**	**Level 1.0** The minimum degree of competency expected of teachers and learners with respect to technology, computers, educational programs, office productivity software, the Internet, and their synergistic effectiveness as a learning strategy.

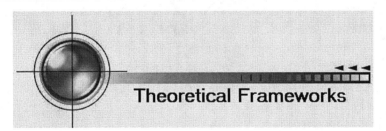

Theoretical Frameworks

Definition and Historical Origins

Literacy represents the most modest level of technology-based learning. At this echelon of the taxonomy, literacy is defined as *"the minimum degree of competency expected of teachers and students with respect to technology, computers, educational programs, office productivity software, the Internet, and their synergistic effectiveness as a learning strategy."*

Level 1.0 involves an awareness of technology as a personal tool for learning as well as a content area worthy of mastery in its own right. Albert Borgmann (1984) offers a schema that is very appropriate for classifying theories of technology. He proposed that educational literature be classified into two main groups: substantive and instrumental. Psychologists who comprise the former group hold that technology is the "key to better schools and better education; it can and will break down traditional barriers to effective and successful school reform" (Public Agenda Foundation, 1995). The latter group builds upon the common notion that technologies are merely tools that learners use in order to achieve other learning outcomes. The former classification serves as the basis for technology as its own content area; the latter provides for technology as a tool for learning.

For the Taxonomy for the Technology Domain, all that is required at this initial level is to recall appropriate information about technology in a timely enough manner to effectively use and understand technology.

Standards for Technology Literacy

The National Educational Technology Standards (NETS) for students (NETS*S) and teachers (NETS*T) offer broad categories of foundation skills entitled "basic technology operations and concepts" for students and "technology operations and concepts" that closely parallel the tasks desired for students and teachers at the literacy level of the taxonomy. The Collaborative for Technology Standards for School Administrators (TSSA) provides the technology literacy tasks appropriate for administrators. Table 1 provides a general set of skills appropriately cataloged for students, teachers (as learners, experts, and scholars), and administrators that appear in the referenced literature.

Student literacy calls for a host of competencies with a focus on learning. Literacy requires demonstrated knowledge and skill in the use of computer and other technologies as they apply to the classroom. For students, keyboarding is often cited as a literacy skill. So is a developmentally appropriate and technically accurate vocabulary. Using input devices (mouse, keyboard, remote control) and output devices (diskettes and printers) to access and accumulate educational materials is also an appropriate literacy. Finally, the correct use of key software applications (primarily word processing) is also considered a basic competency at this level of the taxonomy.

Table 1. Literacy Standards for Students, Teachers, and Administrators

Literacy Competency	Student Standards	Teacher-as-Learner Standards	Teacher-as-Expert Standards	Teacher-as-Scholar Standards	Administrators
NETS*S					
Basic operations and concepts	x				
• Students demonstrate a sound understanding of the nature and operation of technology systems.	x				
• Students are proficient in the use of technology.	x				
NETS*T					
Teachers demonstrate a sound understanding of technology operations and concepts.		x	x	x	
• demonstrate introductory knowledge, skills, and understanding of concepts related to technology		x	x	x	
• demonstrate continual growth in technology knowledge and skills to stay abreast of current and emerging technologies.		x	x	x	
TSSA					
Educational leaders inspire a shared vision for comprehensive integration of technology and foster an environment and culture conducive to the realization of that vision.					x
• facilitate the shared development by all stakeholders of a vision for technology use and widely communicate that vision.					x

For teachers, some of the more popular literacies include knowledge of terminology, fundamental computer operations, and introductory word processing. Teachers should be able to demonstrate literacy through practical applications of classroom computer systems and peripherals. Specific skills at this level include: diagnosing common hardware problems; using word processing and desktop publishing to prepare classroom materials; interpreting and communicating information using spreadsheets and databases; connecting to the Internet and online services, sharing files via networks, and using electronic mail; and, setting up and operating videocassette players, CD-ROM players, closed circuit television, and other electronic devices.

Educational leaders are expected to model the effective use of technology including literacy skills common to both teachers and students. In addition, administrators must use these newly acquired skills to foster viable learning communities that support continuous faculty and staff development in technology; engage in sustained, job-related professional learning themselves using technology; maintain an awareness of emerging technologies and their potential uses in education; and, use technology to advance organizational improvement (Collaborative for TSSA, 2003).

Research has found that a minimal set of technology competencies often embraces universal issues surrounding the access and use of technology to enhance learning across the curriculum; the application of technology to enhance teaching, planning, assessing, reporting, and personal professional development; the use of technology to enhance planning, communication, financial management, and the flow of information within an organization; formulating and implementing a strategic plan for technology; and, the effective assimilation of technology change (ISTE, 2003).

Achieving each of these goals is essential to technological literacy. While literacy forms the foundational skills for using technology as a lifelong tool for learning, its power to affect learning is tied inexorably to the appropriate application in the classroom as rendered in the next section of the chapter.

Practical Applications

Literacy Technologies and Action Statements

Numerous tools for addressing technology literacy standards are shown in Table 2 and should be considered when constructing learning objectives targeting Level 1.0 of the Taxonomy for the Technology Domain.

Action statements such as those in Table 3 provide clearly stated criteria for successful learning as well as observable and measurable assessment method-

Table 2. Appropriate Literacy Technologies

Accessory programs	Hardware operations	Online help feature
Audiovisual equipment	Icons	Operating systems
Computer terminology	Internet	Paint and draw tools
Desktop operations	Keyboard commands	Peripheral device operation
Digital images	Mechanical devices	Programming Languages
Educational software	Menu operations	Toolbars
File transfer	Mouse	Utilities
Floppy diskette	Netiquette	Windows
Hard disk drives	Network operations	

Table 3. Action Statements for Technology Literacy

Access *online data*
Capture *digital pictures*
Cut, copy and paste *text and images*
Copy, move, and delete *files*
Demonstrate mastery of *output devices*
Download and incorporate *text and images*
Electronically transfer *files*
Employ *search engines*
Format *documents, presentations*
Identify appropriate *technologies*
Input *data, URLs*, etc.
Label basic computer technologies
Launch *software applications*
Modify *text* color, size, font, etc.
Navigate *educational software*
Open, save, close, drag files
Point and click to launch applications
Recognize strengths and weaknesses of *technologies*
Select *educational technologies*
Share *files* electronically
Save/store selected *files*
Scan *images*
Type, edit, print *documents*

ology. The use of action statements assist in providing realistic expectations on the part of students, teachers, and administrators. Appropriate action verbs are underlined once while the *instructional technology* introduced is italicized.

Domains of Teaching and Technology Literacy

The cognitive, affective, and psychomotor domains of education impact the literacy level of the new taxonomy for technology directly. Students, teachers, and administrators are exposed to technology literacy at various junctures in their professional careers. Students participate in formal education or training classes, teachers via pre-service and in-service workshops, and administrators in professional training sessions. Each is exposed to goals and objectives that address appropriate technology literacies.

Cognitive Domain

Literacy in the cognitive domain is manifested by a focus on the earliest mental activities associated with learning with technology. In this domain, learners build accompanying schemata for using technology as a tool for acquiring knowledge. As a result, technology literacy skills encountered in the cognitive domain are found mostly at lowers levels for students, teachers and administrators.

Knowledge of literacy skills provides the foundations for using technology as a tool for learning. Committing technical vocabulary to memory is a cognitive literacy skill—so is recognizing the parts of a computer. Both skills support the organization of ideas necessary to explore the higher levels of technology. Literacy skills at this level include practicing, using, and assessing scenarios involving educational technologies appropriate for classroom curriculum. Technology supports all aspects of education including not only teaching but administration as well and calls for mastery of a wide assortment of technology literacies.

Using literacy technologies and action statements offered earlier, the following examples for the cognitive domain were identified or constructed for practical demonstration purposes. Appropriate *action verbs* are underlined once while the *instructional technology* introduced is italicized. The first objective reveals a *student* technology-based learning objective.

Cognitive domain: "Students will complete module six of the Word Processing Skills for Elementary Students CDROM software program. To demonstrate mastery of *output devices*, they will save *word documents* to the class *hard drive folder*, <u>copy</u> *files* to a *floppy diskette* to be provided, and <u>print</u> two copies of their paper."

For teachers, a technology objective often focuses on technical knowledge in the classroom. An appropriate *teacher-as-learner* objective might look like this.

Cognitive domain: "Following the in-service workshop, teachers will <u>post</u> student achievement standardized test scores taken from a simulated *database* provided by the workshop instructor. Data must be <u>ordered</u> into the correct *spreadsheet* cells (rows and columns) with less than two mistakes. Participants must <u>use</u> proper *statistical formulae and functions* to correctly analyze and report the scores."

Charged with the implementation of technology, *administrators* frequently participate in training sessions involving cognitive objectives such as the one shown below.

Cognitive domain: "Using the Technology Planning Guide, administrators will <u>construct</u> a draft table of contents for a school/district/corporate training office *technology plan* for review by senior decision-makers. Projects must <u>identify</u> appropriate *instructional technologies* as well as required elements outlined in the Guide."

Affective Domain

At this lowest level of the Taxonomy for the Technology Domain, affective technology skills are limited. At approximately the same degree of intensity as the cognitive domain, affective literacies are likely to occur with students, teachers, and administrators who are seeking to establish their receptiveness to new information (receiving). They could involve technologies that help student become aware, listen, acknowledge, and attend to various learning needs such as appropriate classroom behavior, time demands, or school priorities. Affective technologies might also offer a variety of learning materials grounded in various instructional strategies and addressing several learning styles.

Affective *student* literacies might include learning how to use educational software for math, science, social studies, or language arts. An affective learning objective at the literacy level is shown here:

Affective domain: "Given the Rules for Engaging in a Synchronous Class, students will <u>differentiate</u> appropriate *netiquette* propriety in an online learning environment and <u>become aware</u> of how these *protocols* differ from the traditional classroom environment."

Literacy demands preparation that might include the following *teacher-as-expert* workshop objective.

Affective domain: "From a list of the top five advantages of technology for adult learners (i.e., access, time, commitment, specialization, and choice), corporate trainers will <u>select</u> *educational technologies* that foster receptivity to instruction for adult learners who evidence a propensity for auditory, visual, or kinesthetic learning."

Administrators must consider the affective receptivity of staff, parents, community members, corporate leaders, curriculum designers, departments of education, etc. when adopting technologies. In professional training sessions for *administrators*, the following objective might appear.

Affective domain: "Given the total cost of ownership (TCO) model, principals and financial managers will <u>acknowledge</u> the strengths and weaknesses of various *instructional technologies* and <u>recommend</u> appropriate *technologies* (based on costs, revenues, expenses, and other financial outlays) for potential clients of the school district or corporation."

Psychomotor Domain

At the literacy level, the application of technology is most prominent in the psychomotor domain where understanding technology focuses primarily on the development of the physical skills necessary to use technology efficiently, if not effectively. Technology literacy encourages learners to demonstrate mastery of basic reflexive movements (imitation) while advancing toward mastery of more complex abilities (manipulation) not yet considered skillful. Some find simply setting up and operating equipment a daunting obstacle to using technology. For still others, perhaps their strongest challenge is maintaining an awareness of emerging technologies and their potential uses for teaching, learning, and management.

An example *student* technology-based learning objective demonstrates literacy in the psychomotor domain.

Psychomotor domain: "Given a series of hands-on exercises, students will demonstrate mastery of *multimedia hardware and software* by mimicking *mouse* operations necessary to launch *word processing and paint and draw applications*. Students must be able to type their name as *text* and *graphics* within the 40 minute class period."

To support the use of technology by a *teacher-as-scholar*, professional development programs assume a minimal level of literacy to successfully integrating technology into the classroom. The following example demonstrates a suitable psychomotor learning objective for a technology-based workshop at level 1.0.

Psychomotor domain: "Teachers will employ an *Internet-based search engine* of their choice to input the *uniform resource locators* (URLs) for three Web sites that concentrate on topics appropriate for integration into existing standards-based content area curriculum. The paths taken to locate these sites will be copy and pasted into an *electronic notepad* and submitted to the workshop instructor for validation."

Administrators are no strangers to the psychomotor domain when it comes to technology. A professional training session for school *administrators* and corporate trainers includes the following psychomotor learning objective at literacy level.

Psychomotor domain: "Administrators will receive a hands-on demonstration of checkbook software to access their *online budget accounts*, modify their default *passwords*, and reproduce electronic third quarter budget *statistics* within 45 minutes."

Technology Literacy and the Psychologies of Learning

Educational psychology examines the teaching-learning process from several perspectives. Behaviorism views learning from the viewpoint of the environment; as a result, much of our technology literacy is acquired via stimulus → response → reinforcement. Cognitivism sees learning as a series of building blocks; so, technology literacy represents the first tier of a classification system providing the minimum skills and competencies to ensure later success. Finally, humanism considers learning from the viewpoint of the learner rather than the teacher. For the humanist, learning does not occur until the learner says it occurs. Technology literacy for such advocates is important because it provides a meaningful foundation for further learning.

Behaviorism

Behaviorally, the acquisition of technical literacy is readily understood and fairly easy to demonstrate. Point-and-click an icon to launch a software application. Tap the F10 function key to save a revised document. Click a blue hyperlink to connect to a favorite Web site. Nearly all forms of computer-assisted instruction (drill and practice, simulations, and tutorials) involve a measure of behavioral responses to technology stimuli. The stimulus-response-reinforcement paradigm, reinforcement schedules, and practical applications of behavior modification all play a major role in the acquisition of technology literacy.

Below is a learning objective appropriate for *student*-centered literacy following the precepts of behaviorism. Appropriate action verbs are underlined once while the *instructional technology* introduced is italicized.

Behaviorism: "Students must achieve at least a novice-level certification during the practical evaluation of the *CD-ROM-based typing exercise* attaining minimal performance standards (25 words per minute) with less than five mistakes."

A *teacher-as-scholar* workshop might present many behavioral learning objectives targeting the literacy level of the taxonomy. Here is one such objective taken from the workshop syllabus of the SUCCESS program (Tomei, 2003) loaded with action verbs and technologies.

Behaviorism: "Teachers will <u>download</u> at least four *images*, <u>highlight</u> and paste two *text* selections, and <u>point-and-click</u> to <u>launch</u> at least two *file transfers*; <u>save</u> these *digital components* on both the available *hard disk drive* and a *floppy diskette*; and, <u>print</u> a hard copy of these items for instructor review."

Professional development sessions tender many behavioral lesson objectives at the literacy level. While most of these objectives are similar to student and teacher literacies, here is one example of a session goal unique to *administrators*.

Behaviorism: "Administrators will <u>use</u> the available *online help features* to <u>cut, copy, and paste</u> an *electronic classroom attendance roster* from the *online student database management system* to an *electronic spreadsheet* without error and <u>print</u> a draft *roster report* for instructor review."

Cognitivism

Technology literacy is often integrated into curriculum via the cognitive approach. As an alternative to teaching the mechanics of point-and-click, keyboarding, and vocabulary, the cognitivist provides ordered scaffolding for incorporating new concepts and information into a learner's existing knowledge base. For example, keyboarding, point-and-click, and mousing are presented not as individual skills but as part of a much larger schema called "input skills." Later, additional technologies (at higher levels of the taxonomy) are assimilated into this organizational construct. A "process skills" scheme introduces the literacies of software manipulation, Internet navigation, and use of online help features. Finally, "output skills" add to the expanding technology literacies in the form of saving files, printing reports, and displaying results.

Together, input, process, and output skills form a fundamentally sound organizational structure for learning technology at the literacy level. The learning objective demonstrated below shows how cognitive psychology approaches the mastery of technology for a *student* at the literacy level.

Cognitivism: "Students will be able to recognize and <u>label</u> basic *computer terminologies* to the point where they can correctly <u>match</u> at least *10 hardware and software items* with their correct definitions within 30 minutes."

Teachers-as-expert might find themselves adding to their technology literacy by participating in an in-service workshop hosted by their school and guided by the technology coordinator. Cognitively, a learning objective typical of the process schemata might look like the one depicted below.

Cognitivism: "Teachers will <u>use</u> the *GradeIT gradebook software program* to <u>process</u> at least 12 simulated student *database records* into their course assignment book maintained on their *personal digital assistants* (PDAs), <u>assign</u> at least four examination grades, and <u>track</u> attendance electronically for at least two weeks without error."

Personal digital assistants (PDAs) are fast becoming standard equipment for educators. The following objective was gleaned from a workshop attended by *administrators* learning the newest handheld technology. It reveals a real-world application of the cognitive input schemata for developing this technology literacy.

Cognitivism: "Administrators will <u>utilize</u> a *personal digital assistant* to <u>create</u> their own individual nine-month *appointment calendar* for both personal and professional schedules for next academic year without error."

Humanism

When compared to the other schools of educational psychology, the research has not embraced humanism as a sufficient media for communicating technology literacy. However, even at this level, the humanistic notion that teachers are the primarily facilitators of the learning process merits consideration.

Some educators find the humanistic role in teaching more suited to advancing the future of instruction than more traditional models. The good news is that, since technology is certainly a tool for tomorrow, humanism opens up many new possibilities for learning. Even at the literacy stage, students, teachers, and administrators deal with a diversity of concerns, learning styles, backgrounds, and talents. The bad news, however, is that the facilitative role is not always supported by technology, given the inherent obstacles of institutional inertia. Still, there are applications of humanism at the literacy level that warrant examination.

The following example displays a learning objective for *student* literacy that attempts to instill the beliefs of humanism. The literacy chosen is a simple behavior of using the Web (a literacy skill) for classroom interaction (humanistic application).

Humanism: "Students will <u>demonstrate</u> compliance with the school's *Internet Acceptable Use Policy* by <u>participating</u> in a guided practice *synchronous chat* with other students in their class."

Teachers learn early how to employ humanistic principles when using technology. Sharing files and using electronic mail via school/training networks often involve personalized applications as seen in the following *teacher-as-learner* example objective.

Humanism: "Teachers will be provided five megabytes of online network folder to <u>store</u> *selected files* (text documents, spreadsheets, images, etc.) into a shared folder for peer review. <u>Edit</u> the *documents*, return them to the *shared folder*, and send an *e-mail* to the writer informing them of your completed review."

The following objective is typical of an appropriate *administrator* application of humanistic technology at the literacy level. Recall that the Technology Standards for School Administrators recommend the application of technology to enhance professional practice.

Humanism: "School administrators (training managers) will complete a 45 minute self-paced presentation on the advantages and disadvantages of the *interactive white board* in the classroom. Administrator/managers will <u>advocate</u> for a *technology plan*, budget, and implementation schedule for integrating these boards into grade-level/training curricula for next academic/fiscal year."

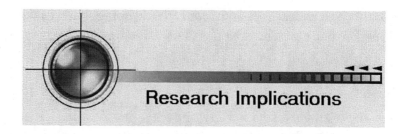

Research Implications

Literacy

Domains of Teaching

Literacy

Psychologies of Learning

Research Phase I: Literacy and the Domains of Teaching and Psychologies of Learning. Research has found that the literacy level of the Taxonomy for the Technology Domain is served best by the psychomotor domain, less so the cognitive and affective realms (Tomei, 2001). At this level of the taxonomy, psychomotor learning promotes approximately 80 percent of cited technology-based lesson plans encompassing understanding of computer terms and concepts, operation of computer hardware, use of basic computer applications, and a general awareness of simple technologies.

The literacy level of the Taxonomy for the Technology Domain is equally advanced by the behavioral and cognitive psychologies (an approximate 40-40 split of reviewed technology-based lesson plans) and less (the remaining 20%) by a humanistic approach (Tomei, 2001). At this level of the taxonomy, literacy is acquired either by properly reinforcing an understanding of the concepts of technology or by helping the learner acquire a schemata for adapting technology into their existing cognitive structure.

Research Phase II: Literacy and Technology-Based Learning Objectives

The purpose of the Phase II study was to determine the levels of the Taxonomy for the Technology Domain most commonly addressed in technology-based lesson plans. The inquiry selected some 300 lesson plans and categorized over 1,440 learning objectives by their representative level of the taxonomy (Table 3).

Table 3. Student Learning Objectives by Taxonomy Level

Level of Taxonomy	Totals	Percent Within Levels
Literacy	610	42.3
Collaboration	176	12.2
Decision-Making	380	26.4
Infusion	188	13.2
Integration	57	3.8
Tech-ology	30	2.1
Totals	1441	100.0

As reported, a preponderance of the objectives examined (80%) occurred at the lower three levels of the taxonomy. For purposes of this chapter, it is important to note that 42.3% of all learning objectives examined were found to represent the Literacy level.

Conclusion of Technology Literacy (Level 1.0)

Thanks in large measure to technology, 21st century educators are teaching their students to become proficient, responsible and ethical users of technology. Tomorrow's students will use technologies not as yet created, perhaps not even dreamt of. In order to prepare them to be ready to accept that challenge, learners must become technologically literate. At the next level of the Taxonomy for the Technology Domain, many of these same technologies become a source of increasing competency for interpersonal collaboration.

References

Borgmann, A. (1984). *Technology and the character of contemporary life.* Chicago: University of Chicago Press.

Collaborative for Technology Standards for School Administrators. (2003). *Technology Standards for School Administrators, TSSA Draft* (version 4.0). Retrieved from the World Wide Web: *cnets.iste.org/tssa/view_standards.html*

International Society for Technology in Education (ISTE). (2003). *Educational Technology Standards and Performance Indicators for All Teachers, National Educational Technology Standards for Teachers.* Retrieved from the World Wide Web: *cnets.iste.org/teachers/t_stands.html*

International Society for Technology in Education (ISTE). (2003). *Technology Foundation Standards for All Students, National Educational Technology Standards for Students.* Retrieved from the World Wide Web: *cnets.iste.org/students/s_stands.html*

Public Agenda Foundation. (1995, October). *Assignment incomplete: The unfinished business of education reform.* New York.

Tomei, L.A. (2001, April 30). Using a taxonomy for the technology domain. *Penn Association of Colleges and Teacher Educators.*

Tomei, L.A. (2003). *The SUCCESS program overview.* Unpublished Manuscript, Duquesne University.

Annotated Bibliography

Additional citations for Technology Literacy

Blacker, D. (1994). Philosophy of Technology and Education: An Invitation to Inquiry. Illinois State University. Retrieved from the World Wide Web: *http://www.ed.uiuc.edu/EPS/PES-yearbook/94_docs/BLACKER.HTM*

Huth, C., & Ravenstahl, H. (2002). *NETS standards based scope and sequence for technology education, Grades K-8.*

Riley, R.W. (1996, June). Getting America's students ready for the 21st century: Meeting the technology literacy challenge. A Report To The

Nation On Technology and Education United States Department Of Education. Retrieved from the World Wide Web: *http://www.ed.gov/ technology/plan/nattechplan/*

Chapter 7

Technology
Collaboration
(Level 2.0)

Collaboration Sharing Ideas	**Level 2.0** The ability to employ technology for effective interpersonal interaction.

Definition and Historical Origins

The effective use of technology includes written communication, the professional exchange of information, and interpersonal collaboration. As the second level of the Taxonomy for the Technology Domain, *Technology Collaboration (Level 2.0)* is defined as *"the ability to employ technology for effective interpersonal interaction."*

Shortly after mastering the literacy skills necessary to effectively and efficiently use technology, most students, teachers, and administrators quickly advance to matters of electronic communications in pursuit of new learning opportunities, expanded interpersonal interaction, and lifelong professional development.

At the second level of the Taxonomy for the Technology Domain, collaboration entails a mastery of technology tools for writing and interpersonal cooperation, sharing information electronically, and communicating via e-mail. Skills acquired during the previous literacy level are extended here in written form (word processing, desktop publishing), by responding to directed personal interchange (electronic mail), and by participating in and interpreting interpersonal electronic dialogs (via synchronous and asynchronous discussions, chat rooms, and online bulletin boards).

Standards for Technology Collaboration

Collaborative skills are given their own category in the National Educational Technology Standards (NETS) for students (NETS*S). Specifically, ISTE recommends introducing skills that foster student use of telecommunications technologies to interact with others in the virtual learning community. Word processing skills, along with technology communications tools such as the Internet, e-mail, synchronous and asynchronous communications, are included as suitable collaborative competencies. The ISTE standards also advocate a skill set that includes a variety of media and formats to share ideas effectively with various audiences (ISTE, 2003).

Somewhat less pronounced are the NETS*T standards for teachers that include collaboration under their suggested Productivity and Professional Practice guidelines. According to ISTE, teachers should use technologies to engage in ongoing professional development and lifelong learning and communicate with constituents in support of student learning (ISTE, 2003).

The Collaborative for Technology Standards for School Administrators offers two key competencies under Productivity and Professional Practice. The first includes technologies for communicating with educational, community, and electorate partners involved in the learning process in order to sustain faculty and staff development and improve overall productivity (Collaborative for TSSA, 2003).

Table 1 compiles collaboration skills appropriate for students, teachers, and administrators.

Student collaboration involves all manner of technologies spanning the inventory of state-of-the-art hardware and software. Collaboration often does not happen without the equipment that underlies telecommunications. As a result, students need a minimal level of competency with telephones, modems, networking, Internet service providers, and cable connectivity.

To communicate collaboratively, students need to know more than simple word processing, mouse operations, and keyboarding tasks — which are all literacy skills at best. They must understand file structures and sharing, page setups, editing, and hardcopy printing options — skills that foster the understanding and communication of ideas. Students must be able to share ideas by integrating images, sounds, and video into otherwise uninspired textual content, develop organizational schemata such as graphic organizers, tables of contents or indexes, and present ideas in novel formats such as columns, tables, hypertext, and distinctive fonts. Finally, collaboration involves a multiplicity of venues for students, teachers, and administrators.

Learning management systems (LMS) offer a growing venue for hosting instructional material. For example, Blackboard version 6.0 offers a menu of collaborative features including simultaneous and concurrent synchronous sessions and small "break-out" groups. Its virtual classroom environment simulates an online lecture hall atmosphere while the lightweight chat feature is perfect for online office hours (Blackboard Learning System, 2003). It provides free-form chat, chat lectures, question-and-answer chats, archives, white boarding, class tours, and group Web browsing. Another popular LMS, WebCT provides an environment for interacting with course participants, small groups, or on a one-to one basis. Its online classroom promotes virtual discussions through whiteboards, student home pages, calendars, and student tips tools (WebCT, 2003). In addition to the technologies identified already, teachers must also be comfortable with advanced telecommunications, more sophisticated desktop publishing software, and cutting-edge learning environments.

Administrators, too, must use a host of collaborative tools to maintain their professional relationship with the numerous constituencies that comprise today's academic clients. In my book, the *Technology Facade*, the "people" involved directly and indirectly in instructional technology programs in the school are crucial to success — and involvement means communications. Teachers, students, parents, community members, administrative staff, and

Table 1. Collaboration Standards for Students, Teachers, and Administrators

Collaboration Competency	Student Standards	Teacher-as-Learner Standards	Teacher-as-Expert Standards	Teacher-as-Scholar Standards	Administrators
NETS*S					
Technology communications tools	x				
• Students use telecommunications to collaborate, publish, and interact with peers, experts, and other audiences.	x				
• Students use a variety of media and formats to communicate information and ideas effectively to multiple audiences.	x				
NETS*T					
Teachers use technology to enhance their productivity and professional practice.		x	x	x	
• use technology resources to engage in ongoing professional development and lifelong learning.		x	x	x	
• use technology to communicate and collaborate with peers, parents, and the larger community in order to nurture student learning.		x	x	x	
TSSA					
Educational leaders apply technology to enhance their professional practice and to increase their own productivity and that of others.					x
• employ technology for communication and collaboration among colleagues, staff, parents, students, and the larger community.					x
• create and participate in learning communities that stimulate, nurture, and support faculty and staff in using technology for improved productivity.					x
• engage in sustained, job-related professional learning using technology resources.					x
• maintain awareness of emerging technologies and their potential uses in education.					

local business leaders as well as outside consultants, institutions of higher learning, and corporate organizations play a pivotal role in the application of technology (Tomei, 2002).

A scope and sequence for collaboration skills encompasses all grade levels. At lower grades, the task list typically focuses on word processing as a vehicle for sharing ideas and establishing interpersonal communications, along with simpler communications tools such as the Internet and e-mail that are readily mastered by youngsters. At mid-level grades, more complex word processing, e-mail, and Web applications are practiced through rehearsal and repetition. By secondary school, students have typically mastered a host of collaboration skills and expanded their bag of learning tools with synchronous and asynchronous experiences in online chat rooms and bulletin boards. The application of collaborative competencies is expected to continue as learners use these tools to enhance their experiences via audio and videoconferencing, satellite learning, and the Internet. Ultimately, colleges and universities expand the frontier of technology-based course delivery as it combines with the distance learning experience to address the diverse learning needs of the adult student via technology.

Collaboration, then, becomes the first level of the Taxonomy for the Technology Domain to provide student, teacher, and administrator with a technology-based, external window to the outside world encouraging an individual perspective to the more universal applications of technology as a tool for personal growth.

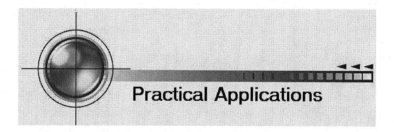

Practical Applications

Collaboration Technologies and Action Statements

Collaboration entails working together toward a common goal, whether or not technologies are involved. The common goal for all learners is to master information and academic content and to acquire the skills necessary for

Table 2. Appropriate Collaboration Technologies

Audio-conferencing	Images, sounds, and video	Public domain forums
Brainstorming software	Internet	Satellite technologies
Cell phones	Intranet	Telephones
Chat rooms	Learning management	Video-conferencing
Desktop publishing software	systems	Voice mail
E-learning environments	List-servers	Virtual classroom
Electronic mail	Media players	Virtual meeting rooms
Electronic address lists	Modems	Word processing
Electronic recording devices	Networks	
File transfer protocol	Newsgroups	
Graphic organizers	Online bulletin boards	

successful lifelong learning. For this goal to be realized, educators must plan units of study that take full advantage of the collaborative technologies available (Table 2) and increase opportunities to learn and apply skills as they relate to the curriculum and individual learning needs.

For the student, teacher, and administrator, elements of successful collaboration include a shared philosophy along with a vision to put these goals into effect. Collaborative technologies foster open, interactive, and effectual interpersonal communication in today's digital learning environment.

Table 3. Action Statements for Technology Collaboration

Communicate *digital information*
Create a desktop-published *online newsletter*
Develop, edit, and submit *digital reflections*
Edit, revised, and resubmit a *word-processed term paper*
E-mail *electronic news/progress* with parents/families
E-mail fellow students
Forward new *hyperlinks* containing academic content
Investigate online *Web sites*
Interact *electronically* with other students
Participate in a *chat session*
Post current events in a *newsgroup*
Post messages to a *bulletin board*
Share information electronically
Subscribe to an appropriate *list-server*
Survey comments via the *Web*
Upload senior class project assignments to the school's *intranet Web site*
Work together via *chat rooms* in student groups

For consideration, Table 3 offers a list of <u>action verbs</u> (underlined once) and *instructional technologies* (italicized) for the second level of the Taxonomy for the Technology Domain.

Domains of Teaching and Technology Collaboration

The cognitive, affective, and psychomotor domains of teaching directly impact the second level of the new taxonomy as well as the first. As we shall see, the greatest use of collaborative tools is found in the affective domain. Considerably more refined psychomotor skills are required to effect collaboration: skills include highlighting, dragging, and multiple clicking text, use of right and left mouse buttons to initiate pop-down menus; mousing over miniature hot spots and hyperlinks, and customizing menu toolbars. A cognitive schema becomes an expeditious tool for interacting at this level. For example, although word processing is the most widely used application for the masses, office productivity packages themselves (with their spreadsheets, databases, graphics presentation, and more) contribute to a common suite of icons, menus, commands, toolbars, function keys, and key combinations standardized throughout the software suite. Such cognitive scaffolding makes it possible for users to easily transition between applications using similar keystrokes for like functions.

For better or worse, learners inextricably link communications with technology. Specifically, they communicate by writing with computers, keyboard operations, and color laser printers, speaking with cell phones, voice mail and electronic recording devices, and listening with earphones, media players, sound bytes, and video clips. Technology collaboration has become a natural manifestation of everyday communications.

Cognitive Domain

In the cognitive domain, constructing knowledge is essential if learning with technology is to occur. According to Bagley and Hunter (1992), learners are empowered to actively construct knowledge when using collaborative technologies. Technology provides resources for problem solving, thinking, and reflection — which are all cognitive constructs. Students spend more time sharing ideas with their peers and communicating with teachers when they have the collaborative skills found at the second level of the taxonomy.

With the teacher at the helm, collaboration supports the extension of student dialogue far beyond the classroom walls. Teachers at this level of the taxonomy embrace the use of networks (Internet, libraries, etc.) as a means to facilitate real-world investigations. They mold learners who are able to share goals, data, findings, analyses, and recommendations without barriers. Teachers who master this level adapt to the increase in student interaction and many actually begin to encourage student dialogue outside the classroom experience (Sandholtz et al., 1997).

Administrators use collaborative technologies to maintain the status quo or as a stimulus for change. Coincidentally, both are principle roles of the effective administrator. An array of Web-based technologies including school sites, intranets, databases, public domain forums, and electronic mailing lists, help educational organizations solve problems and achieve their strategic goals. Administrators reach out to constituencies, provide education and information services, support issues, and build strategic, mission-critical strategies using these technologies. Specifically, technology collaboration helps organizations increase public awareness and involvement, communicate important issues in a timely manner, generate concern and action on issues important to their mission, showcase news and minimize rumors pertaining to school matters, and provide value-added tools for tax-paying constituents.

Many of the technology applications described here encourage extensive student-to-student, student-to-teacher, and administrator-to-constituent communications. Word processing alone is insufficient. In this domain, a wealth of collaborative technologies must come into play to produce much needed changes in the school, classroom, and community.

From the inventory of appropriate collaboration technologies and action statements provided earlier, the following examples are exhibited below. Appropriate action verbs are underlined once while the *instructional technology* introduced is italicized. The first technology-based learning objective is suitable for students.

Cognitive domain: "Following the astronomy lesson entitled, The Night Sky, students will compose a short *expository paper* following correct conventions for grammar, spelling, and punctuation. They will use the K12-Science *List-service* to share with other students in at least two other countries in an appropriate discourse to compare what they see in the night sky at their respective longitude and latitude."

For the *teacher-as-scholar*, collaborative technologies often focus on opportunities for scaffolding interpersonal communication. An objective appropriate for professional development in a particular certification area is shown here.

Cognitive domain: "Teachers will <u>work together</u> using *synchronous and asynchronous communications* to locate sites appropriate for advancing lifelong learning and professional development in their specific academic content areas. Each participant must identify at least five *Internet Web sites*, two *list-services*, and two *bulletin boards* specifically addressing their instructional certification area and share these technologies via the school's Best Practices *intranet site*."

In the cognitive domain, *administrators* should be ready to compare and contrast available technologies for collaboration vis-à-vis the span of clients impacting education. A training session on collaborative technologies would include cognitive objectives such as the one shown below.

Cognitive domain: "After reviewing the Glossary of Collaborative Technologies, administrators will <u>work cooperatively</u> in assigned groups to produce a *Web-based primer* not to exceed five pages comparing and contrasting features, capabilities, and cost of *Web-based tools* appropriate for <u>reaching patrons</u> of the school and school district *electronically*."

Affective Domain

At this level of the Taxonomy for the Technology Domain, affective technology skills are integral to sharing ideas and advancing interpersonal communications. Collaborative technologies have the potential to transport student thinking to new levels of personal interaction. Teachers often use affective technologies to learn more about their students and present more effective instructional lessons. Administrators find these technologies a "virtual suggestion box" to gauge employee morale, solicit better practices, and provide electronic bulletins. Undoubtedly, more discussion of the pros and cons of technologies at this level of the taxonomy is necessary. For now, some examples of how students, teachers, and administrators might present collaborative skills in the affective domain are in order.

Affective *student* collaboration is the most predominant application of technology at this level of the taxonomy. Word processing supports collaboration. Electronic mail supports collaboration. Online communications supports collaboration. In addition, virtually every type of learner and every academic content area fall within the scope of these technologies. Selecting one affective learning objective as an example is difficult. The following instance, then, demonstrates a case in point only.

Affective domain: "Each student will <u>team up</u> with an *electronic pen-pal* in Spanish 101. Students will <u>send conversational</u> *e-mails* written in language appropriate for the classroom topic area under consideration. Students will also receive a minimum of five *e-mails* and using *digital translation software*, prepare your reaction to the message for classroom discussion."

At this level of the taxonomy, the *teacher-as-expert* serves a facilitative role in the classroom using technology to commend, volunteer, discuss, practice, acclaim, and augment learner exploration of content material. The following in-service workshop objective demonstrates the affective application of collaboration.

Affective domain: "Using an *online learning management system*, teachers will <u>investigate</u> various *collaborative tools* to foster <u>interaction</u> among students; learn how to create <u>student groups</u> and provide space for <u>team projects</u>; explore *communications options* for group work, including *bulletin boards*, *whiteboards* and *chat rooms*; and, <u>adopt</u> policies appropriate for creating student *home pages*."

Collaboration and *administrators* go hand-in-hand. In the affective domain, they are charged to establish and nurture learning communities. Often, collaborative technologies are the means to that end. Good writing skills are essential for effective communication to a constituency of peers, employees, partners, and colleagues. The professional preparation of administrators might include an affective learning objective like the one shown next.

Affective domain: "Using *word processing* and *desktop publishing software*, administrators will <u>compose</u> a comprehensive Student Handbook reflecting the adopted policies of the school board with respect to attendance, grading and assessment, and participation in sports. The handbook must <u>reflect teamwork,</u> be patterned after the Brochure Publication template, evidence grammatically correct content, and be free of any and all spelling errors (*spellchecker*)."

Psychomotor Domain

At this second level of the new taxonomy there are fewer applications of collaborative technologies to be found in the psychomotor domain. Students routinely practice using e-mail to communicate with other students. They master the repetitious tasks necessary to create, save, and upload documents created in a word-processing program. They navigate successful through the online maze of available Internet sites, chat rooms, bulletin boards, and list-servers.

Analogous to Bloom, Krathwohl, and others, the Taxonomy for the Technology Domain in general and collaborative skills specifically underscores the sequential, interdependent, consecutive nature of its antecedent taxonomies. To be successful with collaboration presumes competency from level 1.0.

A collaborative *student* learning objective in the psychomotor domain focuses student activity on acquiring, assembling, and manipulating information. One such objective is shown below.

Psychomotor domain: "Students will <u>request,</u> *via e-mail*, current economic indicators from their state representative. Following receipt of this information, students will chart a supply and demand curve, <u>share</u> that <u>information</u> *synchronously* with their group using the *online chat room*, <u>produce</u> a <u>visual chart</u> and <u>text-based</u> executive summary, and <u>deliver</u> the <u>information</u> *digitally* to the instructor."

Working collaboratively, teachers are better prepared to take advantage of one another's strengths and accommodate their weaknesses. Together, they reduce individual planning time while greatly increasing the available pool of ideas and materials. They become more adaptable and self-reliant. Teacher collaborations succeed in large measure by mastering specific skills, many of them in the psychomotor domain. Task-related training bolsters the confidence of a *teacher-as-learner* to work with one another outside the classroom. Addressing these competencies, a proper psychomotor learning objective at level 2.0 follows.

Psychomotor domain: "Academic teams will <u>work collaboratively</u> to design an assessment instrument for their respective content areas. Using *Web-based rubrics*, teachers will <u>input</u> item <u>questions</u> to an *online quiz* (or <u>click and drag</u> selected question items from a library of teacher-created quizzes), integrate automatic scoring and recording of grades; assess and track student progress; and, <u>share</u> reports *asynchronously* with students and parents."

Administrators are advocates for effective practices in the use of technologies. In *School Districts: What Leaders Can Do To Support Their Schools*, the Center for Reinventing Public Education (2003) at the University of Washington identified collaboration among administrators as one of its top five common strategies for improving education. According to the study of schools in the State of Washington, "collaboration by school level, as well as between elementary and middle schools, was cited as a factor in schools' ability to raise test scores." *Administrators* are encouraged to master and use collaborative technologies in the psychomotor domain. An example follows.

Psychomotor domain: "Principals and curriculum directors will <u>cooperate</u> with staff and students to develop, edit, and submit digital and hard copy contributions for inclusion in the monthly *virtual school newspaper* that will be <u>uploaded</u> to the school's *Home Page* on the Internet and <u>accessed</u> by all interested district constituents."

Technology Collaboration and the Psychologies of Learning

Behaviorism (specifically classical conditioning) ties the learner's response directly to a conditioned stimulus and, as such, has not been found to be particularly relevant to collaboration. The goal of collaboration is to work together effectively and that takes initiative, individuality, and personalization and not a predictable response to a specific stimulus.

Likewise, certain theories of cognitive development, characterized chiefly by the precepts of age-stage development and proximal learning, place unnecessary boundaries on the use of technology for collaboration. Humanism takes center stage in the application of technology collaboration. Students, teachers, and school administrators work together more effectively using technology-based collaborative tools in order to address student needs and disseminate timely information.

Behaviorism

Competency with respect to collaboration is difficult to envision without returning to the fundamentals of classical and operant conditioning. Both Pavlov and Skinner contributed to the behavioral underpinnings of this psychology that call for overtly sequencing instruction to ensure successful learning outcomes. The next example learning objective evidences a unit of instruction for *students* seeking to acquire the skills of technology-based interpersonal communications following the principles of behavioral learning.

Behaviorism: "Over the course of the fall semester, students will be exposed to the *collaborative tools* of the Internet to include electronic mail, gopher, list-server, newsgroups, file transfer protocol, chat rooms, and bulletin boards. Following this introduction, they will demonstrate their mastery of technology as collaboration by <u>sending</u> an *e-mail*, <u>accessing</u> a *gopher site*, <u>subscribing</u> to an appropriate *list-service*, <u>reviewing</u> a *newsgroup*, <u>transferring</u> <u>files</u> via the school *network*, <u>participating</u> in a *chat session*, and <u>posting</u> a message to a *bulletin board*."

An appropriate *teacher-as-expert* objective at the technology collaboration level might present an in-service workshop objective containing sequenced instruction characteristic of behavioral learning objectives.

Behaviorism: "Mathematics teachers will explain their understanding of geometry through <u>group work</u> and <u>produce</u> a *multi-media* information *presentation*, *spreadsheets*, and posters depicting the concepts of circles; angles and triangles; and lines and planes, and <u>share</u> those <u>materials</u> *electronically* with their peers by uploading the materials to the school's *intranet*."

Following the behavioral pattern of sequencing, *administrators* staff an important district Strategic Master Plan through the various constituencies using collaborative technologies indicated in the following training workshop objective.

Behaviorism: "Administrators will <u>solicit comments</u> via *interactive collaborative resources* of the school's Web site regarding the Strategic Plan from district constituents. Specifically, administrators will <u>post links</u> to the draft Plan on the school's *home page*, electronic *bulletin board*, and list-server. Comments will be <u>reviewed and edited</u> by senior district officials and school board members as *word-processed documents*."

Cognitivism

Collaboration techniques actively share data, information, knowledge, perceptions, or concepts when working together toward a common goal. Specific cognitive-based collaborations address interactions where cognitive processes predominate. In the cognitive domain, then, technologies for collaboration are found as general purpose and general support tools, tools to facilitate autonomous group processes, and tools to facilitate shared-group processes. General purpose and support tools represent the most common expressions of collaborative technologies. They foster collaboration via e-mail, video and audio conferencing, databases, bulletin boards, news groups, and Web pages. They support asynchronous communication while others exploit synchronous interaction.

Tools to facilitate autonomous group processes address many of the obstacles to successful collaboration that exist even when people meet face to face. Commercially available tools include virtual meeting rooms and software promoting brainstorming, negotiations, review and editing, and idea generation. Finally, tools to facilitate group processes provide visual interactivity for sharing lesson content such as Web-based white boards and e-learning environments.

Students benefit directly from cognitive-based collaborative tools. A well-designed technology program includes learning objectives encouraging *student* development of schemata for using these technologies to participate in learning opportunities outside the four walls of the traditional classroom.

Cognitivism: "Students will <u>recognize</u>, <u>classify</u>, and <u>organize</u> proper *communication protocols* before <u>sending</u> *e-mail* to their *online pen-pals*. Such protocols will include an awareness of *network etiquette*, the possibility of receiving unsolicited e-mail (and appropriate steps to take to resolve the situation), and the dangers of infecting computers with a virus received as an *e-mail attachment*."

Teacher communication takes so many different forms that offering a subset of collaborative tools in the cognitive domain is often unproductive. Technology collaboration supports both formal and informal learning environments. Teachers might find themselves targeting goals in school improvement plans through the use of effective technology or participating in an online professional learning community. As a result, all *teachers-as-learners* need cognitive-based, organizational underpinnings to promote their collaborative skills. A comprehensive program of study in instructional technology would include a learning objective like the one below.

Cognitivism: "Given a review of the fundamental capabilities and features of the *Internet*, teachers will <u>model</u> the most appropriate *technologies* as they pertain to a variety of classroom situations. At a minimum, a synopsis of the following *collaborative tools* will be included: *electronic mail, list-servers, telnet, file transfer, World Wide Web*, and *online learning management systems*."

Besides mastering minimal collaborative competencies, *administrators* need a host of additional interpersonal communications skills to ensure success. As instructional leaders, they invest in quality professional development programs within the school, leveraging limited dollars to reach all teachers within the school building. Using collaboration, they increase standards-based, research driven professional learning opportunities for teachers, provide ongoing continuous support for teachers integrating technology, build teaming opportunities that help develop common practice, and facilitate leadership abilities and the awareness of essential components of quality leaders. Towards that end, professional leadership seminars include the following cognitive collaborative learning objective in their technology-oriented programs.

Cognitivism: "Upon completion of this workshop series, the participants should be able to inspire a <u>shared vision</u> for the effective use of *technology for teaching and learning*, <u>portray</u> the latest educational *technology research* and how it applies to best practices in the classroom, and ensure school-based support structures are in place for maximizing teaching and learning with technology."

Humanism

Well-designed technologies for collaboration create experiences fostering self-knowledge in several ways. First, collaboration makes content more realistic, more useful, and certainly more credible. Electronic mail, bulletin boards, and Web sites extend the classroom to experts in the field who share the passion, commitment, and wisdom of actual episodes. Real stories, shared via collaborative technologies, come through loud and clear, producing immediate veracity regarding academic content along with an ease to internalize the content material.

Humanism, then, becomes the predominant psychology for the application of collaborative tools for teaching and learning. Technology collaboration enriches the curriculum as a vehicle for collecting and distributing rich sources of information. It supports learning by providing an additional media for transferring information and thereby reducing administrative overhead associated with routine communications.

Collaborative tools incite interaction among active learners and strengthen opportunities for human interaction rather than replacing those opportunities. They support many specific activities related to teaching and learning including: e-mailing faculty with "just in time" questions; enhancing reflection and critical thinking skills by removing face-to-face communications barriers; creating a more comfortable learning environment by setting a conversational tone that models effective teaching; and, by bringing in economic, cultural, and international communities for collaborative discussions.

Student collaboration in support of humanistic learning is sustained by e-mail and online discussions enhancing communication between the instructor and among students. These technologies expand traditional classroom-based courses and make interactive distance learning possible. Here's one such learning objective.

Humanism: "Students will <u>liaise</u> *synchronously* (via online chat rooms) and *asynchronously* (via electronic mail) to <u>discuss the impact</u> of technology on human resources, financial markets, and the environment. Together students from Korea, Egypt, Finland, and the United States will complete a <u>team project advocating a solution</u> to a real-world problem during a *videoconference session* led by the instructor."

Teachers adhere to humanistic principles when collaborating electronically. Fewer technologies are more suitable to personalizing the learning experience, improving student curiosity and concentration, motivating students to learn more, inspiring creativity, and enhancing communication among all educational partners. Below is an example learning objective taken directly from a *teacher-as-scholar* professional development program using collaborative tools for sharing ideas.

Humanism: "Teachers are expected to <u>share</u> the progress of their individual research agendas to peers and colleagues *online*. They will employ the Scholars' ListService to <u>post</u> periodic research abstracts; <u>communicate</u> via e-mail with reviewers assigned by the ListService; encourage <u>reviewer interaction</u> with *Web-based inquiries*; and, <u>place</u> their final manuscripts on the service *Web site*."

Administrators become role models by using collaborative technologies for communicating with faculty and by launching their own professional development and research agendas. Effective leaders use e-mail to expedite notices, feedback, and remarks with their constituents. The following objective is typical of an appropriate *administrator* application of humanistic technology collaboration.

Humanism: "School administrators will <u>design</u> the major components of an *interactive school intranet* containing *communications instruments* for teachers, parents and students, community members, and professional educational organizations. As a minimum, the site must include Web-based *synchronous and asynchronous communications tools* as well as provisions for linking to digital, *personalized audio-video files* (e.g., sound bytes and video clips, streaming video, etc.)."

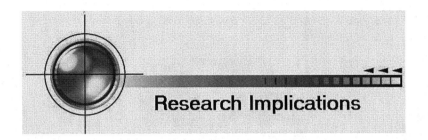

Research Implications

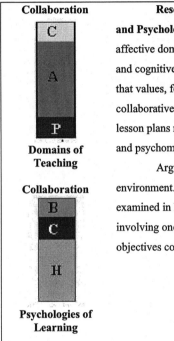

Collaboration

Domains of Teaching

Collaboration

Psychologies of Learning

Research Phase I: Collaboration and the Domains of Teaching and Psychologies of Learning. Research supports the preeminence of the affective domain and, to a lesser degree, the importance of the psychomotor and cognitive domains for technology collaboration. Tomei (2001) found that values, feelings, and emotions bear significant influence on teaching collaborative technology skills. At this level of the taxonomy, over 70% of lesson plans reviewed incorporated affective learning objectives. Cognitive and psychomotor objectives shared the remaining 30%.

Arguably, collaboration thrives best in the humanistic learning environment. Tomei (2001) found that over half of the lesson plans examined in his investigation were directed at collaborative technologies involving one or more humanistic objectives. Behavioral and cognitive objectives comprised the remaining plans.

Research Phase II: Collaboration and Technology-Based Learning Objectives

As a reminder, the inquiry selected some 300 lesson plans and categorized over 1,440 learning objectives by their representative level of the taxonomy (Table 3).

The Phase II study determined that collaborative technologies accounted for approximately 12% of technology-based lesson objectives. What is not shown above is the finding that all grade levels and academic content areas examined contained at least one collaborative objective, by far the highest representative of any of the taxonomy levels.

Table 3. Student Learning Objectives by Taxonomy Level

Level of Taxonomy	Totals	Percent Within Levels
Literacy	610	42.3
Collaboration	176	12.2
Decision-Making	380	26.4
Infusion	188	13.2
Integration	57	3.8
Tech-ology	30	2.1
Totals	1441	100.0

Conclusion of Technology Collaboration (Level 2.0)

Collaboration is all about people. Under the best of circumstances, technologies make available the automated tools, an organizational framework, and the distance-based opportunities to support interpersonal interaction between two people, between teacher and learner, or between educators and constituents. At its worst, we find that collaborative technologies simply do not work the way people do. Technology oftentimes confines the natural human communication process. Therefore, caution in the implementation of any technology for collaboration is always sound advice.

At the next level of the Taxonomy for the Technology Domain, decision-making technologies are introduced and with them a discussion of the tools necessary to use technology in new and concrete situations.

References

Bagley, C., & Hunter, B. (1992). Restructuring constructivism and technology: Forging a new relationship. *Educational Technology*.

Blackboard Learning System (Release 6). (2003). Blackboard Inc. Retrieved from the World Wide Web: *www.blackboard.com/products/ls*

Center for Reinventing Public Education. (2003). School districts: What leaders can do to support their schools. University of Washington. Retrieved from the World Wide Web: *www.partnership4learning.org/plsum/plsumdistricts.html*

Collaborative for Technology Standards for School Administrators. (2003). Technology Standards for School Administrators, TSSA Draft, version 4.0. Retrieved from the World Wide Web: *cnets.iste.org/tssa/view_standards.html*

International Society for Technology in Education (ISTE). (2003). Educational Technology Standards and Performance Indicators for All Teachers, National Educational Technology Standards for Teachers. Retrieved from the World Wide Web: *cnets.iste.org/teachers/t_stands.html*

International Society for Technology in Education (ISTE). (2003). Technology Foundation Standards for All Students, National Educational Technology Standards for Students. Retrieved from the World Wide Web: *cnets.iste.org/students/s_stands.html*

Sandholtz, J.H., Ringstaff, C., & Dwyer, D.C. (1997). *Teaching with technology: Creating student-centered classrooms*. New York: Teachers College, Columbia University.

Tomei, L.A. (2001, April 30). *Using a taxonomy for the technology domain*. Penn Association of Colleges and Teacher Educators.

Tomei, L.A. (2002). *The technology facade: Overcoming barriers to effective instructional technology*. Boston MA: Allyn & Bacon Publishers.

WebCT Campus Edition. (2003). Course Management System, Product Tour. Retrieved from the World Wide Web: *www.webct.com/products/viewpage?name=products_demo_webinars*

Annotated Bibliography

Additional citations for Technology for Decision-Making

Blacker, D. (1994). Philosophy of Technology and Education: An Invitation to Inquiry, Illinois State University. Retrieved from the World Wide Web: *www.ed.uiuc.edu/EPS/PES-yearbook/94_docs/BLACKER.HTM*

Borgmann, A. (1984). *Technology and the character of contemporary life.* Chicago: University of Chicago Press.

Huth, C., & Ravenstahl, H. (2002). NETS Standards Based Scope and Sequence for Technology Education, Grades K-8.

Liu, G. (2002). Smart Ways to Disseminate Information to Build Collaboration in the School: Web-Based Collaboration and the Constructivism. Computer and Network Center. National Chiao Tung University.

Public Agenda Foundation. (1995, October). *Assignment incomplete: The unfinished business of education reform.*

Riley, R.W. (1996). *Getting America's Students Ready for the 21st Century: Meeting the Technology Literacy Challenge - June 1996. A Report to the Nation on Technology and Education.* United States Department Of Education. Retrieved from the World Wide Web: *www.ed.gov/technology/plan/nattechplan/*

Chapter 8

Technology for Decision-Making (Level 3.0)

Decision-Making Solving Problems	**Level 3.0** Ability to use technology in new and concrete situations to analyze, assess, and judge.

Theoretical Frameworks

Definition and Historical Origins

Decision-making technologies literally launched the instructional technology revolution. As such, the third level of the Taxonomy for the Technology Domain centers on problem-solving and its application is defined as *"the ability to use technology in new and concrete situations to analyze, assess, and judge."*

The introduction of a single software package in the early 1980s heralded the age of the microcomputer and transported forever this technology from the workroom of hobbyists to the work desk of nearly everyone. By January 1979, the Apple II personal computer experienced stalled sales. The fascination with hardware was over and users were beginning to ask the $64,000 question, "Now what do I do with this computer?" Fortunately, the answer was found not in hardware but in a software program so important and so useful that it literally sold new computers. In the book, *Accidental Empires*, the author explains the phenomenon this way:

> *"VisiCalc was a compelling application — an application so important that it, alone, justified the purchase of computers. Such an application was the last element required to turn the microcomputer from a hobbyist's toy into a business machine. No matter how powerful and brilliantly designed, no computer can be successful without a compelling application. To the people who bought them, mainframes were really inventory machines or accounting machines, and minicomputers were office automation machines. The Apple II was a VisiCalc machine" (Cringely, 1992).*

Decision-making tools in general came to expand the usefulness of technology in ways no one had ever imagined before, especially at a time when mainframe computers were the only access to most users. Today, strategic decision-makers work in dynamic environments that are increasingly difficult to address using the traditional pencil and paper means of analysis. Specifically, the onslaught of vast amounts of data is increasingly sophisticated, often conflicting, and usually distracting. Planning for the future demands more creative and sophisticated decision-making tools capable of simulating real world dilemmas and exploring "what-if" scenarios.

The Taxonomy for the Technology Domain includes a wide assortment of technologies for decision-making. In addition to the original spreadsheet application, other such technologies include visualization tools such as brain-storming and graphic organizer packages, computer-assisted design, simulation tools, database and statistical analysis applications. Spreadsheets are now subsumed under the more general heading of impact analysis tools and take in financial, medical, and environmental as well as educational investigations.

Finally, interactive groupware (Web-based, town-meeting tools) facilitates whole class and small group decision-making. It is at this third level of the taxonomy that many new technologies come into play as recommended competencies for students, teachers, and administrators.

Standards for Technology Decision-Making

Two categories of decision-making technologies provide the ISTE NETS*S standards for students (ISTE, 2003). Technology research tools and problem-solving/decision-making tools comprise a total of five specific skill sets for learners (Table 1).

Teachers at all levels of development are encouraged to master technologies for decision-making in the form of assessment and evaluation tools. According to NETS*T (ISTE, 2003), teachers-as-experts should use technology to facilitate a variety of assessment and evaluation strategies. Although there is plenty of research regarding computers in elementary and secondary classrooms, the teacher-as-scholar needs to function at this level of the taxonomy to explore the use of technology as a decision support tool. Traditionally, technologies have surfaced more as a laborsaving, management tools for the teacher-as-learner (Merrill et al., 1996). New decision-making tools include grade book software for student record keeping, automatic score averaging, and printouts of student progress reports as well as database software to provide a test generation inventory. Students and teachers together must seek an understanding of how technologies for decision-making can help them acquire new knowledge.

Administrators, on the other hand, need these technologies to effectively dispatch the responsibilities of their office. The Collaborative for Technology Standards for School Administrators (2003) intersperses decision-making tools liberally throughout its standards for leadership. Leadership entails research, data analysis, implementation, integration, monitoring, and allocation (words taken directly from the TSSA standards) all of which culminate in effective decision-making. For the educational administrator, effective decision-making in turn implies the successful use of technology.

Table 1 provides the level 3.0 decision-making skills appropriate for teachers, students, and administrators.

Decision-making technologies include: electronic portfolios and professional development plans, e-mail for just-in-time deliberations, software for student

Table 1. Decision-Making Standards for Students, Teachers, and Administrators

Decision-Making Competency	Student Standards	Teacher-as-Learner Standards	Teacher-as-Expert Standards	Teacher-as-Scholar Standards	Administrators
NETS*S					
Technology research tools	x				
• Students use technology to locate, evaluate, and collect information from a variety of sources.	x				
• Students use technology tools to process data and report results.	x				
Technology problem-solving and decision-making tools	x				
• Students use technology resources for solving problems and making informed decisions.	x				
• Students employ technology in the development of strategies for solving problems in the real world.	x				
NETS*T					
Teachers apply technology to facilitate a variety of effective assessment and evaluation strategies.		x	x	x	
• Use technology resources to collect and analyze data, interpret results, and communicate findings to improve instructional practice and maximize student learning.		x	x	x	
Teachers use technology to enhance their productivity and professional practice.		x	x	x	
• Continually evaluate and reflect on professional practice to make informed decisions regarding the use of technology in support of student learning.		x	x	x	

grading, evaluation, and anecdotal classroom observations, and exemplars of instructional materials that incorporate technology as an empowerment tool. Leader-educators extol electronic decision-making tools for developing curriculum content, monitoring faculty development and preparation of in-service programs, and reviewing and recommending educational technologies (hardware and software purchases).

Table 1. Decision-Making Standards for Students, Teachers, and Administrators (continued)

Decision-Making Competency	Student Standards	Teacher-as-Learner Standards	Teacher-as-Expert Standards	Teacher-as-Scholar Standards	Administrators
TSSA					
Educational leaders apply technology to enhance their professional practice and increase their productivity and that of others.					x
• Use technology to advance organizational improvement.					x
Educational leaders ensure the integration of technology to support productive systems for learning and administration.					x
• Develop, implement, and monitor policies and guidelines to ensure compatibility of technologies.					x
• Implement and use integrated technology-based management and operations systems.					x
• Allocate financial and human resources to ensure complete and sustained implementation of the technology plan.					x
• Integrate strategic plans, technology plans, and other improvement plans and policies to align efforts and leverage resources.					x
• Implement procedures to drive continuous improvement of technology systems and to support technology replacement cycles.					
Educational leaders use technology to plan and implement comprehensive systems of effective assessment and evaluation.					x
• Use technology to collect and analyze data, interpret results, and communicate findings to improve instructional practice and student learning.					x
• Assess staff knowledge, skills, and performance in using technology and use results to facilitate quality professional development and to inform personnel decisions.					x
• Use technology to assess, evaluate, and manage administrative and operational systems.					x

Following the precepts of the Taxonomy for the Technology Domain, technology for decision-making implies mastery of the previous two stages. Before electronic tools are applied to problems, prior to developing strategic visions for education, and ahead of any efforts to advance particular solutions to practical real world problems, students, teachers, and administrators must come to grips with a minimum level of literacy and collaboration. Only then will decision-making tools advance the technology domain in ways unimagined only a few short decades ago.

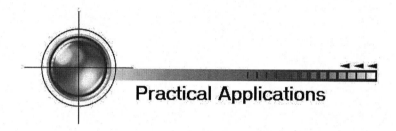

Practical Applications

Decision-Making Technologies and Action Statements

Tools for decision-making abound at level 3.0 of the Taxonomy for the Technology Domain (Table 2). Hardware and software assist teachers, administrators, and policymakers in evaluating students' skills and weaknesses; improving the performance of students with diverse abilities and needs; building local capacity to provide online professional development for teachers and staff; and, helping administrators effectively integrate of technology into their schools and districts.

Students use technologies for decision-making to monitor their own performance. Teachers use them to gauge the effectiveness of educational programs, teaching methods, and curriculum. Administrators use these resources to determine the effectiveness of programs, goals, and reform efforts and to uncover problem areas and their causes. Collectively, the action statements in Table 3 offer a comparative handful of decision-making technologies for consideration. Appropriate <u>action verbs</u> are underlined once while the *instructional technology* introduced is italicized.

Table 2. Appropriate Decision-making Technologies

Anecdotal classroom observations Artificial intelligence Brainstorming software Chart wizard Computer-aided design Computer-assisted design Computer decision support systems Computer simulation software Database applications	Electronic surveys Expert decision systems Grade book software Graphic organizer software Interactive groupware Internet search operations Online evaluation rubrics	Simulation tools Spreadsheets Statistical analysis applications Student grading and evaluation Troubleshooting

Table 3. Action Statements for Technology Collaboration

Analyze interactive *help prompts* and *error messages*
Assess data via *statistical analysis software*
Choose *software menu* and *tools options*
Debate and evaluate alternatives for new *technologies*
Decide using *spreadsheet analyses*
Defend *computers in a laboratory* environment
Defend *computers in the classroom* environment
Develop a computer-based *decision support systems*
Establish an historical *student tracking system*
Interpret *charts/graphs*
Isolate, diagnose, and trouble-shoot hardware problems
Report using *database* capabilities
Track student achievement via *grade book software*

Domains of Teaching and Technology Decision-Making

The preponderance of decision-making tools has been found to lie more or less equally in the cognitive and affective domains. Cognitively, decision-making is defined as the act of information processing, transforming knowledge and information into action (Galbraith, 1974; Orton & Weick, 1990). Decision-makers in the classroom must possess a reasonably accurate mental image of the educational process and its interaction with the world in order to make decisions effectively. Such is the cognitive role of technology for decision-making.

The proper application of affective decision-making skills often leads to agreement, even on the toughest issues. Technologies offer more options and alternatives upon which to base decisions and advance a higher degree of personal and professional involvement. Decision-making tools promote information gathering, summarizing possible conclusions, identifying possible alternatives, and uncovering the most desirable courses of action. These technologies monitor the effectiveness of the decision-making process — important skills for the affective domain of teaching. For the affective educator, it is important to realize that students, teachers, and administrators do not have to agree on the reasons behind a decision, but they must agree on the facts as presented and the solution to be implemented. This last statement describes in large measure the affective role of technology for decision-making.

Learners make decisions in different ways depending on how much time they have to decide. If an immediate response is required, decisions might be made on a psychomotor level. Often characterized as "instinctive" or "reflex" responses, psychomotor decision-making is typically focused on avoiding danger or seizing a short-lived opportunity. As a result, there are fewer documented examples of decision-making learning objectives in the psychomotor domain.

Decision-making technologies provide a wealth of resources for teachers-as-learners, teachers-as-experts, and teachers-as-scholars. The Taxonomy for the Technology Domain explores this phase by advancing technology-based analysis, synthesis, and evaluation skills for students, teachers, and administrators.

Cognitive Domain

Students must come to master certain decision-making tools in order to expand their own personal schemata of problem solving. Teachers use simulations to provide hands-on experience with problem situations that are difficult to create or involve safety factors. They use data and resources from the Internet to design student tasks. Spreadsheets, dynamic software, and computer simulation software are also useful tools for posing real-world problems.

In studies investigating the effectiveness of teaching decision-making skills to students, three specific deficiencies were identified (Shanteau et al., 2003). First, most students do not make effective or efficient use of available information. Too often, they extract exceedingly large amounts of incoherent information before making judgments. Technology helps to overcome this shortcoming. Second, deficiencies in decision-making usually lie in the extrapolation of data to risk and uncertainty, that is, in the application of the decision to the real world. Here again, technologies for decision-making help. Third, weaknesses were reported in students' abilities to evaluate alternatives and to choose from appropriate alternatives. Technologies for decision-making remediate such limitations.

When students do use technological tools, they often spend time working in configurations that alter the role of the traditional classroom teacher, turning the instructor from "the sage on the stage" to the "guide by the side." Yet, truly excellent teachers continue to play a role in technology-rich classrooms making just-in-time decisions that ultimately affect student learning.

For example, the teacher always retains responsibility for when, how, and even if technology is used. Calculators or computers in the classroom afford the teacher opportunities to observe students moving the focus of their thinking from the mechanics of calculations to interpretation of the results. Thus, decision-making tools aid in assessment, thereby allowing teachers to examine the thinking process used by students in their investigations and ultimately enriching the instructional experience.

Administrative decision-making centers around more traditional analytical approaches commonly associated with program evaluation, action research, and institutional assessment, continuous improvement, educational evaluation, and student assessment. With the passage of the No Child Left Behind (NCLB) Act, administrators must accept an even greater share of the responsibility for meeting legislated reporting requirements. Report preparation and submissions must be made more effective, equitable, and efficient. Given the demands on administrators, technologies for decision-making represent a viable channel for meeting imposed deadlines.

This first example demonstrates a *student* learning objective in the cognitive domain and involves decision-making tools found in previous tables. Appropriate <u>action verbs</u> are underlined once while the *instructional technology* introduced is italicized.

Cognitive domain: "Students will <u>choose</u> the proper features of *chart wizard* within the spreadsheet software to create different types of charts and graphs (to include column chart, bar chart, line chart, and pie chart) from the financial data collected. From this *visual presentation*, students will <u>predict</u> the impact of an increase and decrease in prime interest rates to the profit margin of their pseudo-business."

In the classroom, the *teacher-as-expert* uses technology to enhance student learning opportunities by selecting or creating tasks that take advantage of what technology does best — graphing, visualizing, and computing. The objective below prepares teachers to model these technologies.

Cognitive domain: "Given five *educational software* packages in a major academic content area (math, science, social studies, language arts, or fine arts), the teacher will construct an online rubric for evaluating education software and <u>compare</u> the results to applicable state academic standards to <u>evaluate</u> the strengths and weaknesses of each package and <u>propose</u> the package that best supports (i.e., price and content coverage) the technology-*based learning objectives* of the curriculum."

Data-driven decision-making tools are fundamentally changing education as *administrators* seek to understand what really works with students. In turn, their knowledge of these tools might just address the school-based support structures necessary to ensure compliance with emerging mandates. Here is a cognitive objective for all administrators to consider.

Cognitive domain: "Using the Department of Education (DOE) Toolkit for Teachers, the *database* of historical student assessments, and the SPSS *statistical analysis package*, administrators will <u>measure</u> student learning outcomes in both reading and mathematics, <u>index</u> academic achievement at the elementary and middle school, and <u>forecast</u> the school's graduation rate for 2014."

Affective Domain

Decision-making tools in the affective domain run the gamut as students, teachers, and administrators increased their goal setting and decision-making skills. Such technologies promote the decision-making process and predict immediate and long-term consequences to individual, family, and community.

Numerous research projects are underway to explore the affective implications of incorporating decision-making tools into student curriculum. The Affective Computing Research Group at the MIT Media Lab, for example, focuses on creating personal computational systems endowed with the ability to sense, recognize, and understand human emotions. They are also interested in developing computers that assist and support personal decision-making skills as well as the intelligence and ethics to appropriately manage, express, and otherwise utilize these "emotions" (Picard, 2003).

The following learning objective was taken from a lesson plan for ninth grade *students* and demonstrates the application of technology for decision-making in the affective domain.

Affective domain: "Contrasting four-month weather data from last fall, winter, and spring, students will <u>interpret</u> the electronic *spreadsheet chart/ graph data* and its impact and <u>rationale</u> for their decision as to an appropriate month to schedule school intramural games during the upcoming school year."

Teachers-as-learners are often introduced to technology-based materials containing few mistakes or shortcomings. As a result, learning that naturally occurs when their own students encounter confusion, frustration, a host of other associated affective responses is missing. Technology for decision-making facilitates this aspect of learning and does so with less risk emotionally, physically, or financially to the learner or the teacher. The learning objective that follows is characteristic of a lesson involving such technology.

Affective domain: "Using Internet search engines to <u>disclose</u> target instructional *technology career paths*, teachers will prepare an electronic compendium (i.e., historical *database*) of successful leaders in the IT discipline. Participants will characterize the management styles and personal value systems of exceptional leaders and the possible career paths in the field of instructional technology that satisfy their own professional development ambitions."

For many, analyzing the decision-making process in any organization is key to understanding how it functions. The study of decision-making in educational organizations has a long tradition, yet research has often yielded contradictory results. Decision-making is often viewed as a social activity involving groupthink, committee work, and consensus-building depending on the nature of the problem, context of the school, traits of individuals, the availability of information, and other factors. *Administrators* prepare to lead these efforts by familiarizing themselves with available technologies for decision-making such as those shown in the objective below.

Affective domain: "During the administrator's workshop, participants will build a *computer-based decision support system* in response to the legislative reporting requirements of the No Child Left Behind Act. Administrators must understand the concepts of group decision-making, develop an agenda for timely completion of the project, and demonstrate the merits and implications of *technology-based expert systems* to assist the group in deciding the necessary elements of the reports."

Psychomotor Domain

Citations involving technologies for decision-making in the psychomotor domain are few and far between. Even those that address motor skills do so only in general terms. For students, psychomotor skills are found mostly in early childhood curriculum. Hardware troubleshooting offers the only competencies found in the review of teacher competencies. None were found specifically for administrators, although the argument is made here that administrators should possess troubleshooting skills similar to teachers.

For those lesson objectives that were discovered during the research, the argument could be made that they more closely align with technology literacy (Level 1.0) than decision-making. As a result, the learning objectives in the psychomotor domain shown below are offered only for consideration. In other words, better examples are needed before making the case that decision-making tools in the psychomotor domain represent a viable classification within the taxonomy.

A decision-making *student* learning objective in the psychomotor domain might involve gross and fine motor skills required to effectively use an electronic spreadsheet. The learning objective below, found at the K-3 (early childhood) grade level, demonstrates this skill.

Psychomotor domain: "Students will be able to <u>practice</u> appropriately sufficient *motor skills* to execute aspects of <u>spreadsheet</u> operations including, but not limited to: <u>point and click</u>, *highlight* text, <u>drag</u> contents of a spreadsheet cell within a worksheet, between worksheets, and between standalone spreadsheets."

Troubleshooting workshops provide the best decision-making objectives in the psychomotor domain. Such sessions often provide a minimum set of motor skills necessary to diagnose, isolate, and resolve problems with classroom computers and computer peripheral devices, projectors, and audio and video recorders and players. Teachers who, by trial and error, attempt to overcome the problem acquire most of these skills on-the-job. Others acquire these skills by witnessing another's — often their own students — attempts at troubleshooting. Regardless, the following learning objective cites a troubleshooting workshop for established *teachers-as-scholars* and demonstrates an aspect of decision-making in the psychomotor domain.

Psychomotor domain: "All classroom teachers will be able to <u>reproduce</u> basic *troubleshooting techniques* related to classroom technologies. At a minimum, participants will <u>isolate</u>, <u>diagnose</u>, and <u>refine</u> possible solutions to selected classroom technology malfunctions, software setup and installations, *configuring peripherals*, and minor *repairs*."

Without delving too deeply into other psychomotor skills, *administrators* should possess similar psychomotor competencies with regards to classroom technologies, perhaps at a more competent level. Here is a learning objective for consideration.

Psychomotor domain: "Principals and administrators will demonstrate a level of competence in <u>troubleshooting</u> the following classroom technologies: computers and associated *peripheral devices*, *projectors*, *scanners*, *digital cameras*, and *network connections*."

Technology for Decision-Making and the Psychologies of Learning

The ability to discern which students are learning and which are not has become the behavioral basis for tailoring instruction to meet individual learning needs. The No Child Left Behind (NCLB) Act of 2001 holds states, districts, and schools accountable for student achievement. It requires regular assessments to document progress, supported by data maintained for record keeping purposes and reported in the aggregate (combined) and disaggregate (separated by groups and subgroups) by school. Effective teachers use this data daily to make their own informed decisions.

The U.S. Department of Education has published a Toolkit for Teachers summarizing the provisions of No Child Left Behind, answering common questions, and providing information on where to find additional resources. In this document, published in 2003, each district receiving Educational Technology State Grants funds is required to spend at least 25% (an estimated $159 billion at President Bush's current requested funding level) on high-quality professional development in the integration of technology, including "the best analytical tools to ensure early and ongoing assessment of every child's progress" (US DOE, 2003).

In the 1950s and 1960s, cognitive-based research on decision-making focused on clearly structured problems that were within the range of technological sophistication even for its time. Computer programs were written to discover proofs for theorems or to propose scenarios for transporting goods across country.

During the 1960s and 1970s, the next target was to find methods for organizing large quantities of information clearly in the cognitive realm. As the role of technologies for decision-making continued to advance further over the next several decades, a preponderance of cognitive technologies appropriate for student learning, teacher application, and administrative use surfaced.

Technologies for decision-making often demand expert decision systems, large databases, artificial intelligence, computer-aided design and a fairly well-developed understanding of the decision-making process that lends itself well to computer simulation, both for purposes of testing its empirical validity and for augmenting humanistic problem-solving capacities by the construction of expert systems.

Behaviorism

Behaviorism as a psychology for learning relies on orderly discovery. According to Skinner, learning is promoted by controlling responses to desired stimuli in a series of sequential steps that include defining the objective(s), identifying a set of possible actions, gathering support information, testing each alternative, assessing positive and negative consequences, making a final decision, and implementing that decision.

Decisions imply feedback. Eventually, as correct decisions are rewarded and incorrect decisions fail, target skills and knowledge are reinforced. What better way to learn decision-making? Some call it "trial and error," but proponents of behaviorism prefer the term "acquired skill." The following example learning objective demonstrates how a *student* acquires decision-making skills using behavioral principles.

Behaviorism: "Students will <u>enter data</u> into an electronic *spreadsheet* <u>recording</u> how much *digital data* can be stored on selected media, to include a *3.5 floppy*, *CD-ROM*, *zip disk*, *mini-disk*, and *DVD*. Students will <u>react</u> to <u>interactive help</u> prompts and error messages (e.g., free-form text question, available options, search features, and online index) to resolve problems."

New technologies are introduced daily, offering the teacher more effective methods for gauging classroom learning outcomes. An appropriate *teacher-as-learner* objective might address a new behavioral tool for assessing student understanding in the classroom. Here is one such behavioral objective that uses software for group response and information gathering to facilitate and enhance classroom interaction.

Behaviorism: "Teachers will <u>encounter</u> a series of five *videotaped episodes* simulating actual leadership scenarios. Using the electronic *"ranking wizard,"* they will <u>create lists</u> of issues, priorities or goals and <u>rank them</u> against three specific criteria using either a static scale (1-10) or a "paired comparison" approach. Teachers will learn how to <u>operate</u> the classroom-based *digital group response system* by responding to each situation and <u>transmitting</u> *electronic feedback* to small group discussion forums using data collected from the responses."

At the decision-making level of the taxonomy, an appropriate *administrator* objective might address an NCLB reporting requirement such as the one covered in a recent principal's workshop (US DOE, 2003).

Behaviorism: "Middle school principals <u>collect</u> and <u>record</u> seventh grade math scores from the state assessment of mathematics knowledge and skills into the school's NCLB *database*. After studying these results, the principal identifies children who may need extra help to succeed. Using *grade book software*, the principal records the same students' scores at the end of the eighth-grade school year. By comparing the two sets of scores, the principal determines which students have had the most success. Using *statistical analysis software*, a <u>comparison</u> is performed of end-of-the-year average score for each class with the scores and standard deviations for all the eighth-grade students in the school, the district, and across the state."

Cognitivism

For cognitivists, the process itself associated with decision-making is most important. Success for the cognitive decision-maker is based on facts readily measured either from actual data or real world simulations. Technologies at this level deal with the validity, applicability, and scalability of information used to model decision processes.

Teaching students to become effective decision-makers is a task extending far beyond the K-12 curriculum. However, it must begin in the earliest grades to grow into an effective strategy for lifelong learning. The old adage, "Give a man a fish and you feed him for a day. Teach a man how to fish and you feed him for a lifetime," most assuredly holds true for decision-making and technology. For example, while at the literacy and collaboration levels of the taxonomy, the *student* learns how to use electronic mail to communicate, the following objectives demonstrates advanced uses of e-mail to support decision-making at level 3.0.

Cognitivism: "Students will <u>model</u> effective practices for managing *multiple e-mail accounts* including configurable *toolbars*, customize *address books*, and *electronic mailbox* transfers and storage. They will <u>choose</u> *e-mail options* (menus and tools) that limit the size of messages to be downloaded, automatically move messages to appropriate folders based on their subject, and specify the amount of time before deleting unwanted messages from the server."

Teachers are asked to apply their understanding of technology to practical classroom situations. For decision-making, they merge their knowledge of learning theories with decisions regarding curriculum, academic content, and available learning environments. Here is an example of a learning objective written for a *teacher-as-scholar* sharing a finding on how to effectively apply decision-making technologies.

Cognitivism: "Teachers will <u>review</u> learning theories as they apply to *instructional technology* and <u>argue</u> to implement either *computers in a laboratory environment* or *computers in the classroom* as the most appropriate venue for learning technology. The argument must include both pros and cons for the position taken and must address a one-computer classroom and a multi-computer classroom. Be sure to <u>speak to</u> various *technologies* to the pedagogical foundations of educational psychology."

Good administrative decision-making is multi-faceted and complex. Even a decision on a seemingly simple matter can have a serious impact on the public at large. So, it is important for administrators to internalize a process for making decisions that is fair and consistent.

The Office of the Queensland (Australia) Ombudsman monitors administrative practices of the country's public agencies and has developed a comprehensive guide to assist elected and appointed officials in making the best possible decisions. They divide the decision-making process into three components: locating existing decision-impacting guidelines (i.e., legislative provisions, policies, and past practices); making the decision (i.e., statutory obligations, de-conflicting interests, and timeliness); and, communicating that decision to the public. The office recommends a number of technologies to effectively execute this process. Here is an *administrative* learning objective taken from their guide (Queensland Ombudsman, 2003).

Cognitivism: "School principals will <u>create</u> a comprehensive *electronic online survey* to <u>assess</u> *technology skills, literacies and competencies* of teachers and administrators and <u>propose</u> *distance-based alternatives.* Administrators will use this data to <u>formulate instructional strategies</u> necessary to implement a training schedule for teachers and administrators in *basic classroom technologies.*"

Humanism

From a humanistic perspective, there are many factors that contribute to good decision-making. For example, self-esteem is a major factor in making good decisions. Some people are easily pressured into choosing wrong decisions. It takes education and courage to gain the self-esteem necessary to become confident in making decisions. Yet everyday, millions of administrators make decisions that drive the educational process, student achievement, and faculty and staff productivity. A suite of very sophisticated tools has been developed over the years to support the decision-making experience. However, to fully understand this process, it is imperative to differentiate between what technology can do and what people can do.

Technology excels in certain areas, specifically, storing and moving data, manipulating data, creating visual representations of data, and following rules. People, on the other hand, are better at recognizing relevant information, finding new sources of information, understanding the context for information, bringing together information to form judgments, and making decisions. By recognizing these inherent differences between technology and human intelligence, and by understanding how computer intelligence and its strengths support human decision-making, technology for decision-making finds its place in humanistic learning strategies.

Student use of technology for humanistic decision-making, as confirmed by the research, is not found that often in the classroom. However, use of technology at this level of the taxonomy is emerging rapidly thanks to the expansion of the Internet and the World Wide Web. The following example shows a learning objective prepared for secondary social studies *students.* Dependency on the skills and competencies at the two previous levels of the taxonomy are evident.

Humanism: "Student groups will research reasons <u>for and against</u> the legalization of gambling and visually arrange these ideas in the form of a *graphic* *organizer* using a *cluster map*, *spider map* or design your own style to best fit the group's ideas or needs. Finally, students should use available *groupware* (software and hardware for shared interactive environments) to advocate <u>for</u> either side of the discussion."

Teachers often find it difficult to hold fast to humanistic principles when using technology for decision-making. For many, standardization imposed by technology flies in the face of personalized choices. While most academic decisions involve the curriculum, most humanistic decisions naturally involve students. The example learning objective below was taken from a *teacher-as-expert* workshop.

Humanism: "Teachers will <u>formulate</u> a *digital version* of the Classroom of the Future prepared with Computer-Aided Design / Computer-Aided Manufacturing *(CAD/CAM) software* to <u>promote</u> *educational technologies* supporting student learning outcomes in a cooperative learning environment."

Administrators become role models by using collaborative technologies for communicating with faculty, launching their own professional development and research agendas via online collaboration, and using e-mail for notices, feedback, and commentary with their constituents. The following objective is typical of an appropriate *administrative* application of humanistic technology for collaboration.

Humanism: "Administrators will <u>establish</u> a *virtual feedback technique* to determine the on-going *technology training needs* of district support staff to include secretaries, classroom aides, human resources and business office personnel. Administrators will use this data to <u>influence</u> the **technology-based instructional strategies** necessary to implement the training schedule for support staff in basic technologies."

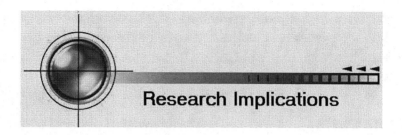

Research Implications

Decision-Making

Domains of Teaching

Decision-Making

Psychologies of Learning

Research Phase I: Decision-Making and the Domains of Teaching and Psychologies of Learning. The nearly two thousand lesson plans examined in Tomei's (2001) review contained over 3,500 references to decision-making technologies. Of those, nearly 40% were in the cognitive domain. Most offered a mental image of the problem at hand and established the relationship between effective decision-making on the one hand and the need for knowledge and information on the other. Correspondingly, close to the same number of learning objectives was noted in the affective domain. Decision-making technologies involve those who have a stake in the topic, know something about it, or will be affected by the outcome. Citations of decision-making tools in the psychomotor domain were negligible, relegated almost entirely to early childhood curricula for students and hardware troubleshooting for teachers. None were found for administrators, although the argument could be made that they should share such knowledge with their teacher counterparts in this particular area.

Even though behavioristic technologies have historically impacted decision-making, cognitivism remains the predominant domain for learning. In *Using A Taxonomy For The Technology Domain*, Tomei (2001) found well over half (about 70%) of the lesson plans incorporating decision-making objectives used cognitive technologies. Behavioral and humanistic lessons share the remaining incidents equally.

Research Phase II: Decision-Making and Technology-Based Learning Objectives

As a reminder, the inquiry selected some 300 lesson plans and categorized over 1,440 learning objectives by their representative level of the taxonomy (Table 3).

Table 3. Student Learning Objectives by Taxonomy Level

Level of Taxonomy	Totals	Percent Within Levels
Literacy	610	42.3
Collaboration	176	12.2
Decision-Making	380	26.4
Infusion	188	13.2
Integration	57	3.8
Tech-ology	30	2.1
Totals	1441	100.00

The Phase II study determined that decision-making technologies ranked second only to literacy for incidents in technology-based lesson objectives. Over 26% of the learning objectives examined were classified in support of solving problems. Similar to previous levels, decision-making has its own claim to fame in that these technologies were found in nearly every one of the 300 lesson plans reviewed. No other level reported such widespread application.

Conclusion of Technology for Decision-Making (Level 3.0)

Before assimilating decision-making tools into the classroom, it would be wise to consider several questions posed by the 1997 House of Representatives sub-committee on the impact of new information technologies on their own decision-making process. They explored several key questions. How do decision-making tools impact the committees and House processes? Which of these technologies has the greatest effect on decision-making? What are the most likely decisions to be assisted by technology? Finally, how can decision-making technology promote better understanding among those in the legislative process? (HR Subcommittee on Rules & Organization of the House, June 26, 1997).

Translated to academic-speak, educators ask similar questions related to technology for decision-making. First, is technology the best way to teach students how to make all types of decisions? What decision-making tools are most appropriate for the many types of decisions we must teach our students to make? How can these technologies for decision-making promote increased student learning outcomes over a lifetime of learning? What technologies are most appropriate for students, teachers, and administrators to promote more effective learning, teaching, and management?

This chapter answers these questions by offering a host of tools addressing a variety of decision-making scenarios. Some of the technologies explored the need to track trends in attendance, test scores, finances and student demographics. Others assist with school assessment reporting and accountability, suggesting ways and means to organize data for making informed decisions about curriculum, instruction, staffing, and professional development. Still other technologies advocate alternatives for examining student achievement, professional development of faculty and staff, and student and teacher effectiveness. Regardless, the technologies proposed in this chapter represent only some of the tools for deciding among the ever-increasing number of alternatives surfacing as a result of the explosion of information and the need to more quickly arrive at resolutions.

Next, Level 4.0 of the Taxonomy for the Technology Domain examines how technology moves beyond literacy, beyond collaboration, even beyond decision-making into the realm of applying technology to new and unique situations.

References

Collaborative for Technology Standards for School Administrators. (2003). *Technology Standards for School Administrators, TSSA Draft*, version 4.0. Retrieved from the World Wide Web: *cnets.iste.org/tssa/view_standards.html*

Cringely, R.X. (1992). *Accidental empires*. Reading, MA: Addison-Wesley.

Galbraith, J.R. (1974). Organization design: An information processing perspective. *Interfaces*, 4.

International Society for Technology in Education (ISTE). (2003). *Educational Technology Standards and Performance Indicators for All Teachers*. National Educational Technology Standards for Teachers. Retrieved from the World Wide Web: *cnets.iste.org/teachers/t_stands.html*

International Society for Technology in Education (ISTE). (2003). *Technology Foundation Standards for All Students*. National Educational Technology Standards for Students. Retrieved from the World Wide Web: *cnets.iste.org/students/s_stands.html*

Merrill et al. (1996). *Computers in education*. Boston: Allyn & Bacon.

Orton, J.D., & Weick, K.E. (1990). Loosely coupled systems: A reconceptualization. *Academy of Management Review*.

Picard, R. (1997). Affective computing. Cambridge, MA: MIT Press.

Queensland Ombudsman. (2003). *An easy guide to good administrative decision-making*. Brisbane Queensland, Australia.

Shanteau, J., Grier, M., Johnson, J., & Berner, E. (2003). Teaching decision making skills to students. *Teaching decision making to adolescents*. Hillsdale, NJ: Lawrence Erlbaum.

Tomei, L.A. (2001, April 30). Using a taxonomy for the technology domain. *Penn Association of Colleges and Teacher Educators*.

U.S. Congress, House of Representatives, Subcommittee on Rules and Organization of the House, Committee on Rules. (1997, June). *Impact of New Information Technologies on Decision-Making in the House of Representatives*. (Transcript, Thursday, June 26, 1997). Washington, DC.

U.S. Department of Education. (2003). *No Child Left Behind: A Toolkit for Teachers*. Retrieved from the World Wide Web: *www.ed.gov/teachers/nclbguide*

U.S. Department of Education. (2003). *Using Data to Influence Classroom Decisions*. Retrieved from the World Wide Web: *www.ed.gov/teachers/nclbguide/datadriven.doc*

Chapter 9

Technology Infusion (Level 4.0)

Infusion Learning with Technology	**Level 4.0** Identification, harvesting, and application of existing technology to unique learning situations.

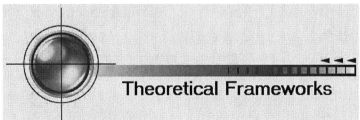

Theoretical Frameworks

Definition and Historical Origins

The fourth level of the taxonomy, technology infusion, is sub-titled, "learning with technology." Following the mastery of technological literacy (understanding technology), collaboration (technology to share ideas), and decision-making (technology to solve problems), "*identifying, harvesting, and applying existing technologies to unique learning situations*" characterizes the next logical step in the development of skills and competencies for teachers and learners.

The evolution of technologies over the last five decades has dramatically expanded classroom options for engaging the learner at all levels of instruction. Technology has matured quickly from overhead, 35mm slide, and 16mm film projectors to multimedia computers, audiovisual communications, and the Internet to undeniably impact every aspect of learning. Today, information processing and communication networks are making open learning communities an increasingly viable alternative to the more traditional forms of education.

Any examination of technologies stirs up an array of sentiments. On the one hand, technology for learning is imbued with an inherent optimism and hope for educational reform. Unbridled enthusiasm greeted Apple Computer in 1983 as they initiated their experimental Apple Classrooms of Tomorrow program with plans to help teachers and schools understand what can happen in classrooms when powerful technology and effective instruction are brought together. Educators applauded the 1996 Federal Telecommunications Act establishing the "E-Rate" to defray the telecommunications costs of schools and libraries. It surprised no one when the Web-based Education Commission was established by Congress to develop policy recommendations to maximize the educational promise of the Internet at all educational levels. A 2002 report, *The Power of the Internet for Learning*, states, "The question is no longer if the Internet can be used to transform learning in new and powerful ways. The Commission has found that it can" (U.S. Education Commission, 2002).

Yet, for all its promises, instructional technology has also disappointed. By 1992, only 14 states had adopted technology-based standards as part of the growing accountability movement. Even with expenditures exceeding $6 billion in school computers, a National Center for Educational Statistics study revealed in a 2000 study that only 31% of new teachers feel "very well prepared" to integrate technology into their curriculum (NCES, 2000).

After reflecting on these successes of technology infusion, placing the failures in a proper context, and analyzing past trends and future predictions, several important concerns emerge regarding the use of technology for learning. For one, does the research justify the cost/benefits of classroom technologies? What has been the impact of infused technologies on the different socio-economic and cultural groups and their equal access to technologies? How can the school prepare teachers to fully utilize these technologies? How can they afford the variety of technologies necessary to address so many different learning styles?

The potential for using different technologies to facilitate the learning process is virtually unlimited. Technologies make it possible to visualize problems formerly confined to printed text and link with diverse learning communities usually restricted to the traditional classroom. Infused technologies simulate new worlds that simply do not exist except in the imagination and foster student participation in learning goals once thought too dangerous and too costly.

Standards for Technology Infusion

The ISTE NETS*S standards for students provide only one foundation standard addressing technology for learning (ISTE, 2003). The implications of this standard, however, have a far reaching impact on the minimum competencies recommended for all students, both at this level of the Taxonomy for the Technology Domain and the next.

As expected, technology infusion standards for teachers are somewhat more encompassing. Teachers-as-learners are encouraged to adopt technology as a viable strategy for developing learning environments and experiences. Teachers-as-experts are expected to use technology to address diverse needs of students and to develop their students' higher order thinking skills. Teachers-as-scholars find technology a critical skill as they advocate for the practice of instructional technology.

Administrators focus on technology infusion in their daily interactions with both students and teachers. The TSSA encourages administrators to promote continuous innovation in learning with technology by supporting instruction and technology-enriched learning environments (Collaborative for TSSA, 2003).

A collection of student, teacher, and administrator competencies at level 4.0 of the Taxonomy for the Technology Domain is provided in Table 1.

Infusion includes the broadest catalog of technologies so far in the new taxonomy. It includes the more traditional classroom resources such as video and audio equipment (telephones, radio, televisions, tape players, etc.) as well as more state-of-the-art hardware (desktop and laptop multimedia computers, LCD projectors, digital still and video cameras, VHS videotape camcorders). In addition, an array of peripheral devices is proposed, including zip drives, scanners, CD players and writers, and intelligent white boards. Finally, the high end of technology for learning considers Web-based tools such as learning management systems, videoconferencing equipment, and other distance-based learning resources.

Table 1. Infusion Standards for Students, Teachers, and Administrators

Infusion Competency	Student Standards	Teacher-as-Learner Standards	Teacher-as-Expert Standards	Teacher-as-Scholar Standards	Administrators
NETS*S					
Technology productivity tools	x				
• Students use technology tools to enhance learning, increase productivity, and promote creativity.	x				
Technology research tools	x				
• Students evaluate and select new information resources and technological innovations based on the appropriateness for specific tasks.	x				
NETS*T					
Teachers plan and design effective learning environments and experiences supported by technology.		x	x	x	
• apply current research on teaching and learning with technology when planning learning environments and experiences.			x	x	
• identify and locate technology resources and evaluate them for accuracy and suitability.			x	x	
• plan for the management of technology resources within the context of learning activities.			x	x	
• plan strategies to manage student learning in a technology-enhanced environment.					
Teachers implement curriculum plans that include methods and strategies for applying technology to maximize student learning.		x	x	x	
• facilitate technology-enhanced experiences that address content standards and student technology standards.		x	x	x	
• use technology to support learner-centered strategies that address the diverse needs of students.		x	x	x	
• manage student learning activities in a technology-enhanced environment.		x	x	x	
Teachers apply technology to facilitate a variety of effective assessment and evaluation strategies.		x	x	x	
• apply technology in assessing student learning of subject matter using a variety of assessment techniques.		x	x	x	
• apply multiple methods of evaluation to determine students' appropriate use of technology resources for learning, communication, and productivity.		x	x	x	

Table 1. Infusion Standards for Students, Teachers, and Administrators (continued)

Infusion Competency	Student Standards	Teacher-as-Learner Standards	Teacher-as-Expert Standards	Teacher-as-Scholar Standards	Administrators
TSSA					
Educational leaders ensure that curricular design, instructional strategies, and learning environments integrate appropriate technologies to maximize learning and teaching.					x
• identify, use, evaluate, and promote appropriate technologies to enhance and support instruction and standards-based curricula leading to high levels of student achievement.					x
• facilitate and support collaborative technology-enriched learning environments conducive to innovation for improved learning.					x
• provide for learner-centered environments that use technology to meet the individual and diverse needs of learners.					x
• provide for and ensure that faculty and staff take advantage of quality professional learning opportunities for improved learning and teaching with technology.					

The goal of infused technology is to help students, teachers, and administrators become responsible independent learners. To produce their best work, learners must interact cooperatively to seek and share information, become critical thinkers, and have fun and enjoy learning. Since everyone is a learner, this book has a vested interest in exploiting level 4.0 of the taxonomy to its fullest potential.

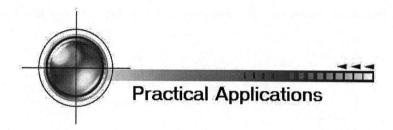

Practical Applications

Infusion Technologies and Action Statements

As educators respond to the challenges of infusing technology into teaching and learning, they must also become aware of the important distinction between using technology and infusing technology. The applications of a technology-infused curriculum range well beyond any single academic discipline or any one instructional technology. Teaching students how to learn with technology, preparing the professional teacher, and developing administrative acumen are key components in such pedagogical shifts. Table 2 reflects the infused technologies.

Table 2. Appropriate Infusion Technologies

Cable network programs	Radio broadcast programs	Video clips of current events
CD-based publications	Satellite downlink programs	Visual-based lesson materials
Digital classroom presentations	Simulation education software	Web-based conference proceedings
Distance learning programs	Sound bytes of famous speeches	Web-based lesson home pages
Digital student workbooks		
Electronic journals and magazines	Spreadsheet of real-time data	Web-based lesson materials
	Text-based materials	Web Quest lessons
Graphics presentation software	Videoconference lessons VHS videotape camcorders	
Laser disk programs	Video and audio equipment,	
LCD Projectors	including telephones, radios,	
Learning management systems	television, tape players, videocassette player	
Multimedia computer cart	Videoconferencing	
Peripheral devices, including scanners, CD players and burners	equipment	

Table 3. Action Statements for Technology Infusion

Adapt *technologies* to academic standards
Arrange classroom *Web pages*
Burn a CD-ROM with *digital lesson materials*
Capture *textual content, visual images, auditory sound bytes,* and *video clips*
Construct the *visual elements* of a technology action plan
Download *text citations* and *digital images*
Employ internet *multimedia search engines*
Harvest (select, download, and print) *digital content*
Harvest *sound bytes* and *video clips* to enhance instruction
Harvest *textual content* for remedial instruction
Incorporate curriculum-appropriate *educational software*
Insert links to classroom *Web sites*
Investigate selected *Web-based educational sites* for academic content
Supplement lessons with original *audiotape presentations*
Utilize *Web design and editing software*

Table 3 exhibits common action verbs for level 4.0 of the Taxonomy for the Technology Domain. Appropriate action verbs are underlined once while the *instructional technology* introduced is italicized.

Domains of Teaching and Technology Infusion

The first chapter set the stage for the taxonomy by establishing the notion of educational domains for teaching and reviewing the fundamentals of the cognitive, affective, and psychomotor domains. The cognitive domain focused on acquiring knowledge in stages from recall to evaluation. The affective domain concerned individual attitudes and values. The psychomotor domain examined physical skills with observable actions.

The second chapter concentrated on the psychologies of education, namely, behavioral, cognitive, and humanistic theories of learning. Whether you believe learning is the result of a reaction to environmental stimulus, the total of one's schemata for organizing information, or the personalization of content to satisfactorily employ the Taxonomy for the Technology Domain, a working knowledge of the psychologies of learning is required.

Infused technology is well grounded in the principles of learning. As such, this particular section on the domains of teaching takes a back seat to the follow-on section on the psychologies of learning. Conversely, in the next chapter, Technology Integration focuses on technologies for teaching and reduces the emphasis on learning.

If this explanation is confusing, that is, if your understanding of domains and psychologies as presented in this text is insufficient for you to proceed, it is suggested that you review Chapters 1 and 2 before going further. For without this shared starting point, subsequent discussions of level 4.0 and level 5.0 of the new technology taxonomy may appear speculative and unsubstantiated. As a reminder, this explanation (and admonishment) appears again in Chapter 10, Technology Integration.

Cognitive Domain

Teachers use technology for infusion as a tool to identify instructional materials previously unavailable. By locating new classroom materials (most of which is digital in format), they select from among a growing inventory of text, visual, and Web-based resources focused on the learning styles of students and augmented by their own particular teaching strategy.

Administrators as well play a key role in how technology is infused into the curriculum. We know from the research that the tendency in schools today is to consider technology more as its own content area to be covered in "computer class" than for its potential as an alternate strategy for teaching and learning. The primary application of technologies in the cognitive domain centers on teaching with computers rather than teaching about them. Administrators must come to appreciate this distinction and help to overcome its inherent limitations.

Significant examples using the technologies and action statements provided earlier reveal proper use of infused technologies in the cognitive domain. Remember, the key characteristics of infused technologies in the cognitive domain include the identification, harvesting, and use of *existing* technologies to adapt (i.e., assimilate or accommodate) teaching strategies to a unique learning situation. The following *student* example is provided for consideration. Appropriate action verbs are underlined once while the *instructional technology* introduced is italicized.

Cognitive domain: "During the fall quarter, students will <u>gather research</u> concerning the greatest battles of the American Civil War. After <u>fabricating</u> the key characteristics of the greatest battle, they will select, <u>download,</u> and <u>harvest</u> *digital content* that best represents new information via *text, visual, and Web-based materials* and adds further content to lessons presented earlier in social studies class."

In the example above, students themselves locate new teachable materials. The *teacher-as-expert*, too, uses technology infusion to distinguish innovative and unique instructional resources. In the following example, classroom teachers seek out appropriate content materials on the Internet to present to their students who need remediation or enrichment pertaining to a particular lesson. An objective for such an in-service session appeared in the workshop syllabus of a summer institute for teaching with technology.

Cognitive domain: "Teachers will <u>employ</u> Internet *search engines* to locate and <u>harvest</u> *textual content, visual images, audio sound bytes,* and *video clips* that address current science and space-related standards for eighth grade curriculum. Selected resources will be <u>burned</u> onto a *CD-ROM disk* containing remedial and enrichment materials depicting the U.S. Space Shuttle Program."

Principals and curriculum directors are often called upon to sponsor in-service workshops for their faculty and staff. Too often, the instructional materials used in these workshops, if any, are reproduced handouts copied minutes before the start of the session. As a result, the dry, uninteresting, uninspiring content is usually discarded soon after dismissal. Alternatively, infused technologies provide stimulating resources for in-service programs and help teachers compete with television, game stations, and DVD movies for the attention of their students. In the cognitive domain, *administrators* would do well to use the following learning objective to guide their next in-service practicum.

Cognitive domain: "The principal will demonstrate the use of *classroom technologies* to address particular academic state standards in math, science, social studies, and language arts. The technologies to be examined include the *LCD projector, multimedia cart, wireless Internet-capable laptops, vid-*

eocassette player, laser disk software, closed circuit television, cable network channels, satellite downlink programs, and the *videoconferencing learning network.*"

Affective Domain

Anyone wishing to establish the effectiveness of technology as a teaching tool in the affective domain has to look no further than *Mister Rogers' Neighborhood* and *Sesame Street*, both shown on public television stations. The focus of *Mister Rogers' Neighborhood* was primarily affective and research has demonstrated positive effects on the self-esteem of children as a result of these broadcasts. *Sesame Street's* emphasis on socialization and affective development has garnered positive outcomes in terms of school readiness in math, reading, and social skills (Seels et al., 1996).

For student applications at this level of the taxonomy, there is strong evidence that technology infusion in the affective domain is most effective when it is intentionally gathered for a particular lesson, addressing individual learning styles, and directed at specific learning objectives. Also critical is teacher involvement in the selection, utilization, and integration of the technology into the curriculum (Anderson & Collins, 1988), a powerful assumption at this level of the taxonomy.

The most current research into affective infused technologies focuses on three particular areas. In practice, these three areas also represent the most number of occurrences of affective objectives found during the Tomei study. From a teacher's perspective, these areas involve coaching students to take responsibility for their actions, specifically, setting goals and objectives, study time management, and personal self-awareness skills. Also, affective goals for teachers and administrators address working in groups and the related skills involving respect for other's values, decision-making, resolving conflict, and working with peers who have different values and expectations.

Student learning objectives, such as the one shown below, reflect the affective dimensions of feelings, emotions, and self-esteem. Infused technologies influence these dimensions by adding previously unavailable learning resources to the repertoire of individualized instructional materials.

Affective domain: "Students will <u>explore</u> selected *Web-based sites* pertaining to the Viet Nam anti-war demonstrations of the 1960s. Students will <u>characterize</u> the doves (opponents of the war) and hawks (advocates for the war) and prepare a five-minute speech <u>defending</u> one of the two positions, *harvesting* appropriate *sound bytes* and *video clips* to support their views."

Teachers must identify potentially appropriate technology-based materials that specifically compliment their own instructional strategies. From the inventory of available infused technologies, the *teacher-as-learner* has the option of choosing affective materials to receive, respond, value, organize, and characterize their own learning behavior. The following objective demonstrates the affective application of technology at this level of the taxonomy.

Affective domain: "Teachers will review the audiovisual training package entitled, *Strategies for Bullying Prevention*, to include a *videotape* and *visual-based classroom presentation* after which they will <u>participate</u> in a facilitator-led group discussion. In addition, they will use a *tape recorder* to transcribe the events surrounding a personal bullying incident experienced in school and <u>relate</u> the way it <u>affects</u> them as classroom teachers."

An administrator's role in the affective domain closely parallels cognitive applications. This time, however, the affective domain concentrates on technologies that help students attach value to the social and emotional aspects of the lesson. Here, the *administrator* attends a workshop that introduces infused technologies addressing the affective goals of internalizing motivation.

Affective domain: "The administrator will participate in a *distance learning* seminar with in-service teachers throughout the district on the anticipated outcomes of the proposed Student Homework Incentive Program (SHIP). Using two-way *videoconferencing*, participants will <u>formulate</u>, <u>characterize</u>, and <u>share opinions and values</u> regarding the five unique scenarios for <u>inducing</u> internal student <u>motivation</u> for the program in their classroom."

Psychomotor Domain

A renowned study in active learning (Korwin & Jones, 1990) measured increases in knowledge attributable to hands-on technology-based activities. The study examined specific questions regarding the effectiveness of psychomotor activities versus stand-alone classroom lecture presentations. It found significant increases in teaching effectiveness when using infused technologies grounded in the psychomotor domain. Although the study focused on technology-based objectives, its findings were later generalized to any academic content.

The results of this research have significant implications for general education and technology-enhanced instruction. Psychomotor activities enhance teaching effectiveness by improving short- and long-term memory retention through greater use of visual, auditory, tactile, and motor memory storage areas of the brain.

A *student* learning objective in the psychomotor domain infuses technologies that provide opportunities for students to physically evidence their mastery of a particular learning objective, such as the one found in a fifth grade physical science lesson.

Psychomotor domain: "Students will complete the guided response exercise to physically trace the correct path of an alternating and direct electric current using the *intelligent white board, LCD projector*, and a *graphics presentation software* package to the satisfaction of the instructor."

Learning objectives in the psychomotor domain involve motor skills that presuppose an existing knowledge base and describing how to perform a procedure is not the same as being able to actually perform that skill. Here is an example in-service objective prepared by a *teacher-as-scholar* to augment the skills of pharmacy candidates with infused technologies in the psychomotor domain.

Psychomotor domain: "To ensure that pharmacy candidates appreciate the importance of meticulous record-keeping, instructors will introduce the Pharmacy Inventory of Controlled Substances — a *spreadsheet* with enabled protection/security options along with the Patient Profile prototype *database* — to <u>input</u>, <u>sort</u>, and <u>maintain</u> accurate patient profiles and medication records in the computer data base."

Research reveals that skill acquisition is much more than a sequence of movements simply performed in a repetitive way. While students and teachers often remain at this lower level of the psychomotor domain, *administrators* move quickly to tasks performed automatically in an effort to increase productivity.

Canada, for example, invests considerable resources in programs for its young learners by focusing on psychomotor skills (Shipley, 1997). Administrators are required to implement the comprehensive, three-part psychomotor skills program. At level one, students demonstrate critical elements of basic psychomotor skills in selected simple situations (imitation). Audio and video recording technology is often used to validate level one skills. Level two examines increasingly complex psychomotor skills in increasingly complex situations (manipulation and precision). Multimedia computers and simulation software provide opportunities for evidencing mastery at this level. For level three, students must perform in progressively unpredictable situations (naturalization). Often, distance learning technologies (videoconferencing, satellite downlinks, etc.) present these simulated scenarios. To accomplish these goals, *administrators* might implement the learning objective shown below with the help of infused technologies in the psychomotor domain.

Psychomotor domain: "Principals and physical education department chairs will <u>operate</u> *recording technology*, *simulation software*, and off-site *distance education programs* to provide an outcome-based plan of play and learning for K-3 early childhood students. Progress and achievement is <u>tracked</u> as students move on to more complex play activities."

Technology Infusion and the Psychologies of Learning

Behaviorism as a theory of learning poses many interesting questions in its attempt to offer the suite of infused technologies that satisfy the stimulus-response-reinforcement equation. One question is overriding here. Do students, teachers, and administrators mistakenly seek technology infused activities based on the SRR model because they are easier to produce in the electronic/computer environment?

To teach cognitively using infused technologies means addressing certain key characteristics of good instruction. For example, a well-designed cognitive lesson is self-paced, yet constructed, regulated, and controlled by the intrinsically motivated learner. Infused technologies promote this psychology of learning by offering a variety of safe, cost-effective, and abundant mental models for developing the target schemata for living in the real world.

Humanism is the third alternative. Infused technologies here address three basic strengths of humanistic education. First, students should be able to have some choice in what they want to learn. The underpinnings of technology infusion address this strength. Second, the goal of education should be to foster students' desire to learn and teach them how to learn. Infused technologies are innate motivators of immediate feedback. Finally, humanists believe that grades, particularly objective testing of a student's ability to memorize, are subordinate to self-evaluation. Instead, measuring student learning outcomes is buoyed by technologies selected especially for individual student styles.

Behaviorism

To properly acquire instructional materials for learning, successful students, teachers, and administrators are often called on to master a sequence of steps. *Computers for Dummies*, a popular series of introductory technology books, contains over 30 behavioral tutorials on basic skills and competencies. Each tutorial offers a step-by-step course of action for solving a host of technical problems best described as infused technology. The learning objectives presented in the next several paragraphs demonstrate technology infusion as a behavioral teaching strategy. We will begin with *students*.

Behaviorism: "Students will <u>follow the sequence</u> of steps to harvest (i.e., <u>download and save</u>) at least two *text citations* and four *digital images* from Internet sites pertaining to the dinosaurs and the theories of extinction. Employing the concepts and tools of *Web harvesting*, the materials will be inserted (<u>cut/copy/paste</u>) into a two-page (minimum) text-based document using *word processing software* and printed in enough copies to distribute to each member of the class."

An appropriate *teacher-as-learner* objective employing infused technology involves an undergraduate course objective containing the following behavioral learning objective.

Behaviorism: "Given a model for visual-based instructional materials, teachers will <u>locate and harvest</u> a minimum 15-slide *digital classroom presentation*. As a minimum, the harvested materials will be <u>organized sequentially</u> to address specific state standards in their academic subject areas, contain <u>stimulus-response</u> slides assessing <u>observable and measurable</u> student learning, and include *audio and visual feedback*."

Administrators access an assortment of infused technologies to aid in supporting administrative, staff, and curricular planning. The following example objectives was found in a workshop on the use of the Inspiration™ and Kidspiration™ software packages to promote administrative planning.

Behaviorism: "Using *graphic organizer software*, administrators will <u>construct</u> the *visual elements* of a technology action plan to include the necessary <u>consecutive steps</u> to upgrade a school's *computer lab* with new *desktop computers*, improvements to *network connectivity*, addition of classroom *projection capabilities*, and replacement of *ergonomic lab furniture*."

Cognitivism

At the infusion level, cognitive technologies address three dominant learning strategies. First, students must be able to learn from technology. While apparently over-simplistic in its message, if technology-based instructional materials match a particular student's style of learning, successful learning often does occur. If it does not, technology should not be mandated. Second, technology must be considered simply another learning style. As with every other instructional strategy, technology is better suited for some learners than for others. It is the responsibility of the teacher to match the strengths and weaknesses of technology to recognized individual student needs. Lastly, there is the mandate to select infused technologies that are carefully organized and sequenced to accommodate schemata for understanding. Learners should receive material in the most efficient delivery media. In many cases, that means technology-based applications harvested from a variety of resources and combined to address the particular learning styles of individual students.

Students benefit from carefully selected cognitive-based technologies for learning. The abundance of electronic resources encourages teachers to seek a variety of resources appropriate for a diversity of learning strategies, many of which are created by other teachers and content area experts as remedial or enhancing activities. Digital text, visual, and Web-based instructional materials represent content from numerous sources and are offered online as initiating, developmental, and concluding activities appropriate for classroom instruction. For example:

Cognitivism: "Following the economics classroom <u>lecture and discussion</u> on purchasing goods and services, payment methods, and consumers' basic rights, students will <u>examine</u> selected Web *lesson home pages* at www.ecommerce.com/ projects and, using the accompanying *digital student workbooks*, <u>formulate</u> the components of an *online e-business* of their choice."

Alternately, *teachers-as-scholars* appreciate the strengths and weaknesses of infused technologies as targets for research in the evolution of new teaching strategies addressing individual student needs. At the outset of a workshop, teachers are encouraged to develop their skills to search, identify, bookmark, and harvest infused technologies appropriate for their own classrooms. The text-based objective found in the workshop is characteristic of using infused technologies to build a cognitive lesson.

Cognitivism: "Teachers will <u>model</u> successful *text-based instructional materials* by <u>harvesting</u> a minimum-length, ten-page *digital student hyperbook* appropriate for their academic subject area. The selected materials must <u>augment the instruction</u> with resources that either <u>remediate</u> or <u>enrich</u> the target lesson."

When it comes to technology infusion, administrators remain attuned to the benefits of cognitive-based instructional materials. They have an obligation to stay abreast of technological innovations and look beyond the ordinary to help teachers identify, evaluate, and implement resources in this domain. *Administrators* possess the broadest familiarization and most receptiveness to new ideas. One illustrative case in point is provided here:

Cognitivism: "School principals and curriculum directors will host a series of training sessions in curriculum specific classroom technologies that <u>impact student learning</u> including, but not limited to: *video and audio equipment*, state-of-the-art *computer hardware and software*, peripheral devices such as *zip drives, scanners, CD players and writers*, and *intelligent white boards*; and Web-based *learning management* and *distance learning systems*."

The recommended objective above typifies the three highest levels of the cognitive domain. At the application level of Bloom's taxonomy, the example objective asks teachers to use a concept in a new and unfamiliar situation. Higher at the analysis level, teachers separate technology-based material or concepts into component parts so that its organizational structure may be used to target specific learners. At the highest level of evaluation, teachers make judgments about the value of the digital materials.

Humanism

Humanistic teachers are eclectic by nature. They prefer to use different teaching styles along with a variety of instructional media and delivery methods. They gleam with the successes realized by individually tailoring instruction to the learner.

The fact that technology infusion provides such different modes does not, however, mean the traditional classroom teacher is no longer the driving force in the classroom. Rather, the humanistic teacher continues to determine course content and strategy and remains the most valuable instrument in the learning process. Technology in the classroom should always facilitate teaching, relying "heavily on improvisation, on freedom to follow up ideas that excite interest, and on unexpected happenings that illustrate the problems. Learning technologies should be designed to increase and not reduce the amount of personal contact between faculty and students on intellectual issues" (Glick, 1990).

The humanistic classroom, then, should be a model for flexible learning environments. With the ability to present information in a variety of ways, access to varied information sources is possible with maximum flexibility for interaction between and among the teacher, the student and the content. To achieve such flexibility, classrooms combine a wealth of infused technologies, only some of which are considered in this text.

Technology infusion impacts the humanistic learner in many forms and fashions. Students use technology to develop their interpersonal skills by provoking and facilitating interaction among active learners, often intensifying human interaction rather than merely replacing it with machines and programs. They use technology to understand another's perspective, characteristic of the humanistic classroom. There are so many possible applications of infused technology that the findings of the Tomei study with regards to infused technology-based lesson objectives was, frankly, very disappointing. Future research at level 4.0 of the Taxonomy for the Technology Domain will continue to expand faster than perhaps any other classification level. For now, here is one such *student* learning objective.

Humanism: "Students will listen to an original audiotape presentation of H.G. Wells' *War of the Worlds*. Using the Halloween *Web site*, students will discuss the confusion caused by the radio broadcast and how consumers respond to the media around them today. Students will assemble *digital testimonies* from reputable authorities discussing theories of whether the duping of the American public by the broadcast was intentional, whether it was something that could have happened only in the 1930s, or whether Americans have become too sophisticated in their consumption of news to be deceived by the media."

For the humanistic teacher, instruction is tailored to the content needs of the learner. Technologies are useful only if they are academically appropriate. Self-discovery is part of learning. Teachers-as-experts provide the necessary resources for their students to make personal decisions based on their own values and sense of identity. The following objective has each of these characteristics:

Humanism: "Given a model for *Web-based instructional materials*, teachers will harvest, at minimum, a three-page *Web virtual tour* appropriate to

<u>support</u> a specific state standard in their academic subject areas. The selected Web pages must include <u>student-centered</u> *online activities*, <u>personal</u> *Internet exploration exercises*, and student evaluation and feedback."

A new vision for educational leadership was captured in the *Standards for School Leaders*, developed by the Interstate School Leaders Licensure Consortium — a consortium of some 30 states and major professional organizations advocating for the discipline of school administration. The consortium's standards call for "re-culturing" the profession of school administration and provide a platform for sweeping changes in *administrator* preparation programs and certification of school leaders. Fortunately, they also provide comprehensive resources for inclusion in workshop program agendas like the one shown below.

Humanism: "School administrators will subscribe to selected resources from among the following *electronic media*: annual reports and newsletters (*electronic journals*), digital research and best practices journals (*CD-ROM-based publications*), text books and hard-copy journals, conference proceedings (*Web-based conference proceedings sites*), and district daily newsletters (delivered via *e-mail list-servers*)."

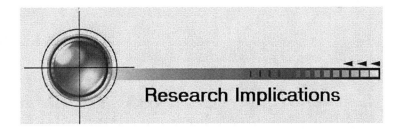

Research Implications

Students, teachers, and administrators pursue teaching by sharing technologies equally throughout the three traditional domains. Technology infusion questions fundamental assumptions, promotes new ideas and change, and encourages partnerships that eliminate geographical boundaries. In short, this step of the taxonomy, more than any other, encompasses equally the cognitive, affective, and psychomotor domains of learning.

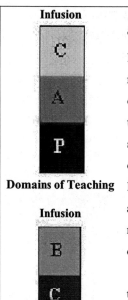

Infusion

Domains of Teaching

Infusion

Psychologies of Learning

Research Phase I: Infusion and the Domains of Teaching and Psychologies of Learning. Unfortunately, not many lesson plan objectives are found at this level of the taxonomy regardless of the domain or psychology. Of the lesson plans examined, Tomei (2001) found a mere 13.2% contained references to infused technologies. From those, only 3.9% of the math, science, language arts, or social studies lessons investigated contained objectives particular to enhanced technology-based learning. (The remaining 8.3%, as we shall see later in the chapter, address teaching demands.) As a result, it is difficult to cite meaningful examples here. Perhaps in further research or editions of this text, additional incidents will be available.

Of the lesson plans examined, only 8.3% boasted infused technologies addressing the psychologies of learning (Tomei, 2001). A follow-up edition of this text or further research will undoubtedly identify more lessons at this level of the Taxonomy for the Technology Domain. For now, the behavioral, cognitive, and humanistic learning objectives that were identified are explored in greater detail here.

Research Phase II: Infusion and Technology-Based Learning Objectives

The inquiry selected some 300 lesson plans and categorized over 1,440 learning objectives by level of the taxonomy (Table 3). Only 13% of the objectives reviewed were categorized as Infusion objectives.

Infused technologies barely outperformed collaboration. However, unlike collaboration technologies that were evenly spread among all grade levels and academic content areas, infused technologies fluctuated considerably among grade levels and content areas.

Table 3. Student Learning Objectives by Taxonomy Level

Level of Taxonomy	Totals	Percent Within Levels
Literacy	610	42.3
Collaboration	176	12.2
Decision-Making	380	26.4
Infusion	188	13.2
Integration	57	3.8
Tech-ology	30	2.1
Totals	1441	100.00

Conclusion of Technology Infusion (Level 4.0)

Schools invest huge sums of money outfitting their classrooms with technologies under the assumption that they will somehow enhance the educational experience. Research, however, remains inconclusive as to the definitive effect of technology on student achievement. It is too easy to be lulled onto the technology bandwagon, blindly installing state-of-the-art multimedia computers, video and audio equipment, and sophisticated learning management systems and distance learning resources before sufficiently considering their role in the instructional process.

Technology infusion provides opportunities never before available to classroom teachers and administrators. This chapter offers an initial examination into the value of technology at this higher level of the taxonomy. At the next level, integration takes technology to its ultimate conclusion to explore possible applications for teaching with technology.

References

Anderson, D.R., & Collins, P.A. (1988). *The impact on vhildren's education: Television's influence on cognitive development.* ERIC Document Reproduction Service No. ED 295-271. Washington, DC: Office of Educational Research and Improvement.

Collaborative for Technology Standards for School Administrators. (2003). *Technology Standards for School Administrators, TSSA Draft*, version 4.0. Retrieved from the World Wide Web: *cnets.iste.org/tssa/view_standards.html*

Glick, M. (1990). Integrating computing into higher education: An administrator's view. *Educom Review, 25*(2).

International Society for Technology in Education (ISTE). (2003). *Educational Technology Standards and Performance Indicators for All Teachers.* National Educational Technology Standards for Teachers. Retrieved from the World Wide Web: *cnets.iste.org/teachers/t_stands.html*

International Society for Technology in Education (ISTE). (2003). *Technology Foundation Standards for All Students, National Educational Technology Standards for Students.* Retrieved from the World Wide Web: *cnets.iste.org/students/s_stands.html*

Korwin, A.R., & Jones, R.E. (1990, Spring). Do hands-on, technology-based activities enhance learning by reinforcing cognitive knowledge and retention? *Journal of Technology Education, 1*(2).

National Center for Education Statistics (NCES). (2000). *Teacher use of computers and the Internet in public schools: Stats in brief.*

Seels, B., Berry, L.H., Fullerton, K., & Horn, L.J. (1996). Research on learning from television. In D. H. Jonassen (Ed.), *Handbook of research for educational communications and technology.* New York: Macmillan.

Shipley, D. (1997, Spring). Play: For development and for achieving learning outcomes. Interaction. *Canadian Child Care Federation.*

Tomei, L.A. (2001, April 30). Using a taxonomy for the technology domain. *Penn Association of Colleges and Teacher Educators.*

U.S. Education Commission. (2002). *The power of the Internet for learning: Moving from promise to practice.* U.S. Department of Education.

Annotated Bibliography

Additional citations for Technology Infusion

Huth, C., & Ravenstahl, H. (2002). *NETS Standards Based Scope and Sequence for Technology Education, Grades K-8.*

Lemke, C. & Coughlin, E. (1998). *Technology in American schools: Seven dimensions for gauging progress.* Milken Family Foundation.

Murphy, J. (2001, November). Six Standards for School Leadership. American Association of School Administrators. The School Administrator Web Edition. Retrieved from the World Wide Web: *www.aasa.org/publications/sa/2001_11/murphy_standards.htm*

Reeves, T.C. (1998, February 12). *The impact of media and technology in schools.* The University of Georgia.

Tomei, L.A. (2002). *The technology facade: Overcoming barriers to effective instructional technology.* Boston: Allyn & Bacon Publishers.

Chapter 10

Technology Integration (Level 5.0)

	**Level 5.0** The creation of new technology-based materials, combining otherwise disparate technologies to teach.

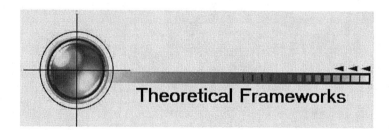

Definition and Historical Origins

As this critical level of the taxonomy, technology integration provides for "teaching with technology." In the previous chapter, infused technologies centered on learning. At level 5.0, the focus is on *"creating new technology-based materials by combining various technologies to teach."*

Within an effective educational setting, technology becomes an enabling tool for teaching and takes many forms at this level of the taxonomy. A prime function of integrated technologies is to provide learners with knowledge of specific subject areas. Traditionally, students learn from technologies used as delivery tools to communicate messages just as they learn from teachers. But at this level of the taxonomy, learners will create "new technology-based materials, combining otherwise disparate technologies to teach."

Likewise, integrated technology tools promote meaningful learning. They engage learners in the construction of new knowledge and the expansion of personal understanding. Computer-based tools such as databases, spreadsheets, hypermedia construction, networks, the Internet, and online learning environments serve as extensions of the mind. Learners enter into an intellectual partnership with technology by creating their own instructional materials.

Lastly, a key purpose of integrated technology is to enhance professional productivity. Technology assists administrators with a variety of responsibilities such as keeping student records, scheduling classes, creating school budgets, organizing library cataloguing and circulation, improving communication and collaboration between educators, and providing tools such as computerized grade books, templates and test/worksheet generators.

It has been said that meaningful learning occurs whenever technologies actively engage the learner. Technologies aptly integrated into the curriculum achieve conversation—not reception, articulation—not repetition, and collaboration—not competition. The applicable characteristics of technology integration are introduced in this chapter.

Standards for Technology Integration

The ISTE NETS*S technology standards for students is noticeably weak in its campaign for student-initiated technology integration. But, they do advocate for "students' use of productivity tools to ... produce creative works" (ISTE, 2003). Similarly, very few instances were found encouraging students to create their own instructional materials based on technology-enhanced resources. When these enticements were uncovered, they occurred mostly at the top levels of the K-12 curriculum. Yet, ask any classroom teacher (at least from grades 5 and up) and they will probably tell you that it is the younger student who is most likely to use technology to create new instructional materials. The skills necessary to integrate technology are mastered at earlier and earlier grades every year. The bar is being raised for students and teachers to participate in level 5.0 of the new Taxonomy for the Technology Domain.

Similar to the previous level of the taxonomy, technology integration standards for teachers are more inclusive. The general topic of planning and designing learning environment and experiences includes a host of mandates for identifying, designing, and applying technologies to enhance teaching and address the diverse needs of students.

Learning and teaching, along with assessment and evaluation, pose the primary mandate for administrators for the TSSA. Between these two categories of standards, nine specific requirements are enumerated (Collaborative for TSSA, 2003). It is clear from this mandate that school boards, superintendents, principals, curriculum directors, and supervisors of instruction are also charged with successfully integrating technology into the classroom.

The student, teacher, and administrator competencies — and there are many of them — at level 5.0 of the Taxonomy for the Technology Domain are provided in Table 1.

Level 5.0 of the Taxonomy for the Technology Domain includes tools for creating individualized instructional materials. As such, traditional and state-of-the-art classroom resources represented here include technologies meant to increase a teacher's range of instructional strategies.

Table 1. Integration Standards for Students, Teachers, and Administrators

Integration Competency	Student Standards	Teacher-as-Learner Standards	Teacher-as-Expert Standards	Teacher-as-Scholar Standards	Administrators
NETS*S					
Technology productivity tools	x				
• Students use productivity tools to collaborate in constructing technology-enhanced models, prepare publications, and produce other creative works.	x				
Technology research tools	x				
• Students evaluate and select new information resources and technological innovations based on the appropriateness for specific tasks.	x				

Table 1. Integration Standards for Students, Teachers, and Administrators (continued)

Integration Competency	Student Standards	Teacher-as-Learner Standards	Teacher-as-Expert Standards	Teacher-as-Scholar Standards	Administrators
NETS*T					
Teachers plan and design effective learning environments and experiences supported by technology.		x	x	x	
• design developmentally appropriate learning opportunities that apply technology-enhanced instructional strategies to support the diverse needs of learners.		x	x	x	
• apply current research on teaching and learning with technology when planning learning environments and experiences.		x	x	x	
• identify and locate technology resources and evaluate them for accuracy and suitability.		x	x	x	
• plan for the management of technology resources within the context of learning activities.		x	x	x	
• plan strategies to manage student learning in a technology-enhanced environment.					
Teachers implement curriculum plans that include methods and strategies for applying technology to maximize student learning.		x	x	x	
• facilitate technology-enhanced experiences that address content standards and student technology standards.		x	x	x	
• use technology to support learner-centered strategies that address the diverse needs of students.		x	x	x	
• apply technology to develop students' higher order skills and creativity.		x	x	x	
• manage student learning activities in a technology-enhanced environment.		x	x	x	
Teachers apply technology to facilitate a variety of effective assessment and evaluation strategies.		x	x	x	
• apply technology in assessing student learning of subject matter using a variety of assessment techniques.		x	x	x	
• apply multiple methods of evaluation to determine students' appropriate use of technology resources for learning, communication, and productivity.		x	x	x	

Table 1. Integration Standards for Students, Teachers, and Administrators (continued)

TSSA					
Educational leaders ensure that curricular design, instructional strategies, and learning environments integrate appropriate technologies to maximize learning and teaching.					x
• facilitate and support collaborative technology-enriched learning environments conducive to innovation for improved learning.					x
• provide for learner-centered environments that use technology to meet the individual and diverse needs of learners.					x
• facilitate the use of technologies to support and enhance instructional methods that develop higher-level thinking, decision-making, and problem-solving skills.					x
• provide for and ensure that faculty and staff take advantage of quality professional learning opportunities for improved learning and teaching with technology.					x

Video and audio equipment are categorized as integrated technologies as well as desktop and laptop computers and other high-end distance learning technologies. Telephones, radio, televisions, and tape players represent media for designing integrated lesson objectives and so are office productivity software, Web document-authoring tools, bitmap editing software, and Internet harvesting skills. In addition, a veritable inventory of technologies for integration (most of them software instruments) submits tools to analyze, design, develop, implement, and evaluate instruction, provides for lesson planning and curriculum development, and encourages student evaluation and assessment, professional development, and classroom management.

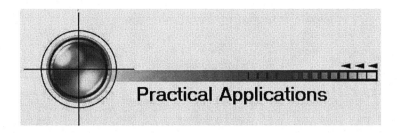

Practical Applications

Integration Technologies and Action Statements

Infused technologies, explained in detail in the previous chapter, consist of instructional materials harvested from various digital sources and incorporated into classroom lessons "as is." They are not altered by the learner except perhaps by changing the host media on which they are delivered. Integrated technologies, however, represent new, innovative, original instructional materials geared specifically to target learners, delivered by target teachers, and addressing a particular target curriculum. An analogy is in order to ensure a complete understanding of this level of the taxonomy. Examine the following scenario:

A teacher has been given the assignment to design a new semester-long instructional unit on the battlefields of the American Civil War. Upon entering the school library, she photocopies images from a particularly visual chapter in one textbook along with a well-researched paragraph or two about Gettysburg from another. The teacher locates an epic Hollywood film on President Lincoln but chooses only 20 minutes of the two-hour documentary. Finally, a series of Web sites are found that provide learners with a virtual field trip of Antietam. Using these materials, she prepares new text handouts, visual presentations, and Web pages to meet her expected student learning outcomes. This scenario delineates, one final time, the distinction between technologies infused (harvested and incorporated intact) and technologies integrated (harvested and modified to create new instructional materials).

Table 2. Appropriate Integration Technologies

Closed circuit television station	Narrated slide show	Virtual tour
Communications technologies	Online mentoring	Virtual publishing
Database wizards	Online research technologies	Web-based design technologies
Digital images, sound, video	Programming languages	Web-based Tools
Desktop publishing software	Software Utility Tools	Classroom Materials Makers
Digital forecasting technologies	Award Certificate Generator	Crossword Puzzle Maker
Electronic intelligent portfolio	Flash Card Generator	Graphic Organizer Maker
Graphic organizer software	Lesson Plan Generator	Makeworksheets.com
Harvested images, sound, video	Teacher Conference Generator	Resume Materials Makers
Hyperbook	Personal Education Plan Generator	Rubric Generators
Hypercard and hyperstudio software	Progress Report Generator	Word Search Maker
Integrated thematic unit	Learning Contract Generator	Worksheet Generators
Interactive Power Point lesson	Weekly Schedule Generator	Web-based Front Door
Internet	Timeline Generator	
Multimedia presentation tools	Sound recorder	
	Videotape recorder (analog)	

The possibilities of integrated technology grow geometrically every academic year. Table 2 attempts to distinguish appropriate technologies for integrating curriculum.

Table 3 presents possible action statements for students, teachers, and administrators. Appropriate <u>action verbs</u> are underlined once while the *instructional technology* introduced is italicized.

Domains of Teaching and Technology Integration

This chapter explores the many uses of technology to create new instructional materials for teaching by combining resources gathered from a variety of sources. A working knowledge of Chapters 1 and 2 is assumed before proceeding.

Table 3. Action Statements for Technology Integration

Arrange a simulated *radio broadcast*
Build new enrichment materials for *technology lessons*
Compose an *electronic grading template*
Compose an *electronic form* to assist at parent teacher conferences
Construct an *electronic portfolio*
Craft an *interactive lesson* using *digital images and video clips*
Create workshop resources to include *text-based publications*
Design a *multimedia pamphlet* for an imaginary public relations business
Develop a *spreadsheet template* to capture lesson observations
Employ *hypercard* and *hyperstudio*-based lesson
Generate an *integrated thematic technology unit* lesson plan
Harvest from educational sites to create a *Web Quest*
Implement custom rubrics for assessing *online student* performance
Incorporate *multimedia* presentation elements
Initiate curriculum-appropriate, *technology-based instructional materials*
Integrate a *Web-based quiz*
Manufacture *text-based, visual-based, and Web-based technologies*
Produce a *"front door"* to a Web-based *virtual tour*
Produce a *hyperbook*
Produce an *interactive lesson*
Program a new *educational software* package
Record a five minute *videotape*
Record a *radio show/closed circuit TV* show
Prototype a customized application using *programming languages*
Teach a lesson via the school's *closed circuit television station*

Cognitive Domain

Since bursting onto the educational psychology scene in the mid-1960s, designing instructional materials for many educators has centered on principles drawn from cognitivism. Cognitive models for instruction emphasize the importance of the learners' processes in constructing knowledge. On par with the input → processing → output model of a computer, the information-processing theory makes the new Taxonomy for the Technology Domain even more important and relevant. In this view, represented by the work of Atkinson and Shiffrin (1968), inputs are sensed, encoded, and stored in short-term and, later, transferred to long-term memory as new information for later retrieval and recall.

When creating instructional materials at this level of the technology taxonomy, teachers would do well to embed learning in realistic and relevant environments, to support multiple learning styles, teaching strategies, and multiple modes of representation, and to further personal ownership in teaching (Driscoll, 2000).

M. David Merrill (2002) proposed a comprehensive framework in the cognitive domain for consideration. In his work, *First Principles of Instruction*, the author proposes four phases to the instructional process: activation of prior experience, demonstration of skills, application of skills, and integration of these skills into real-world activities. As its own cognitive model, these principles of instruction provide an excellent model for promoting problem-centered learning in which instructional materials are provided that engage the learner in solving real-world problems. Merrill's principles capture a program for designing instruction that, when shared with teachers and staff, offer one venue for successfully applying technology in the classroom.

Keeping in mind that cognitivism is the domain of factual knowledge and the intellectual skills to understand and use that knowledge, the following *student* objective is provided for consideration. Note that the example objectives are created using the integration technologies and action statements examined previously. Appropriate <u>action verbs</u> are underlined once while the *instructional technology* introduced is italicized.

Cognitive domain: "Students will <u>design</u>, <u>develop</u>, <u>prototype</u>, and <u>exhibit</u> public relations literature/materials for an imaginary business, Including *word-processed letterhead* and *desktop-published newsletters*; *electronic spreadsheets* of daily sales totals; and, a *visually illustrated annual report* of sales figures for board of directors meetings."

As noted earlier, most of the 57 objectives cited at level 5.0 of the taxonomy were in the cognitive domain. Teachers participating in technology workshops and participants in graduate instructional technology programs would do well to search for courses of study emphasizing teacher-designed, technology-based instructional courses materials.

Text-, visual-, and Web-based resources are within the reach of every teacher whose school is equipped with multimedia computers, office productivity software, and access to the Internet. Text-based handouts, study guides, and worksheets are easily prepared using images and text harvested from the Web and word processed for the classroom. Likewise, visual-based lessons address the demands of the cognitive learner by using harvested images, sounds, text, and video integrated into a Power Point presentation. Web-based home pages, prepared with state-of-the-art editors, reduce the risk of unsupervised Internet exploration while focusing attention on validated content area sites.

Teachers-as-experts design, develop, and implement their own instructional materials using Microsoft Word, Power Point and Netscape Composer. The following objectives present the key elements of integrating technologies into the cognitive domain.

Cognitive domain: "Given a <u>model</u> for *text-based instructional materials*, teachers will <u>harvest</u> a minimum of four pages of *digital text* and at least eight appropriate *digital images* to create a *hyperbook* appropriate to teach academic subject content."

"Given a <u>model</u> for *visual-based instructional materials*, teachers will <u>harvest</u> *digital text*, at least 16 *multimedia elements* (*images*, *sound*, or *video* clip files) to create an *interactive lesson* appropriate to teach academic subject content."

"Given a <u>model</u> for *Web-based instructional materials*, teachers will <u>identify/select</u> at least six unique *Web sites* and create a "*front door*" to a Web-based *virtual tour* of the Internet appropriate to teach academic subject content."

The Children's Internet Protection Act (CIPA) and the Neighborhood Internet Protection Act (NIPA) went into effect on April 20, 2001. These new laws place restrictions on the use of available funding and implement Internet safety policies that block or filter access to objectionable material. *Administrators* (i.e., schools, school boards, and local educational agencies) are tasked with the specific objective exhibited below. Integrated technologies serve to provide these training resources to partner institutions.

Cognitive domain: "Administrators should <u>produce workshops</u> for teachers and staff to address the school's policy for Internet safety of minors. Included in the *self-paced technology-based program* are measures that protect against access through such computers that are (or contain) visual depictions that are obscene, child pornography, or harmful to minors. Potential resources for <u>preparing workshop resources</u> include *text-based online reports* and *publications*, a list of key *Web sites*, and recommended *audiovisual materials*."

Affective Domain

Schools are increasingly responsible for the social agendas of affective issues mandated by various educational units, usually without funding and almost always without the instructional resources to offer the desired content. Contemporary social justice issues embrace bullying and building safe and orderly schools, prayer and religion in schools, and equal access to educational opportunities often provided by guest speakers, films, and videotapes.

Affectively, such lessons are best delivered using materials designed and developed for specific communities, age groups, and target audiences. With sophisticated technology and office productivity software, even students are creating affective materials. Here are three objectives exemplifying appropriate student, teacher, and administrator competencies with respect to teaching and learning with integrated technologies. First, examine this suitable *student* objective in the affective domain:

Affective domain: "From information harvested from the American Society for the Prevention of Cruelty to Animals (ASPCA) Web site, students will <u>design</u>, <u>arrange</u>, and <u>record</u> a five-minute *videotape* offering pet owners some common-sense tips to help them keep their pets safe during Halloween trick-or-treat. The school will <u>schedule a broadcast</u> of the video on their *closed circuit television* station the morning of Halloween."

One of the final projects for pre-service teachers involves a handbook to be used by high school seniors to document graduation requirements. The handbook is used during the final year to track program course completion, assess final grades, and evaluate the final senior project. Parents and administrators are privy to the handbook and afforded an opportunity to review the final version of the mandatory senior project. Copyright laws and proper citations are strictly enforced. The learning objective to help the *teacher-as-learner* master the construction of the senior handbook is shown next.

Affective domain: "Teachers will <u>construct</u> a draft *digital handbook* for high school senior graduation. The handbook includes a *visual synopsis* program of study of all courses required for graduation. A *database* will be provided to <u>capture individual student record</u> of course completions with *standardized input screens* and periodic <u>electronic reports</u>. An *electronic spreadsheet template* will be <u>adopted</u> for computing final grade point average and class standing and a <u>personalized</u> *electronic intelligent portfolio* containing progress reports and evaluation rubrics for the senior project will be <u>assembled</u> throughout the senior school year."

Educators readily admit that bullying is a problem. The question, of course, is what is the best methodology to bring this delicate situation to light? A solid program of information helps identify, defuse, set boundaries, control and eliminate "bullying" behavior. However, the same lesson material used to introduce the topic to students would not be appropriate for teachers or parents to help them deal with problems on a more personal and immediate basis.

Administrators participating in a summer 2003 workshop were charged with preparing just such an in-service program for teachers. They were asked to evaluate the success of the program with pre- and post-student surveys related to incidents of school-related bullying. Development of the program materials using a variety of integrated technologies is demonstrated in the objective below.

Affective domain: "Participants in the administration program will <u>manufacture</u> a *technology-enhanced lesson* entitled, "How to Prevent and Deal With Bullying" for parents and teachers. The lesson should <u>incorporate</u> an integrated thematic unit, *hyperbook*, *interactive lesson*, and *virtual tour* to address the <u>characteristic</u> nature and manifestations of bullying and possible <u>typical responses</u> toward confirmed episodes of harassment."

Psychomotor Domain

In the psychomotor domain, commercially available educational software is more and more prevalent to help develop fine and gross motor skills in learners, especially in young learners. Unfortunately, episodes of lessons and learning objectives in this domain are few and far between. The use of integrated technologies seems constrained at this point in the evolution of instructional technology to checklists, portfolios, and multimedia presentation tools.

Preparing students to design their own learning resources is somewhat akin to the old adage of "teaching a man to fish." By the time students enter secondary school most have been using word processing for years and the Internet for as long as they have been watching television and talking on the telephone. The following objective provides *students* with the tools to create their own diagnostic instruments for solving common computer problems — a reasonable application of integrated technologies in the psychomotor domain.

Psychomotor domain: "Students will successfully demonstrate novice skill level with regards to computer *hardware* and *troubleshooting, software installation, network connectivity*. Students will <u>take</u> *digital camera images* depicting how to dismantle a desktop computer and create a <u>point-and-click</u> *digital slide presentation. Graphic organizer software* will be used to prepare a *visual demonstration* of how to install and test CD-ROM software and how to <u>download</u>, <u>install</u>, and <u>test</u> *Web-based freeware and shareware packages*."

Teacher-made assessment tools include electronic checklists, rubrics and digital portfolios enhanced with technology. The following *teacher-as-scholar* objective demonstrates the advanced use of integrated technologies for the classroom.

Psychomotor domain: "Teachers will <u>build</u> three *online assessment tools* for appropriate student feedback. As a minimum, these tools will <u>accommodate tactile responses</u> and include an *HTML-based checklist* containing student performance of subject matter curriculum content; a rubric containing performance and knowledge criteria <u>produced</u> using *educational software*; and, an *electronic portfolio* documenting long-term student learning outcomes."

In today's fast-paced world, attention to the psychomotor domain is particularly beneficial in programs for the "gifted and talented." Such programs demonstrate high performance academic aptitude, reasoning and divergent thinking, visual or performing arts, and psychomotor abilities — a keen capacity to acquire both gross and fine manipulative skills (India Parenting, 2003; National Association for Gifted Children, 2003; Gogel, 2003).

To encourage administrators to provide learning opportunities for gifted students, principals and directors of gifted programs are encouraged to address the following objectives. Recommended technologies for integration are cited to aid *administrators* in the design and development of necessary instructional resources for the psychomotor domain in this fairly comprehensive example objective.

Psychomotor domain: "Students are expected to grow and excel in four foundation curriculum areas. School board policies should be implemented to provide expanded teacher-preparation time to foster hands-on development of technology-based remedial, enrichment, and professional development materials by faculty, administrators, and staff. *Technology-based remedial materials* include exercises in problem solving, critical thinking, and communication. *Technology-based enrichment materials* include virtual exploration in the relationships of knowledge, themes, issues, and problems that exist within the disciplines. *Technology-based professional development materials* foster continued teacher growth in language arts, mathematics, science, and social studies."

Technology Integration and the Psychologies of Learning

Behaviorally, educators are tasked with creating their own resources using integrated technology tools. Students, teachers, and administrators use the cognitive style to construct materials representing content knowledge. As technologies are increasingly immersed into the culture, educators must ensure that they employ various technologies from a humanistic perspective that serve to enhance learning rather than detract from it.

Behaviorism

Technologies such as online Web-based tools, multimedia applications, and a host of utility software, assist students in the design and development of their own behavioral materials including tutorials, drill and practice, simulations, and instructional games. Teachers create computer-assisted instruction, computer-based education, computer-assisted learning, and computer-based instructional materials. Administrators seek educational innovations at this level such as teaching machines, competency testing, and educational accountability systems. The objective shown for *student* application is a typical example of programming languages used to teach behaviorally at the technology integration level.

Behaviorism: "Using the Visual BASIC programming language, students will program, test, and prototype a *customized application* for calculating quarterly grade point averages. Users of the program must be able to input a minimum of ten assessment scores and calculate the correct GPA for each student as well as report the arithmetic mean, range, and standard deviation for the class."

Interactive lessons are appropriate teaching strategies for "learners of all ages who benefit from concrete, sequential instruction" (Tomei, 2001). The technology objective that follows encourages the *teacher-as-expert* to master the features and commands of Microsoft's Power Point software to prepare an interactive lesson for a high school driver's education course. It shows the strength of applying integrated technologies to create an S $\rightarrow$ R $\rightarrow$ R lesson based on behavioral characteristics.

Behaviorism: "Teachers will construct an *interactive lesson* to test the reaction time of students participating in the second semester of driver's education. Using features of *action buttons, hide slides, slide and bullet transitions*, and *custom animation*, teachers will generate slides that assess the speed at which students respond to various roadside stimuli encountered while driving at night. Students will be expected to point and click at *simulations* of potential road hazards at increasingly shorter time intervals."

For practicing *administrators*, the advantages of preparing behavioral objectives are familiar. They are relatively easy to write and even easier to categorize. They are quickly evaluated using objective criteria that are both observable and measurable. They may be designated for horizontal enrichment or vertical remediation. A behavioral objective using integrated technologies and parsed from the key educational leadership characteristics is offered by Charles Schwahn in his book, *Total Leaders: Applying the Best Future-Focused Change Strategies to Education* (Schwahn et al., 1998). *Author's Note:* Dr Schwahn uses the term "leader" to describe his target learners. With apologies, the term "administrator" is substituted here.

Behaviorism: "Leaders will <u>compose</u> a *text-based checklist* to be incorporated into a *professional development portfolio* evidencing personal growth in the knowledge and understanding and abilities and skills of a leader. As a minimum, the checklist and electronic portfolio must <u>accommodate</u> *digital recording* of artifacts demonstrating satisfactory evidence of systemic leadership, instructional leadership, community and political leadership, organizational leadership, and interpersonal and ethical leadership."

Cognitivism

At level 5.0 of the new taxonomy, the construction of content knowledge is aided by integrated technologies. Instruction must be modeled and gradually incorporated into a curriculum so that its relevance to the learner is readily apparent before it can take on meaningful, long-term importance. Students must be aware of relevant schema and be exposed to strategies that allow them to bridge beyond prerequisite skills to actual learning objectives. Unless the learner appreciates the power of applied knowledge (i.e., what can be done with the knowledge), and accepts a rationale for doing so, it becomes increasingly unlikely that much will be retained beyond the learning event itself.

Student productions, often found in the fine arts curriculum, provide the best examples of objectives written for the cognitive domain using integrated technologies. Here is one such example:

Cognitivism: "Seniors will <u>produce</u> a radio show set in mid-1930's Germany during the rise of the Nazi Party. Using the Internet, selected *reference CD-*

ROM's, and the *sound recorder utility*, students will <u>assemble</u> the script for a five-minute *simulated radio broadcast* defending/denouncing the "Kristallnacht" attack on Jewish businesses. Use the <u>model</u> for propaganda discussed during the semester to <u>evidence your understanding</u> of its principles during the broadcast."

The following examples might appear similar to the *teacher-as-learner* objectives exhibited in the previous chapter, but they are not. Try to distinguish between technologies for infusion and these integrated technologies.

Cognitivism: "Teachers will demonstrate a <u>personal mastery</u> of *text-based*, *visual-based*, and *Web-based technologies* to include *word processing*, *graphics presentation*, and enhanced *Web page editors* to <u>create</u> their own curriculum-appropriate, *technology-based instructional materials*. Using content <u>harvested</u> from the Internet, teachers will <u>design</u>, <u>develop</u>, and <u>implement</u> a *technology-based lesson* including, as a minimum, handouts and worksheets, classroom presentations, and Web home pages for a lesson of their choice."

Administrators deal with school board members, prospective parents, and local public officials on a daily basis. The school's computer labs and classrooms are often the focus of welcome tours as principals proudly point out the wonderful new computers, scanners, digital cameras, and other technologies acquired with the help of various fund-raisers. Next is the inevitable question, "How do you know this investment will pay off in terms of student achievement?" To answer this question, *administrators* are encouraged by the TSSA to create their own mini-presentation using integrated technologies to address the following topics.

Cognitivism: "Administrators will work together to <u>design professional development materials</u> for a district-wide educational technology planning guide to be adopted by member schools who must craft a coherent and focused technology plan. To ensure widest possible dissemination of these resources, the materials should include a *narrated slide show* providing significant research on technology use in the classroom; a *text-based handbook* introducing a quick start overview of the technology planning process, a *spread-*

sheet "what if" analysis of the conditions under which technology is most likely to have a positive impact on student learning; and, an *electronic template* to gather and organize planning data for later inclusion in an actual technology plan document."

Humanism

A shift from lectures to interactive instructional media suggests that technology enhances understanding if it promotes learner involvement rather than restricting it. Here is one such example of a *student* learning objective:

Humanism: "Students will <u>create</u> a *Virtual Museum* for a certain time period in American History. At a minimum, the museum must include a timeline of major events, a biography of important public figures, and a display of key historical events. Students will <u>integrate</u> element of the *digital camera, scanner, harvested images, digital video, music,* and other *audiovisual elements* and <u>incorporate</u> these *multimedia elements* into a *visual-based presentation* for <u>inclusion</u> in their personal intelligent *portfolio.*"

Challenger Learning Centers, located at institutions of higher learning throughout the nation, offer excellent examples of effective humanistic lessons. When classes of students visit a Challenger Learning Center, they climb aboard a virtual space station, conduct fabricated scientific experiments, and work together to solve problems using a host of integrated technologies including the Internet, audiovisual resources, and videoconferencing.

Teachers-as-scholars integrate technologies in anticipation of mission day using program objectives like the one shown here (Challenger Learning Center, 2003):

Humanism: "Operation Montserrat is all about Earth's fragile systems and the interplay between life, land, air and water. The e-Mission *simulation* encourages students to <u>role-play</u> the interaction of scientists by gathering, analyzing and interpreting data to <u>solve real-life problems</u>. On mission day, students join one of four crisis management teams that include Communications (*verbal and printed technologies*); Volcano Predictions and Activity Tracking (*data* *analysis technologies*); Hurricane Tracking (data analysis and *forecasting technologies*); and, Island Evacuation Procedures (*online research* and *communications technologies*)."

Administratively, the role of the school counselor is especially important to the K-12 environment. In the normal course of their responsibilities, counselors are asked to assist students in their exploration of career choices. Such products and services are typically designed to provide developmentally appropriate alternatives for their students. Possible career paths must be research-based, individually tailored to a spectrum of abilities and skills, and meet or exceed standards for quality, integrity, confidentiality, and accessibility. Since the materials created using integrated technologies encompass such individualized focus, the following objective provides a reasonable example of how such materials could be created specifically by counselors and administrators.

Humanism: "Counselors will <u>create their own</u> *multimedia materials* on career awareness for students in grades four through six. They will use *hypercard* and *hyperstudio* software to <u>fashion</u> occupational cards depicting an inventory of possible career occupations as well as *hyperlinks* that allow students to <u>tour a 'neighborhood'</u> and <u>visit people</u> in various occupations. Through their *electronic explorations* of the cards and *virtual tour*, students not only learn about a multitude of occupations but also <u>learn self-awareness, problem solving, listening, and comprehension skills</u>."

Research Implications

With so few integration objectives uncovered during this study, citing meaningful examples is even more difficult than the previous level. Hopefully, future research will find a change in momentum favoring the higher levels of the Taxonomy for the Technology Domain. However, this chapter focuses on those lesson plans in which instructional technologies have produced new materials for teaching and learning.

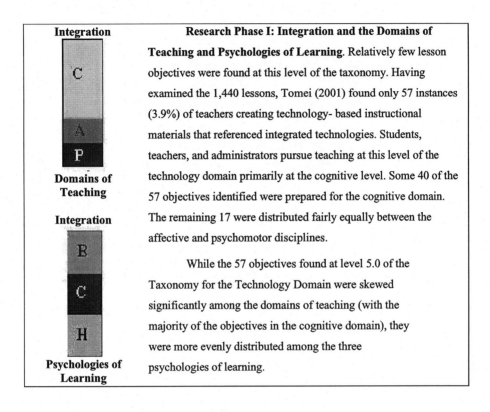

Integration

C

A

P

Domains of Teaching

Integration

B

C

H

Psychologies of Learning

Research Phase I: Integration and the Domains of Teaching and Psychologies of Learning. Relatively few lesson objectives were found at this level of the taxonomy. Having examined the 1,440 lessons, Tomei (2001) found only 57 instances (3.9%) of teachers creating technology- based instructional materials that referenced integrated technologies. Students, teachers, and administrators pursue teaching at this level of the technology domain primarily at the cognitive level. Some 40 of the 57 objectives identified were prepared for the cognitive domain. The remaining 17 were distributed fairly equally between the affective and psychomotor disciplines.

While the 57 objectives found at level 5.0 of the Taxonomy for the Technology Domain were skewed significantly among the domains of teaching (with the majority of the objectives in the cognitive domain), they were more evenly distributed among the three psychologies of learning.

Research Phase II: Integration and Technology-Based Learning Objectives

A mere 4% of the selected 300 lesson plans and 1,440 learning objectives were classified at this level of the taxonomy (Table 3). Integration seems a distant promise of how technology will influence teaching and learning in future classrooms.

There are so few learning objectives noted at the infusion level that further analysis is not merited here. Subsequent analysis is provided in the final chapter to compare the use of infused objectives across grade levels and academic content areas.

Table 3. Student Learning Objectives by Taxonomy Level

Level of Taxonomy	Totals	Percent Within Levels
Literacy	610	42.3
Collaboration	176	12.2
Decision-Making	380	26.4
Infusion	188	13.2
Integration	57	3.8
Tech-ology	30	2.1
Totals	1441	100.00

Conclusion of Technology Integration (Level 5.0)

Imperative in this new classification scheme is an understanding of how infusion differs from integration. In much of the literature, the two terms are used synonymously when discussing instructional technology. For purposes of this taxonomy, they are not considered the same. Technology integration is the final step in the personal application of technology for teaching and learning. In the previous level, everyone was considered a learner. At level 5.0, everyone is considered a teacher. As with the previous level of the taxonomy, everyone reading this book has a vested interest in exploiting integrated technologies to their fullest extent as a lifelong educator. For those interested in locating, harvesting, and incorporating existing technology into the curriculum, a review of level 4.0 is appropriate. For those interested in analyzing, designing, developing, implementing, and evaluating new instructional materials, compiled from components located and harvested from digital resources, level 5.0 is more suitable. The next chapter in the Taxonomy for the Technology Domain expands upon the "study of technology" and considers the effect of technology on the student, teacher, and administrator as have past stages but also explores the educational institution, the community, and society as a well.

References

Atkinson, R.C., & Shiffrin, R.M. (1968). Human memory: A proposal system and its control processes. In K.W. Spence & J.T. Spence (Eds.), *The psychology of learning and motivation: Advances in research and theory*. New York: Academic Press.

Challenger Learning Center at Wheeling Jesuit University. (2003). *E-Mission: Operation Montserrat*. Retrieved from the World Wide Web: *http://www.wju.edu/clc/*

Collaborative for Technology Standards for School Administrators. (2003). *Technology Standards for School Administrators, TSSA Draft*, version 4.0. Retrieved from the World Wide Web: *cnets.iste.org/tssa/view_standards.html*

Driscoll, M.P. (2000). *Psychology of learning for instruction*. Boston: Allyn & Bacon.

Gogel, E.M. (2003). *Do children have a right to be challenged in school?* Association for the Gifted (TAG) Initiatives for Education, Albuquerque, NM. Retrieved from the World Wide Web: *http://www.cectag.org*

International Society for Technology in Education (ISTE). (2003). *Educational Technology Standards and Performance Indicators for All Teachers*. National Educational Technology Standards for Teachers. Retrieved from the World Wide Web: *cnets.iste.org/teachers/t_stands.html*

International Society for Technology in Education (ISTE). (2003). *Technology Foundation Standards for All Students*. National Educational Technology Standards for Students. Retrieved from the World Wide Web: *cnets.iste.org/students/s_stands.html*

Merrill, M. D. (2002). *First principles of instruction*. Educational Technology Research and Development.

National Association for Gifted Children. (2003). *Who Are The Gifted? Characteristics of Various Areas of Giftedness*, Washington, DC. Retrieved from the World Wide Web: *www.nagc.org/ParentInfo*

Schwahn, C.J., Spady, W.G., & O'Neil, G.R. (eds.). (1998). *Total leaders: Applying the best future-focused change strategies to education*. American Association of School Administrators.

Tomei, L.A. (2001, April 30). Using a taxonomy for the technology domain. *Penn Association of Colleges and Teacher Educators.*

Chapter 11

Tech-ology
(Level 6.0)

Tech-ology **The Study of Technology**	Level 6.0 The ability to judge the universal impact, shared values, and social implications of technology use and its influence on teaching and learning.

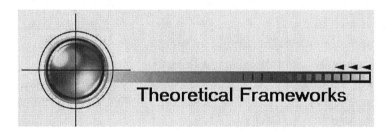

Theoretical Frameworks

Definition and Historical Origins

At the apex of the Taxonomy for the Technology Domain lies the study of technology, an often overlooked, yet uncommonly important venue for the application of technology for teaching and learning. Closely akin to the highest level of Bloom's taxonomy of educational objectives in the cognitive domain,

Tech-ology concerns itself with the *"ability to judge the universal impact, shared values, and social implications of technology use and its influence on teaching and learning."* Given the impact of technology on society over the past six decades, this level of the taxonomy also concerns itself with judgments, recommendations, implications, influences, values, effect, and affect on teaching and learning. Some of the most essential considerations are presented here.

Student Achievement

Since educators first used technology in the classroom, researchers have tried to confirm whether its use has a significant and reliable impact on student achievement. Searching for an answer, they have come to appreciate that technology cannot be treated as a single independent variable. In other words, student achievement is gauged not only by how well students perform on standardized tests but also by their ability to use higher-order skills to critically isolate realistic, logical, and practical solutions to problems. For instance, technology assists in gathering usage and course enrollment data by school. It disaggregates that data based on basis of race, gender, language status, disability status, and income level and analyzes these data to determine the extent of inequities and possible alternatives to remediate these imbalances.

Student Assessment

Judging the impact of any particular technology requires an understanding of the learning goals considered important to students, teachers, and administrators and how the technology is used in the classroom to address these objectives. Technologies impact the types of assessments used to evaluate student achievement and offer a perspective of the complex nature of change in the school environment.

Equal Access

Although there has been a strong push to get educational technology into the hands of teachers and students, many obstacles to implementation remain. Equipment may not be placed in easily accessible locations. Hardware and software often pose problems for teachers in the classroom, and just-in-time technical support may be unavailable. Teachers may lack the time and the incentives to increase their own technology skills.

Removing Barriers to Learning

Technology removes inequities between schools of the inner city and the suburbs, between cities and rural districts. It becomes a force to equalize the educational opportunities of all children regardless of location and social and economic circumstance.

Social Fairness

Technology augments the increasing social agenda laid on schools by government and communities. New technologies provide distinctive curricula addressing local attitudes and the policies to foster improvements in the character and quality of student learning. Digital technologies assist with partnerships that foster grant-writing efforts seeking public and private support, special purpose fund-raising events, private foundation enterprises merging the philanthropic efforts of diverse companies, and individuals who donate equipment, services, software or cash.

Global Awareness

Global education provides students and individuals with the skills necessary for them to meet their responsibilities as citizens of the community, state, and nation in an increasingly interdependent and complex global society. Technologies at this level of the taxonomy encourage knowledge of world cultures and international events and an understanding of the complexities of international systems of economics, politics, and culture. The goal of global education is to expand an individual's perception of the world with an awareness of the multicultural and transnational nature of the human condition. They exhibit an intellectual curiosity about the world that transcends local and national boundaries.

Tech-ology supports each of these noble and ambitious goals, offering a myriad of state-of-the-art resources only some of which are presented in this chapter.

Standards for Tech-ology

Not since the standards for literacy at Level 1.0 are the criterion and benchmarks for technology as clear as they are here at the pinnacle of the Taxonomy for the Technology Domain. The International Society for Technology in Education provides its own category for social, ethical, legal, and human issues related to technology skills and competencies — for both students and teachers. For students, NETS*S addresses issues, practice, and attitudes. For teachers, the NETS*T demands a level of performance from all teachers that includes modeling the proper uses and applications of, and access to, technology across the most diverse audience of target learners (ISTE, 2003).

Students are expected to understand the implications of technology both as a tool for lifelong learning, collaboration, and productivity as well as a content area worthy of its own interdisciplinary knowledge base in its own right. Teachers, likewise, are obliged to master the issues surrounding the potential of technology and to promote its power as a teaching and learning tool throughout their academic careers.

The Collaborative for Technology Standards for School Administrators (Collaborative for TSSA, 2003) incorporates the self-same category of social, legal, and ethical issues into their directives for preparing educational leaders. Actually, many of the specific mandates are exactly the same as students and teachers — with two noted exceptions. The TSSA adds a charge for administrators to infuse and communicate their vision for technology as integral to the mission of learning and teaching. The collaborative also encourages a professional awareness of emerging technologies and their potential to aid sectors of potential learners at both ends of the intellectual spectrum (TSSA, 2003).

A summary of competencies at level 6.0 is offered in Table 1 and includes many of the international, national, state, and professional expectations for judging the universal impact, shared values, and social implications of technology use and its influence on teaching and learning.

Table 1. Tech-ology Standards for Students, Teachers, and Administrators

Tech-ology Competency	Student Standards	Teacher-as-Learner Standards	Teacher-as-Expert Standards	Teacher-as-Scholar Standards	Administrators
NETS*S					
Social, ethical, and human issues	x				
• Students understand the ethical, cultural, and societal issues related to technology.	x				
• Students practice responsible use of technology systems, information, and software.	x				
• Students develop positive attitudes toward technology uses that support lifelong learning, collaboration, personal pursuits, and productivity.	x				
NETS*T					
Teachers understand the social, ethical, legal and human issues surrounding the use of technology in K-12 schools and apply those principles in practice.		x	x	x	
• Model and teach legal and ethical practice related to technology use		x	x	x	
• Apply technology resources to enable and empower learners with diverse backgrounds, characteristics, and abilities		x	x	x	
• Identify and use technology resources that affirm diversity		x	x	x	
• Promote safe and healthy use of technology resources		x	x	x	
• Facilitate equitable access to technology resources for all students		x	x	x	

The world is connected by an increasingly unfettered flow of information stimulated by incredible advances in computer and telecommunications technologies. The flow of information, crossing political, economic and social boundaries, has changed the world, making it a smaller, more interactive place. World events affect us more directly and more immediately than ever before. Because of advancements in technology, issues that once fell primarily in the dominion of domestic affairs — health, the environment, social justice, education, and human and natural resources — are now viewed from a global context. The once clear distinction between foreign and domestic affairs is blurred. The impact of solutions is more globally dynamic and uncertain and, as a result, the solutions more challenging.

Table 1. Tech-ology Standards for Students, Teachers, and Administrators (continued)

Tech-ology Competency	Student Standards	Teacher-as-Learner Standards	Teacher-as-Expert Standards	Teacher-as-Scholar Standards	Administrators
TSSA					
Educational leaders understand the social, legal, and ethical issues related to technology and model responsible decision-making related to these issues.					x
• ensure equity of access to technology resources that enable and empower all learners and educators					x
• identify, communicate, model, and enforce social, legal, and ethical practices to promote responsible use of technology					x
• promote and enforce privacy, security, and online safety related to the use of technology					x
• promote and enforce environmentally safe and healthy practices in the use of technology					x
• Participate in the development of policies that clearly enforce copyright law and assign ownership of intellectual property developed with district resources					x

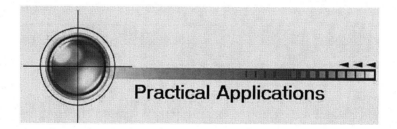

Practical Applications

Tech-ology Technologies and Action Statements

The study of technology and its impact on teaching and learning conjures up an inventory of hardware, software, and applications (Table 2), while simultaneously generating a host of action statements (Table 3) distinct from any found in previous levels of the taxonomy.

Table 2. Appropriate Tech-ology Technologies

Assistive Technologies	Electronic Group Surveys	Telephone Interviews
Bulletin Boards		
Topical	List-Serves	Video Observations
Educational Issues		
Professional Development	Modeling Software	Virtual Communities
Chat Rooms		
Topical	Online Research and	Virtual Learning
Student Debates	Publishing	Communities
Professional Interaction		
	Simulation Programs	Web Sites
Discussion Forums		Political Action
Electronic Field Trips	Statistical Software	Government
		Educational
		Religious

Tech-ology serves to expand on important cultural issues. Use of the various technologies shown in Table 2 promotes individual thinking and, as a result, entails a more sophisticated level of understanding on the part of students, teachers, and administrators.

When considering the technologies and action statements presented below in Table 3, you are encouraged to expand your own vision for blending higher-order thinking levels with the practical tasks advanced therein. Appropriate action verbs are underlined once while the *instructional technology* introduced is italicized.

Domains of Teaching and Tech-ology

New technologies continue to evolve, challenging current thinking, policy and practice. Virtual field trips, unimagined only a few short years ago, enable students to visit cultural and educational sites around the world without ever leaving their classroom. Educational Web sites, now numbering into the millions, steer educators to resources that help with lesson plan design and

Table 3. Action Statements for Tech-ology

Address strategies for ensuring *technology equity* with respect to curriculum enhancements
Address issues of *technology access* inequities
Advocate for and against issues of *technology applications*
Analyze personal liability, intellectual property, and *technology copyright* issues
Argue the ethical technology issues and esthetic point of view
Become involved with *technology planning*
Create opportunities for students to share *electronic diaries*
Develop a vision for improving student *technology competencies*
Set policy for *computer usage* and *Internet access*
Ensure equitable access to various technologies
Recognize the human and social factors that affect technology use
Measure variances in *student and teacher technology skills* and address solutions to narrowing this gap
Find new ways that technology can help students to learn
Identify beneficiaries of *technology grants and funding*
Implement effective *assistive technologies*
Judge moral issues surrounding the use of technology
Consider research findings on technology in education
Share an understanding of what technology skills are important
Support inquiry into *technology impact on society*
Value technology for all students, especially those "at risk"

personal professional development. Authors of these sites often employ as many technologies as possible to address the range of learning styles and teaching strategies encountered in today's diverse classrooms. Teachers and learners tap into videoconferencing resources, satellite content providers, and online and Web-based services for their news, sports, biographies and history, travel, entertainment, as well as academic content. The truly exciting aspect of using technologies for teaching and learning is to consider the dynamic interplay of technology with culture and society.

Cognitive Domain

Cognitivist theory holds that before the first technology is purchased or teachers are asked to participate in their first technology development session, the educational goals for technology should be in place. Initially, goals for basic student curriculum must be established. Then, the targeted technology-based competencies to be taught in schools are needed. Finally, a list of the administrative tasks before technology can successfully promote those learning goals must be adopted.

Cognitivist theory further encourages varied approaches, all of them learner-driven, for solving problems and instructional tasks. Tech-ology encourages multiple representations for teaching rather than relying on single schemas to present new knowledge. It promotes a practical, real-world context for transferring these basic concepts and theories to the learner.

Consistent with the principles of tech-ology, the study of technology encompasses one's own personal schemata of values, impact, and implications. There are technologies available to promote such understanding but, as seen in the example objectives that follow, the majority of efforts lie in addressing questions, simulating scenarios, and imbedding new learning situations into the curriculum. The examples of tech-ology in practice begin with *student*-focused objectives. Appropriate action verbs are underlined once while the *instructional technology* introduced is italicized.

Cognitive domain: "Students must understand the possible *implications of technology* in society. In this lesson, they will conduct an analysis (*spreadsheets, statistical software*) of key questions, such as: "Who pays for this technology and who benefits?" and "What are the specific ethical and moral issues surrounding the use of this technology?" Students will formulate models of cost-benefit analysis from economics, sociology, law and philosophical ethics that analyze personal liability, professional duty, and intellectual property issues."

The thrust of tech-ology for the *teacher-as-expert* from a cognitive teaching perspective is demonstrated in the following objective used by many classroom computer teachers to ensure successful learning outcomes. It is also used by the *teacher-as-scholar* to research and report on measures taken by educators to provide consistent, fair, and equitable access to technology.

Cognitive domain: "Ensure that students have equitable access to various technologies (such as *presentation software, video production, Web page production, word processing, modeling software*, and *desktop publishing* *software*) to produce projects that <u>demonstrate learning</u> in particular areas of the curriculum."

It seems that the most important administrative tasks necessary to successfully promote learning involve an amalgamation of research, partners, and technologies. Research offers many of the potential venues for promoting learning. The proper uses of technologies advances learning on so many levels – levels already applied in previous stages of the Taxonomy for the Technology Domain. The following *administrative* objective discusses a vision for learning and represents the impact of learning at the tech-ology level.

Cognitive domain: "School administrators should develop a <u>clear vision</u> for improving student *learning through technology*. This vision must be well documented (*word processing*) and disseminated (*collaborative technologies*) throughout the district so that teachers, students, administrators, and parents <u>share understanding</u> of what technology skills and abilities are important and how they will be measured. The technology must be used to <u>support learning goals</u> of the school or district."

Affective Domain

Technology in the affective domain represents an emerging area of teaching and learning with unparalleled potential to offer significant benefits to so many inter-disciplines within the field of education. Besides its apparent application in ethical issues, aesthetic appreciation, social impact, and cooperative learning, technology at this level of the taxonomy offers implications for special needs students, improvements to human-machine interface technology, and advancements in online learning environment design. Each of these techniques involves the expression and interpretation of emotion and human responses. Although researchers are still in the experimental stages with these devices, it would be valuable for special educators, in particular, to think about possible implications for the classroom. Below are some examples that provide a background for affective computing technologies at the top level of the Taxonomy for the Technology Domain. The examination begins with a proper *student* objective.

Affective domain: "Students will <u>attend to</u> the ethical issues and esthetic point of view of the creative artist by placing representative original pieces of art on the *World Wide Web* for <u>public access</u>. Students will <u>research</u> both sides of the <u>debate</u>, harvest appropriate *text*, *visual*, and *Web-based support materials* reflecting their <u>advocacy</u> on one side of the issue."

Affectively, *teachers-as-learners* are introduced to the potential of tech-ology to support collaborative classroom learning environments as in the following objective discovered in a 400-level course in instructional technology.

Affective domain: "Teachers will involve students in <u>meaningful learning activities</u> in which *instructional technologies* are used to <u>support inquiry</u>, <u>enhance communication</u>, extend access to resources, <u>guide students</u> to analyze and visualize data, and <u>encourage expression of ideas</u>. Promote the use of *virtual communities* that offer opportunities for students to <u>exchange ideas</u> with other students, teachers, and professionals across the world."

Administrators, likewise, are encouraged in workshops and seminars to explore the possibilities of tech-ology to develop positive working relationships among faculty, staff, and other administrative personnel in hopes of affecting learning outcomes of students at both ends of the intellectual spectrum.

Affective domain: "Administrators will <u>consider</u> the *value of technologies* for all students, especially those considered <u>at risk</u> of educational failure. Offer technologies that help students <u>develop positive cooperative learning relationships</u>, enabling them to work together. <u>Students with special needs</u> may require *assistive technologies* in the form of *computer-based remedial activities*. <u>Gifted students</u> may require *enrichment technologies* to sustain interest and pique intellectual curiosity."

Tech-ology and the Psychologies of Learning

At this highest level of the taxonomy, technology promotes effective interaction between student and teacher, teacher and administrator, and student and administrator. Emerging technologies applied cognitively for instructional purposes advance social interactions and therefore the study of technology and its implications and influences.

Behaviorism

While most technology-oriented behavioral objectives are found at the lower levels of the taxonomy, there are many instances in which behaviorism plays an important role at the more elevated levels as well. At level 4.0 and level 5.0 of the new taxonomy, course objectives that infuse and integrate technology-based instructional materials into the teaching and learning environment provide valuable new knowledge for learners. They monitor their own performance and gain positive reinforcement as they accomplish course objectives.

Although it may be tempting to simply dismiss behavioral objectives at the higher end of the taxonomy, it would be a mistake to ignore its contributions here. Tech-ology accepts the importance of behavioral objectives and provides an impetus for identifying new candidate technologies. Behavioral technologies are recognized in education at all grade levels, inner-city schools, instructional techniques, job training, and interpersonal and intra-personal communications. Certainly, additional areas will continue to emerge now that the Taxonomy for the Technology Domain has exposed the means to categorize these technologies. The behavioral *student* objective shown below typifies the tech-ology level of the taxonomy.

Behaviorism: "Students should be able to <u>recite</u> the rules and <u>recall</u> the appropriate behaviors for using technology in *school computer facilities*. Students shall not lend their *e-mail logins and passwords* to anyone else, create a *computer virus* or place a virus on the network, send a message that is inconsistent with the school's code of conduct, *send messages* that are inappropriate, obscene, sexist, contain obscenities, or contain inflammatory or abusive language, *send messages* under someone else's name; read mail or files without the owner's permission, or interfere with the ability to <u>make effective use</u> of school district *computing and network resources*."

For teachers, the classroom is the most visible platform upon which the study of technology is played out. In addition, schools often host an annual open house, science fair, or video and audio productions. Incorporated into a curricular scope and sequence in a public school district of some considerable size, the following *teacher-as-learner* objective is offered as evidence of behavioral applications at this highest level of the Taxonomy for the Technology Domain.

Behaviorism: "Teachers will <u>generate</u> *technology-based media opportunities* for students to <u>share work</u> publicly through performances (*video* and *videotape*), public service opportunities (*audio* and *audiotape*), parent open houses (*visual presentations*), and *technology-focused school-wide science fairs*. Such occasions will inform and <u>educate</u> parents and community members of the kinds of learning outcomes the school is providing for students."

Administrators serve level 6.0 of the taxonomy by hosting sequential, orderly, behavioral programs promoting technology. The objective shown below was lifted from an educational leadership program encouraging participants (K-12 principals and district superintendents) to create technology programs within their purview built on sound fiscal management, a comprehensive infrastructure, and demonstrated leadership.

Behaviorism: "Ensure that all students have equitable access to effective uses of technology. <u>Develop strategies</u> for addressing a variety of <u>access inequities issues</u> to include <u>writing grants</u> to receive public and private support, <u>conducting</u> special purpose <u>fund-raising events, forming foundations</u> so that companies and individuals may <u>donate</u> much-needed *technologies*, and <u>pursuing strategies</u> for addressing curriculum inequities by evaluating technologies in the same way you evaluate other instructional materials."

Cognitivism

The mathematician Vernor Vinge succinctly described the impact of technology on the cognitive development of learners this way:

> *"The acceleration of technological progress has been the central feature of this century. I argue [that] we are on the edge of change comparable to the rise of human life on Earth" (Vinge, 1987).*

Maximum benefits are likely whenever technology serves to energize and facilitate thinking and knowledge construction (Jonassen et al., 1998). For proponents of this newest taxonomy for the technology domain, learning objectives prepared at the tech-ology level encompass Vinge's vision for the potential of technology. For example, when students actively develop logical rules and apply them to real-world situations using technologies presented in this chapter, critical thinking and logical decision-making processes cannot help but be promoted. In the cognitive domain, Jonassen (2000) suggests the use of technologies to enhance the learner's ability to construct new knowledge.

Tech-ology encourages learners to accept responsibility for technology in the construction of their own knowledge base. Emerging technologies offer many opportunities for accessing information, communication, and collaboration as a powerful means for expression. However, they must be considered in the overarching environment of individual accountability (Fulton & Honey, 2002). Educators have come to expect that technology advancement will leverage changes in the teaching and learning environment. However, technology does not cause learning and it cannot account alone for advancements in successful teaching. How effectively technology works in instruction and learning depends on how well tech-ology is addressed in the cognitive domain.

Examine an objective focusing on *student*-centered exploration of technology advancements by various segments of our society. It provides an excellent demonstration of a developmentally appropriate task at level 6.0.

Cognitivism: "Students will <u>explore</u> the evolution of *technological advances* from the perspective of contributions by a <u>diverse group of people</u>. Students will <u>analyze</u> selected *Web sites* provided by the teacher to identify the contributions of minorities to science, medicine, and technology. Students will write (*word-processing*) a three- to five-page paper providing a short biography, a description of their *technological contributions*, and a summary of how their *innovations* impacted society in the 20th century."

The impact of technology on student achievement serves as an example of the cognitive psychology of learning at the tech-ology level. In this objective, *teachers-as-scholars* evaluate the impact of technology on student achievement.

Cognitivism: "Use appropriate *technology tools* to determine the impact on student achievement of your school's technology program. Consider using *electronic mail, telephone* interviews, *video* observations, and student record *databases* to gather demographic information to include computers in general, skills and competencies with respect to word processing, spreadsheets, databases, graphic applications, presentation software, desktop publishing, and Internet activity."

Between 1995 and 2000, the federal government allocated states over $8 billion to purchase technology hardware and software for schools to fund start-up educational technology programs. That initiative, released through the National Educational Technology Plan, provided the nation with five technology goals. They included: access to information technology, effective use of technology to achieve high academic standards, basic technology and information literacy skills, a call for research and evaluation of technology applications for teaching and learning, and increased digital content and networked applications.

While nine states mandated certification or licensure in technology integration, most failed to define any role in technology for school administrators. Only six states even mention administrators in their statutes addressing instructional technology and even in those states, their role was typically restricted to membership on advisory councils or committees (Daniel & Nance, 2002).

As a result of such studies, institutions of higher education providing administrator preparation programs have opted for a minimum set of technology-based objectives before endorsing their constituents as school leaders. The following objective, taken from a course description from The University of Southern Queensland in *Technology and Educational Leadership*, offers an international scope for what *administrators* should know and understand. While the particular course referenced below contains many course objectives, these best represent the tech-ology level of the taxonomy.

Cognitivism: "On successful completion of this course, educational administrators will be able to participate in <u>informed debate</u> (*videoconference* session) about the <u>significance</u> of *information technology* for educational change, <u>appreciate</u> the administrative challenges to be faced in relation to *technology in education*, comment (via *list-serve discussion forums*) upon the educational and professional <u>implications</u> of *web-supported teaching and learning*, and <u>outline</u> some significant findings from research on technology in education."

Humanism

McCormick and Austin offer five humanistic approaches for seeking to "reach" or "connect" technologically, many of these strategies match perfectly with student, teacher, and administrator objectives. For example, the *student* learning objective below demonstrates how several of the technologies recommended by McCormick and Austin involve designing opportunities for social contacts with students, including electronic opportunities (e-mail, listserves, bulletin boards, and chat rooms) for social exchanges between students and faculty.

Humanism: "Students <u>adopt</u> various *technologies* to <u>broaden their horizons</u> by means of global connections (*Internet* and *virtual learning communities*), electronic visualization (*integrated learning systems*, *simulation* programs, *drill/practice* programs, and *tutorial* programs), electronic field trips (*virtual museums* and *videotapes*), and online research and publishing (*electronic journals*, *CD-ROM publications*, etc.)."

Teachers are encouraged by the authors to provide a sense of organization and consistency by using technologies (electronic calendars, digital learning environments, computer-managed instruction, etc.) to maintain a predictable structure of content and time and display respect for student time via prompt communication (e-mail and telephone). McCormack and Austin encourage teachers to create an atmosphere of sharing (via the collaborative tools discussed at level 2.0 of the taxonomy). Here is an objective that captures all three strategies for the *teacher-as-expert*.

Humanism: "Become familiar with human factors that affect the use of *technology for teaching and learning*. Learn about real-world scenarios that describe how technology use influences student understanding, teacher experience, and administrative support. Analyze the impact of how various technologies (i.e., *computers in the classroom*, classroom-based *visual tools*, access to the *World Wide Web*, etc.) impact teacher release time, professional development opportunities, funding levels, curriculum leadership, etc."

Finally, in this last objective, *administrators* are called on to humanize the classroom environment, making the "high-tech" environment of the classroom a more user-friendly place in which to learn via videoconferencing and digital imagery (McCormick & Austin, 1998).

Humanism: "Advocate for a national *distance education policy*. Propose strategies that bring together diverse populations of both students and teachers. Schedule at least two *videoconference* sessions to establish new ways that technology helps students meet and exceed nationally mandated learning standards."

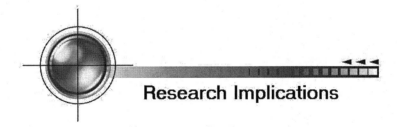

Research Implications

The fewest number of objectives were found at this level of the taxonomy. Of the 1,440 learning objectives examined, Tomei (2001) found a mere 30 incidents (2.1%) addressing technology from a societal, legal, or ethical perspective.

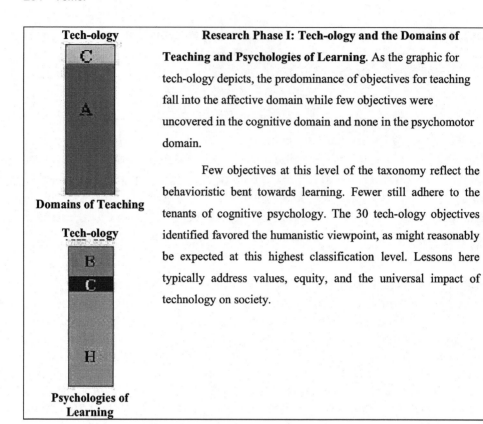

Research Phase I: Tech-ology and the Domains of Teaching and Psychologies of Learning. As the graphic for tech-ology depicts, the predominance of objectives for teaching fall into the affective domain while few objectives were uncovered in the cognitive domain and none in the psychomotor domain.

Few objectives at this level of the taxonomy reflect the behavioristic bent towards learning. Fewer still adhere to the tenants of cognitive psychology. The 30 tech-ology objectives identified favored the humanistic viewpoint, as might reasonably be expected at this highest classification level. Lessons here typically address values, equity, and the universal impact of technology on society.

Research Phase II: Tech-ology and Technology-Based Learning Objectives

Only 2.1 percent of the selected lesson plans classified addressed learning objectives at this level of the taxonomy (Table 3).

As with integration, there were so few tech-ology learning objectives as to make further analysis inconclusive. Some analysis is provided in subsequent chapters to compare objectives across grade levels and academic content areas.

Table 3. Student Learning Objectives by Taxonomy Level

Level of Taxonomy	Totals	Percent Within Levels
Literacy	610	42.3
Collaboration	176	12.2
Decision-Making	380	26.4
Infusion	188	13.2
Integration	57	3.8
Tech-ology	30	2.1
Totals	1441	100.00

Conclusion of Tech-ology (Level 6.0)

In many ways, this highest level of the technology taxonomy parallels the characteristics Bloom attributed to evaluation (level 6) in the cognitive domain, Krathwohl ascribed to characterization (level 5) in the affective domain, and Kibler endorsed as naturalization (level 5) in the psychomotor domain. Tech-ology is marked by reasoning and judgment and requires the learner to value information.

Literacy remains the underlying qualification for advancement up the levels. Students, teachers, and administrators seek tech-ology only after possessing a set of requisite skills and competencies. Collaboration, too, is implicit before judging the merits of technology from a social, ethical, and legal perspective.

Decision-making advances the learner toward tech-ology with a set of tools for handling new situations and unfamiliar problems. Infusion and integration prepare the learner to gather technology resources and convert them into materials suitable for a lifetime of learning.

Tech-ology, then, is the reasonable outgrowth of preparing oneself to use technology for its true ultimate purpose, namely, the betterment of mankind and the advancement of knowledge.

In the previous chapters, the results of a three-year study were unfolded in order to match the emerging levels of the new Taxonomy for the Technology

Domain to documented lesson plans. Learning objectives were offered as examples of how technology contributes to the cognitive, affective, and psychomotor domains of teaching and the behavioral, cognitive, and humanistic psychologies of learning.

In the chapter to follow, a synopsis of the methodology, statement of the problem, findings, and recommendations of the study are provided to redefine technology as a discipline and its potential impact on the future of teaching and learning.

References

Collaborative for Technology Standards for School Administrators. (2003). *Technology Standards for School Administrators, TSSA Draft* (version 4). Retrieved from the World Wide Web: *cnets.iste.org/tssa/ view_standards.html*

Daniel, T.K., & Nance, J. (2002, Spring). *The Role of the Administrator in Instructional Technology Policy*. The Ohio State University P-12 Project.

Fulton, K., & Honey, M. (2002). *Emerging technologies in education*. Educational Technology.

International Society for Technology in Education. (ISTE). (2003). *Educational Technology Standards and Performance Indicators for All Teachers*. National Educational Technology Standards for Teachers. Retrieved from the World Wide Web: *cnets.iste.org/teachers/ t_stands.html*

International Society for Technology in Education. (ISTE). (2003). *Technology Foundation Standards for All Students*, National Educational Technology Standards for Students. Retrieved from the World Wide Web: *cnets.iste.org/students/s_stands.html*

Jonassen, D. (2000). *Computers as mindtools for engaging learners in critical thinking* (2nd edition). Upper Saddle River, NJ: Prentice-Hall.

Jonassen, D. H., Carr, C., & Yueh, H.P. (1998). Computers as mindtools for engaging learners in critical thinking. *TechTrends*.

McCormick, B. P., & Austin, D. R. (1998). *Technology is Only a Beginning: A Humanistic Approach to Reaching Students*. Indiana Higher Education Telecommunication System. Retrieved from the World Wide Web: *old.ihets.org/learntech/distance_ed*

Tomei, L. A. (2001, April 30). *Using A Taxonomy For The Technology Domain*. Penn Association Of Colleges and Teacher Educators.

Vinge, V. (1987). *True Names*. Binary Star Number 5. Reprinted in True Names and Other Dangers. Baen Books. Originally published by Dell, 1981.

Chapter 12

Investigation into the Taxonomy for the Technology Domain

Introduction

This final chapter on the Taxonomy for the Technology Domain provides a discretionary inquiry into the research base of this newest classification system. Similar to the historical evolution of the taxonomies of Bloom (cognitive), Krathwohl (affective), Kibler (psychomotor), Bruce and Levin (technology as media) and SeSDL (communications and information technology), a watershed text such as this is obligated to demonstrate the scholarly basis upon which the new classification schemata is built.

This investigative chapter may be bypassed by readers preferring instead to concentrate on the theoretical foundations and practical applications found in the previous chapters. That is both understandable and anticipated. Certainly, for teachers-as-learners described in the foreword and advanced throughout the predominant chapters of this text, the importance of the new taxonomy lies in its underpinnings on the foundations of educational theory and the principles of teaching and learning that apply to the uses of technology in the classroom. For the teacher-as-expert, the text generates a wealth of relevant applications of the new taxonomy with its six levels based on standards, identified technologies, and possible action statements that serve to move the classroom teacher into the design of appropriate student learning objectives.

This chapter completes the development of the Taxonomy for the Technology Domain for professional educators by considering the teacher-as-scholar as well. From such humble beginnings will come future expansions of the scholarly base from which the Taxonomy for the Technology Domain must eventually mature. It took nearly 50 years of learned scrutiny for Bloom's Taxonomy to emerge as the predominant psychology for instructional design. This final chapter delivers the "opening volley" of a research base that will ultimately support technology as a domain for teaching and psychology for learning in its own right. The investigation exposed herein and the ensuing questions and issues it raises represent the necessary imperative prior to widespread acceptance of this theoretical construct. More is certain to follow.

Recapitulation of Research Phases I and II

You will recall that the results of an initial inquiry into the use of the new taxonomy for preparing technology-based classroom applications was shared as an integral component of previous chapters. The Phase I research offered in each of these chapters sought to establish quantitative support for the use of the taxonomy in real-world learning environments. It described the number of lesson plans found to contain technology-based learning objectives in the cognitive, affective, and psychomotor domains of teaching as well as the behavioral, cognitive, and humanistic psychologies of learning.

Phase II ranked the six levels of the taxonomy by number and percent of technology-based learning objectives uncovered. The weakest representation of objectives was tech-ology (Level 6.0) with only 2.1% of the observed objectives. The strongest representation occurred at the literacy Level 1.0. Over 40% of the objectives were classified at this level.

This chapter expands upon this preliminary data-gathering research to determine relationships between the levels of the Taxonomy for the Technology Domain most commonly addressed in technology-based lesson plans and the grade levels and academic content areas they represented. The investigation sought to establish the viability of the taxonomy as a classification scheme and the legitimacy of technology as its own domain for learning.

Statement of the Problem

The purpose of the investigation was to add value to the body of literature regarding technology and taxonomies by determining the degree of correlation between technology-based learning objectives found in online lesson plans and grade levels. Also examined was the degree of correlation between technology-based learning objectives and certain academic content areas. The study was later delimited to the core subject areas of math, science, language arts and social studies. Further exploration disclosed that the findings, conclusions, and recommendations were sufficient to warrant further investigation.

Methodology

Initially, participants located 30 random lesson plans in four grade levels: primary (N-3), elementary (fourth to sixth), middle school (seventh to eighth), and secondary school (ninth-12th). Collectively over the course of several semesters some 1,441 learning objectives were harvested from hundreds of online lessons reviewed. Only learning objectives that addressed a specific technology competency or involved the use of technology as a tool for learning content area material were extracted for further study. Each learning objective was categorized in one of the six levels of the Taxonomy for the Technology Domain and captured in tabular format by grade levels and academic content area.

For this more comprehensive investigation, four teams were created to handle the tasks of data collection, statistical analysis, research, and writing. Teams collaborated via threaded discussion boards, synchronous chats, telephone contacts, electronic mail, and the more traditional face-to-face meetings.

The *Data Team* compiled the results of the initial inquiry. Team members reviewed a data set consisting of 29 spreadsheets and 1,441 objectives comprising data to serve as a starting point for the investigation. Subsequent reviews discovered duplicate spreadsheets in the data pool that were deleted and further reduced the spreadsheets from 29 to a final 25. Six core content areas were identified before the data team realized the initial study had categorized objectives from multiple academic curricula other than those listed as core areas. The team decided that incidents representing all but the four core areas of math, science, social studies, and language arts would be classified in the "other" category.

After some deliberation, the *Stat Team* opted to use the one-way analysis of variance (ANOVA) to compare groups of data in terms of their mean scores or averages. The team used the Kirkman Web site and its data analysis tool to conduct the ANOVA test and discovered correlations as reported in the Findings section of this chapter.

The *Research Team* uncovered resources addressing (either directly or indirectly) the process of using taxonomies to classify processes in the technology domain. Carefully selected articles were reviewed and presented to guide the project's team efforts.

The *Writing Team* divided the drafting process into its six component elements and created virtual discussion forums using an online learning management environment. After the initial drafts for each section were finished, they were posted to the appropriate discussion forum for review and revision. All sections were compiled into a master document and an overall quality control check was conducted prior to submission to the course instructor.

Findings

The results of the investigation into the Taxonomy for the Technology Domain are depicted first by grade level then by academic content area in a series of tables.

Table 1 provides descriptive data recounting the review of 29 spreadsheets and the classification of 1,441 objectives by grade level. Computed averages (means) and standard deviations are included. Figure 1 supplies a visual graphic depicting the distribution of learning objectives within the taxonomy among grade levels. Table 2 provides the actual ANOVA calculations using an online, Web-based statistical analysis tool provided by Tom Kirkman (2003). Finally, the investigation into the use of the taxonomy continues with respect to academic content areas examined, respectively, in Tables 3 and 4 and Figure 2.

Taxonomy by Grade Level

Table 1 shows a preponderance of the objectives examined (80%) occurred at the lower three levels of the taxonomy (42.3% + 12.2% + 26.4%) *within* the four grade levels. However, there was not much difference in the number of objectives found *among* each grade level.

When comparing the objectives *among* the four grade levels, the computed averages (57.67 – 61.50) and deviations (38.28 – 82.61) show how the objectives are more evenly distributed for secondary lessons than any of the other grade levels examined. Within the levels of the taxonomy, however, there appears to be no consistency with respect to averages (7.50 – 95.00) or deviations (0 – 49.76) within the taxonomy. Therefore, the inquiry could not demonstrate (descriptively) any appropriate distribution *within* the taxonomy levels.

As a result of these initial findings, means and standard deviations were calculated to provide additional descriptive statistics in order to better compare the data sets. As depicted in Figure 2, the data derived in the initial inquiry is considerably more complex. When comparing the objectives *among* the four grade levels, the computed averages (57.67 – 61.50) and deviations (38.28 – 82.61) show how the objectives are more evenly distributed for secondary lessons than any of the other grade levels examined. Within the levels of the taxonomy, however, it would be safe to say that no conclusions can be drawn from the descriptive data calculated. There appears to be no consistency with respect to averages (7.50 – 95.00) or deviations (0 – 49.76) within the taxonomy. Therefore, the inquiry could not demonstrate (descriptively) any appropriate distribution *within* the taxonomy levels.

Figure 1 provides a visual comparison of the means and standard deviations resulting from the review of learning objectives by grade level. The outer-most curve represents the considerable spread of objectives *within* the six levels of the taxonomy. The innermost curve shows how evenly distributed were the objectives *among* the four grade levels examined.

Table 1. Basic Descriptive Results by Grade Level

Level of Taxonomy	Early Childhood (N-3)	Elementary School (4-6)	Middle School (7-8)	Secondary School (9-12)	Percent Within Levels	Mean Within Levels	Std Deviation
Literacy	223	149	129	109	42.2	152.5	49.76
Collaboration	44	44	44	44	12.2	44.00	0
Decision-Making	59	100	119	102	26.4	95.00	25.47
Discrimination	30	38	51	69	13.2	47.00	17.03
Integration	6	12	13	26	3.8	14.25	8.42
Tech-ology	1	3	7	19	2.1	7.50	8.06
Percent Among Grades	25.2	24.0	25.2	25.6			
Mean Among Grades	60.50	57.67	60.50	61.50			
Std Deviation	82.61	56.18	52.14	38.28			

Figure 1. Distribution of Learning Objectives within the Taxonomy (Outer Curve) and Among Grade Levels (Inner Curve)

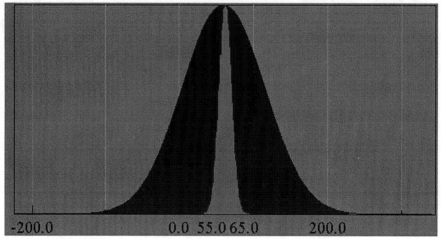

The comprehensive investigation attempted to determine if grade levels exhibited any correlation to the number of objectives in technology-based lesson plans. The investigation sought to determine whether the number of objectives found within each level of the taxonomy increased as the grade level increased, or whether the numbers of objectives found *among* the six levels of the taxonomy increased as the grade level increased. In other words, would it be fair to assume that learning at the higher grade levels included technology-based objectives found at the higher levels of the taxonomy? Would learning at lower grade levels concentrate more on objectives found at the lower levels of the taxonomy?

The investigators computed the aggregated results of the objectives using the ANOVA test to determine correlation. The grade level data is provided in Table 2. The comparison between the actual variation of the group averages is expressed in terms of the *F* ratio: $F =$ (found variation of the group averages) / (expected variation of the group averages). *Within* the six levels of the taxonomy, an *f*-ratio exceeding 20 was found in conjunction with a probability of approximately 0.00. *Among* the four grade levels, the ANOVA test calculated an f-ratio of approximately 0.0046 along with a probability of 0.99.

Table 2: ANOVA Computations for Grade Level Data

Source of Variation	Sum of Squares	Degrees of Freedom	Mean of Squares	F Ratio	Level of Probability	Accept/Reject the Null Hypothesis
Within Levels of the Taxonomy	6.0222 E+04	5	1.2044E+ 04	20.36	0.00	*Reject*
Among Grade Levels	49.125	3	16.375	0.00462	0.9995	*Accept*
Null Hypothesis: There is no significant difference of learning objectives either within the six levels of the taxonomy or among the four grade levels examined.						

If the null hypothesis (that is, there is no significant difference) is correct, we expect F to be about 1. A "large" F, along with a level of probability of zero, indicates the need to reject the null hypothesis. An F-ratio approaching zero with a level of probability close to 1.0 accepts the null hypothesis.

Therefore, the ANOVA calculations were sufficient to establish a significant difference of stratified learning objectives *within* the levels of the taxonomy. However, they were not sufficient to substantiate a correlation *among* the four grade levels.

In summary, the descriptive data provided by Table 1 evidences a significant application of the taxonomy at each of the four grade levels: early childhood, elementary, middle, and secondary school. Objectives are more evenly distributed for secondary lessons than any of the other grade levels examined. The first table shows that a preponderance of the 1,441 objectives examined (80%) occurred at the lower three levels of the taxonomy across all grade levels. Figure 1 visually reveals a possible demarcation. But Figure 2 provided the actual calculations sufficient to establish a significant difference of stratified learning objectives *within* the levels of the taxonomy at each grade level but not *among* the four grade levels. While it was demonstrated that teachers are writing lesson plans with technology-based objectives prepared at all six levels of the taxonomy, they are clearly focusing on technology more as a skill and competency rather than as a tool for learning.

Taxonomy by Academic Content Area

Table 3 shows inquiry results of objectives *among* the four core academic areas (the remainer classified as "other" areas) ranging from 18.4% to 27.8%,

Table 3. Basic Descriptive Results by Academic Content Area

Level of Taxonomy	Math	Science	Language Arts	Social Studies	Other	Percent Within Levels	Mean Within Levels	Std Deviation
Literacy	66	122	160	72	33	31.4	90.60	50.18
Collaboration	26	11	57	30	10	9.3	26.80	19.07
Decision-Making	95	95	59	90	27	25.4	73.20	25.80
Discrimination	21	36	31	32	9	9.0	25.80	10.89
Integration	3	11	8	16	3	2.8	8.20	5.54
Tech-ology	0	4	2	10	2	1.2	3.60	3.85
Percent Among Areas	18.4	24.4	27.8	22.0	7.4			
Mean Among Areas	35.17	46.50	52.83	41.67	14.00			
Std Deviation	37.65	49.98	57.64	32.09	12.93			

with "other" objectives omitted. *Within* each level of the taxonomy the percentage of objectives varied from 1.2% to 31.4%. Some 66% of the objectives examined occurred *within* the lower three levels of the taxonomy (31.4% + 9.3% + 25.4%), which is not as overwhelming a statistic as with grade levels, but noteworthy nonetheless. Similar to the previous grade level findings (ignoring the "other" category) there was not much difference in the number of objectives found *among* each content area.

A significant difference was noted in the number of objectives found *within* each level of the taxonomy examined. Computed averages ranged from a low of 3.60 objectives at the tech-ology level to 90.60 for literacy. Deviations were even more pronounced, spanning 3.85 – 50.18. Among the core content areas much more consistency was uncovered with averages only from 35.17 to 52.83 and standard deviations from 32.09 to 57.64. It would seem from these data that most educators have yet to successfully incorporate higher order thinking into the domain of technology.

The investigation discovered a significant difference in the number of objectives found *within* each level of the taxonomy examined. Computed averages ranged from a low of 3.60 objectives at the tech-ology level to 90.60 for literacy; deviations were even more pronounced spanning 3.85 – 50.18. Among the core content areas much more consistency was uncovered with averages only from 35.17 to 52.83 and standard deviations from 32.09 to 57.64. It would seem from these data that most educators (even those who are familiar with

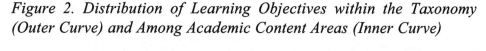

Figure 2. Distribution of Learning Objectives within the Taxonomy (Outer Curve) and Among Academic Content Areas (Inner Curve)

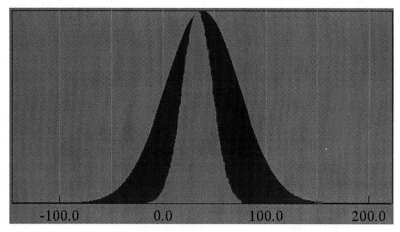

Bloom's taxonomy) have yet to successfully incorporate higher-order thinking into the domain of technology.

Figure 2 compares the means and standard deviations by academic content area. Again, the outer-most curve represents the spread of objectives *within* the six levels of the taxonomy while the innermost curve shows a more even distribution of objectives *among* the four core areas examined. **Author's Note**: Consider the disparity of values on the X-axis when comparing the two graphics (Figure 3, Grade Level versus Figure 7, Content Areas).

The investigation attempted to determine the correlation of technology-based lessons with content-specific lesson plans. The investigation sought to determine whether the number of objectives found within each level of the taxonomy varied with academic content area or whether the numbers of objectives found *among* the six levels of the taxonomy varied with academic content area. In other words, would it be fair to assume that learning in certain content areas included technology-based objectives found at the higher levels of the taxonomy? Or, would learning in certain areas be found more at the lower levels of the taxonomy?

The investigators computed the aggregated results of the 1,441 objectives using the ANOVA test to determine correlation. The academic content area

Table 4: ANOVA Computations for Academic Content Data

Source of Variation	Sum of Squares	Degrees of Freedom	Mean of Squares	F Ratio	Level of Probability	Accept/Reject the Null Hypothesis
Within Levels of the Taxonomy	3.4147E+04	5	6829.0	15	0.00	Reject
Among Content Areas	1.0668E+05	3	3.5560E+04	0.8850	0.466	Accept
Null Hypothesis: There is no significant difference of learning objectives either within the six levels of the taxonomy or among the four academic content areas examined.						

data is provided in Table 4. The comparison between the actual variation of the group averages is expressed in terms of the *F* ratio: *F* = (found variation of the group averages) / (expected variation of the group averages). *Within* the six levels of the taxonomy, an *f*-ratio exceeding 15 was found in conjunction with a probability of approximately 0.00. *Among* the four content levels, the ANOVA test calculated an f-ratio of approximately 0.8850 along with a probability of 0.466. If the null hypothesis (that is, there is no significant difference) is correct, we expect *F* to be about 1. A "large" *F*, along with a level of probability of zero, indicates the need to reject the null hypothesis. An F-ratio approaching zero with a level of probability close to 1.0 accepts the null hypothesis.

The ANOVA calculations were sufficient to establish a significant difference of stratified learning objectives *within* the levels of the taxonomy. However, they were not sufficient to substantiate a correlation *among* the four core academic content areas.

Table 3 evidences a significant application of the taxonomy in each of the core academic content areas examined specifically mathematics, science, language arts, and social studies. Distribution of objectives is fairly even across all areas while a majority of objectives (66%) occurred at the lower three levels of the taxonomy across all content areas. Figure 2 visually revealed a somewhat lesser stratification supported by Table 4 calculations sufficient to establish the significant difference *within* the levels of the taxonomy but not *among* the four academic subject areas. As with the grade level investigation, it was demonstrated that teachers are writing lesson plans with technology-based objectives prepared at all six levels of the taxonomy. However, even with respect to the primary curricular areas employing technologies, these objectives remain clearly focused on skill and competency.

Summary of the Findings

The comprehensive investigation determined the number of objectives at each level of the taxonomy and found that they differed significantly both within the six levels of the new taxonomy and among the grade levels and academic content areas from which the sampled lesson plans were extracted. The study found a significant difference of stratified learning objectives *within* the six levels of the taxonomy at grade level (early childhood, elementary, middle, and secondary school) and *within* the six levels of the taxonomy for four core academic content areas (mathematics, science, language arts, and social studies). It is also important to observe that the study was inconclusive in its exploration of a correlation *among* grade levels or academic subject areas. For these data, the F-ratios and P values were not sufficient to establish the necessary connection.

Recommendations

This chapter presents the results of a limited investigation into the degree to which the levels of the Taxonomy for the Technology Domain are addressed in K-12 technology-based lesson plans across particular academic content areas. So many venues for additional research are possible. For example, this research did not seek to determine if using the Taxonomy for the Technology Domain when preparing instructional objectives produced successful student learning outcomes. In order to establish whether increased student learning occurs as a direct result of using the taxonomy, further study is necessary.

The investigation probed the impact of the taxonomy as a viable classification scheme by examining learning objectives to determine the frequency and distribution of objectives by grade level and academic content area. The results of the investigation surfaced general guidelines for educators planning technology-based lessons. Individual teachers are encouraged to adapt the Taxonomy for the Technology Domain to the specific needs of their classroom and students.

Based on these findings, the following recommendations are offered for further consideration. First, broaden the scope of the original inquiry and investigation. Second, explore additional criteria against which to assess the impact of the technology domain on teaching and learning. Third, design new related studies focusing on taxonomies in general.

Broadened Scope of the Original Inquiry and Investigation

Further study is needed in order to more thoroughly examine the impact of the Taxonomy for the Technology Domain and its potential for increasing student learning. Additional investigation is also in order to confirm the correlation of the taxonomy to lessons taken from a wider spectrum of sources. While the scope of the present study was limited to the examination of core content areas, it would be valuable to investigate other curricular areas and more closely examine their level of correlation.

Exploring Additional Criteria in the Technology Domain

Lessons prepared by novice versus experienced teachers should be compared to offer insight into the impact of teaching experience in the distribution of learning objectives within taxonomy levels. Second, future research should refine the system of data gathering to collect objectives from a wider range of academic content areas in an effort to eliminate the "other" category of the present study. Third, it is imperative that there be complete agreement as to the particular version of taxonomy to be utilized and the interpretations of the terminology to be employed. (See Author's Note below.) This information should also be made available for added clarity. Such caveats in future projects will avoid weaknesses in the findings and inconsistencies detected in the present project.

Author's Note: The Taxonomy for the Technology Domain was revised since the inception of the notion in 1999. The key adjustment impacting this study was the label and definition attached to the fourth level of the taxonomy. Originally labeled as "Discrimination," Level 4.0 encouraged teachers to "select technology-based instructional materials appropriate for individual students" (Tomei, 2001). In its most current rendering, Level 4.0 has been stamped as "Infusion" and defined more generally as "learning with technology." The author admits that the study may have been affected by the terminology and re-definition of this level of the taxonomy although the impact is considered minimal.

New Related Studies Focusing on Taxonomies

A study should be undertaken to determine the extent of teachers' familiarization with taxonomies in general and, more specifically, the Taxonomy for the Technology Domain during the time when they prepared their lesson plans and the resulting impact on student learning following implementation of these technology-infused lessons. Also, a longitudinal study should be designed to assess teachers' general acceptance of the technology taxonomy. The methodology for this proposed study should correlate the taxonomy to lesson plans written before and after teachers are introduced to the taxonomy.

This research also examined the application of technology taxonomy to the K-12 teaching and learning environment only. In order to demonstrate its applicability in the higher education and corporate environments, it is critical that future research should expand its scope into these areas as well.

Conclusion

The existence of objectives at all levels of the Taxonomy for the Technology Domain for both grade levels and academic content areas was adequate to support the Taxonomy for the Technology Domain as a viable classification scheme. Educators should be encouraged by these results to prepare lesson plans that incorporate literacy, collaboration, decision-making, infusion, integration, and tech-ology objectives when planning for successful teaching and learning experiences. In addition, this study advances the need for further statistical investigation of grade levels and/or content areas within the technology domain. The introduction of a new Taxonomy for the Technology Domain has the potential to promote more superior and more complex applications of technology for teaching and learning across all grade levels and curricular areas.

References

Kirkman, T. (2003). *ANOVA: ANalysis Of VAriance Between Groups.* College of Saint Benedict / Saint John's University. Retrieved from the World Wide Web at: www.csbsju.edu/physics/faculty_staff/kirkman.html

Tomei, L.A. (2001). *Teaching Digitally: A Guide for Integrating Technology into the Classroom.* Norwood, MA: Christopher-Gordon Publishers.

Annotated Bibliography

Additional citations for the Inquiry and Investigation into the Taxonomy for the Technology Domain

Armstrong, T. (2000). *Multiple intelligence in the classroom* (2nd edition). Alexandria, VA: Association for Supervision and Curriculum Development.

Bailey, M. (2003). *Education and values: Interface on the Internet. Reconceptualizing teaching and learning in a technocracy.* Retrieved July 4, 2003 from the World Wide Web: *education.ed.pacificu.edu/aacu/workshop/reconcept2B.html*

Bereiter, C., & Scardamalia, M. (n.d.). *Beyond Bloom's Taxonomy: Rethinking knowledge for the knowledge age.* Retrieved from the World Wide Web: *csile.oise.utoronto.ca/abstracts/Piaget.html*

Bloom, B. S., Englehart, M.B., Furst, E. J., Hill, W. H., & Krathwohl, D.L. (1956). Taxonomy of educational objectives. The classifications of educational goals. Handbook 1. In L.A. Tomei (Ed.), *The use of technology in schools: Taxonomy for the technology domain.* Pittsburgh, PA: Duquesne University. Retrieved from the World Wide Web: *www.duq.edu/~tomei/heinz/ taxonomy*

Bruce, B.C., & Levin, J.A. (1997). Educational technology: Media For inquiry, communication, construction, and expression. *Journal of Educational Computing Research, 17*(1). Retrieved July 2, 2003 from the World Wide Web: *www.lis.uiuc.edu/~chip/pubs/taxonomy*

Galant, M. (2003). *Applications of Vygotsky's Theory to Education.* Retrieved from the World Wide Web: *facultyweb.cortland.edu/ andersmd/VYG/APP.HTML*

Huitt, W. (2000). *Bloom's Taxonomy of the cognitive domain.* Retrieved from the World Wide Web: *chiron.valdosta.edu/whuitt/col/cogsys/ bloom.html*

Kibler, R.J., Barker, L.L., & Miles, D.T. (1970). Behavioral objectives and instruction. Allyn & Bacon Publishers. In L.A. Tomei (Ed.), *The use of technology in schools. Taxonomy for the technology domain.* Retrieved from the World Wide Web: *www.duq.edu/~tomei/heinz/taxonomy.*

Krathwohl, D.L., Bloom, B.S., & Massia, B.B. (1964). Taxonomy of educational objectives. The classification of educational goals. Handbook II. In L.A. Tomei (Ed.), *The use of technology in schools. Taxonomy for the Technology Domain.* Retrieved from the World Wide Web: *www.duq.edu/~tomei/heinz/taxonomy*

Levin, J.A., & Bruce, B.C. (2001). *Technology as media: A learner-centered perspective.* Retrieved from the World Wide Web: *lrs.ed.uiuc.edu/j-levin/levin-bruce.html*

Mellon, C.A. (1999). Technology and the great pendulum of education. *Journal of Research on Computing in Education, 32.*

Passig, D. (2001). A taxonomy of ICT mediated future thinking skills. In H. Taylor & P. Hogenbirk (Eds.), *Information and communication technologies in education: The school of the future.* Boston: Kluwer Academic Publishers. Retrieved from the World Wide Web: *www.passig.com/pic/FutureThinkingSkills.htm*

Piaget, J. (2003). *Genetic epistemology.* Retrieved from the World Wide Web: *tip.psychology.org/piaget.html*

Rousseau, J. (ed). (2003). *Technology integration: Role of the teacher as a manager.* TCET Curriculum Integration Module. Retrieved from the World Wide Web: *www.arp.sprnet.org/admin/supt/page2.HTM*

Rowe, H. (2003). *Personal computing: A source of powerful cognitive tools.* Retrieved from the World Wide Web: *www.educationau.eduau/ archives/CP/REFS/rowe_cogtools.htm*

Southwest Educational Testing Laboratory. (1995). *Constructivism and geometry.* Retrieved from the World Wide Web: *www.sedl.org/ scimath/compass/v01n03/3.html*

Tomei, L.A. (1999). *The taxonomy for the technology domain.* Pennsylvania Association of Colleges and Teacher Educators, Annual Conference, Hershey, PA.

Tomei, L.A. (2001). *The use of technology in schools. Taxonomy for the technology domain.* Pittsburgh, PA: Duquesne University. *www.duq.edu/~tomei/heinz/taxonomy*

Tomei, L.A. (2003). *The taxonomy for the technology domain.* Hershey, PA: Idea Group Publishing. Retrieved from the World Wide Web: *www.duq.edu/~tomei/heinz/taxonomy*

Wenglinsky, H. (1998). *Does it compute? The relationship between educational technology and student achievement in mathematics.* Princeton, NJ: Educational Testing Service. Retrieved from the World Wide Web: *kant.citl.ohiou.edu/ACCLAIM/rc/rc_sub/vlibrary/4_abs_e/research_reports/ED425191.htm*

Whitton, D. (1996). *Beyond Bloom.* Retrieved from the World Wide Web: *www.nexus.edu.au/teachstud/gat/ whitton.htm*

Appendix

Contributors

Initial Inquiry. The author commends the graduate students of the Program in Instructional Technology at Duquesne University's School of Education who participated in the initial inquiry into effective teaching of technology skills and competencies in the classroom of the future. Research that validates a broad use of higher order thinking, domains, and educational psychologies more quickly matures the discipline of technology into a successful strategy of teaching and learning. The initial inquiry was conducted over several semesters (Summer 2002 – Fall 2003) as part of the course GITED 511, Technology and Education, under the supervision of the faculty of the Program in Instructional Technology, including Dr. David Carbonara and Dr. Linda Wojnar.

Comprehensive Investigation. The author commends the efforts of the first cohort of Ed.D. in Instructional Technologies doctoral students at Duquesne University's School of Education. The following individuals conducted the comprehensive investigation during the Summer 2003 term of the EdDIT program for course GEDIT 703, Foundations of Instructional Technologies, under the supervision of the course instructor and author, Dr. Lawrence Tomei.

Sean Baldis
Heather Bigley
Jason Brown
Mary Sue Cicciarelli
Jeanette Clement
Leighann Forbes
Eugene Gan
Rubina Iqbal
Mara Linaberger
Darren Mariano
Marie Martin
Sharon McGuire
Edward McKaveney
Robert Mickolay
Jennifer Nightingale

Stephanie Perry
Nicole Roth
Alex Stone
Junko Yamamoto

Glossary

A

Action Statements: To help students, teachers, and administrators develop their host of skills and competencies, each of the six chapters compiles an inventory of appropriate statements (composed of various instructional technologies and appropriate action verbs) used in creating technology-based learning objectives.

Affective Domain: The domain of teaching that describes attitudes, beliefs, tastes, appreciations, and preferences.

Asynchronous Learning: Any learning event where interaction is delayed over time or where the learner and teacher are separated by geography and time. Typical examples include use of electronic mail, bulletin board posts, list servers, and threaded discussion.

B

Behaviorism: As a psychology of learning, behaviorism focuses on the observable effects of the environment to provide the impetus for learning, i.e., learner response to stimulation equates to learning. Learning must be observable, measurable, and repeatable. Behaviorism with respect to technology offers numerous solutions for classroom management, curriculum design, and content presentation.

C

Cognitive Domain: The domain of teaching that refers to mental activities, an approach to teaching that focuses on the process of delivering information and imparting new concepts.

Cognitive Tools: Classroom technologies, learning systems, simulation, and automated performance aids that enhance and extend the teacher in the classroom. Includes smart boards, videoconferencing equipment, digital cameras, projection systems, etc.

Cognitivism: A psychology of learning in which knowledge is viewed as a symbolic mental construct in the learner's mind. Learning is the means by which these symbolic representations are committed to memory. Knowledge is measured by what learners know and not by what they do. The successful cognitive teacher uses technology to help students organize data and link new knowledge to existing information.

Collaboration: Level 2.0 of the Taxonomy for the Technology Domain defined as the ability to employ technology for effective interpersonal interaction.

Computer Assisted Instruction (CAI): Training or instruction where a computer program provides motivation and feedback in place of a live instructor. CAI can be delivered via CD-ROM, LAN or Internet. Creation is done by teams of people including instructional designers, and often has high development costs. Synonymous with Computer Based Training (CBT) and Computer Managed Instruction (CMI).

D

Decision-Making: Level 3.0 of the Taxonomy for the Technology Domain defined as the ability to use technology in new and concrete situations to analyze, assess, and judge.

Distance Learning: Learning where the instructor and the students are in physically separate locations. Can be either synchronous or asynchronous. Can include correspondence, video or satellite broadcasts, or e-learning.

Domains of Teaching: One of two "pillars of instructional technology," the domains offer the necessary grounding in cognitive, affective, and psychomotor teaching.

E

e-Learning: Any learning that utilizes a network for delivery, interaction, or facilitation. This would include distributed learning, distance learning (other than pure correspondence), computer-based training delivered over a net-work, and Web-based training delivered via the Internet. Can be synchronous, asynchronous, instructor-led, computer-based or a combination.

External Link: A uniform resource locator (see URL) that sends the learner to another site on the Internet. The URL for an external link must begin with http://.

F

Foundations of Education: Provide the critical underpinnings for the new Taxonomy for the Technology Domain and include the cognitive, affective, and psychomotor domains of teaching and the behavioral, cognitive, and humanistic psychologies of learning.

H

Harvesting: Skills related to Web browsing, navigation, and file downloads, naming conventions, and file-saving. Harvesting involves the capture of text, images, sound files, video clips, and Web pages from the Internet to a desktop computer for subsequent infusion or integration into a unit of instruction or lesson. The ability to locate, evaluate, and collect information from library resources, CD-ROM publications, online catalogs, and the Internet. Copyright and Fair Use Law restrictions apply.

Humanism: A learning psychology that emphasizes the study of the whole person. Human behavior is viewed through the eyes of the learner rather than the teacher. Learning with technology is influenced by the meanings attached to personal experiences. The more technology aids in "making meaning from information," the more successful the learning experience.

Hyperbook: An instructional resource using the advanced capabilities of word processors and desktop publishing software to integrate text-based practical exercises and activities that guides students through a teacher-authored learning experience.

I

Infusion: Level 4.0 of the Taxonomy for the Technology Domain recognizes technology as a powerful strategy for teaching with technology and is concerned with the identification, harvesting, and application of existing technology to unique learning situations.

Implementing Technologies: More complex tasks require more capable technologies to assist the teacher in demonstration. Such technologies include smart boards, simulation software, and overhead and LCD projection systems.

Instructional Systems Design (ISD): The systematic development of instructional specifications, using learning and instructional theory to ensure the quality of instruction. It is the entire process of analysis of learning needs and goals and the development of a delivery system to meet those needs. It includes development of instructional materials and activities, and tryout and evaluation of all instruction and learner activities.

Integration: Level 5.0 of the Taxonomy for the Technology Domain is concerned with the creation of new technology-based materials, combining otherwise disparate technologies to teach.

Interactive Lesson: An instructional resource using graphics-based visual presentation materials prepared by teachers who wish to control the sequence of the instruction while allowing students to be in charge of the tempo of the lesson.

Internal Link: A uniform resource locator (see URL) that sends the learner to a file present on the same computer, in the same physical directory or on the same physical media as the home Web page. An internal link may connect to another Web page, document or presentation file, or software application.

L

Learning Management Environments: An LME is a system of teaching and learning that uses technology to enhance and make more effective the network of relationships between learners, teachers and designers of instruction through integrated tools for communications and student tracking. Synonymous with Virtual Learning Environment (VLE).

Literacy: Level 1.0 of the Taxonomy for the Technology Domain defined as the minimum degree of competency expected of teachers and students with respect to technology, computers, educational programs, office productivity software, the Internet, and their synergistic effectiveness as a learning strategy.

Low-Tech Devices: Typically portable, low in cost, easy to use, and may be virtually transparent in use. For example, a rubber pencil grip enables a student with poor motor control to grasp a pencil more securely and produce more legible work. Other examples include sticky notes, highlighter pens, removable tape, correction tape, tape recorders, calculators, overhead projectors, film projectors, radio and television, and telephones.

M

Mindtools: Jonassen (1996) describes "mindtools" as a way of using a computer application program to engage learners in constructive, higher-order, critical thinking about the subjects they are studying.

N

Netiquette: Network etiquette, the dos and don'ts of online communication. Netiquette covers both common courtesy online and the informal "rules of the road" of cyberspace.

P

Psychologies of Learning: The second of two "pillars of instructional technology" presented, the traditional schools of educational psychology include behavioral, cognitive, and humanistic learning.

Psychomotor Domain: The domain of teaching concerned with the development of physical skills ranging from simple physical competencies to those that demand complicated muscle coordination.

S

Synchronous Learning: Any learning event where interaction happens simultaneously in real-time and requires learners and teachers to participate at a mutually scheduled time. Typical examples include the traditional classroom, chat room discussions, and videoconferencing.

T

Taxonomy for the Affective Domain: David Krathwohl (in collaboration with Bloom and Mascia) took the lead to produce a parallel taxonomy to explain the development of human attitudes, principles, codes, and values.

Taxonomy for the Cognitive Domain: Benjamin Bloom (et al.) identified six levels of cognitive development, from the simple recall or recognition of facts, as the lowest level, through increasingly more complex and abstract mental levels, to the highest order, which is classified as evaluation.

Taxonomy for the Psychomotor Domain: R.J. Kibler (in conjunction with Bloom and Krathwohl) defined the domain concerned with the physical dimensions of learning from gross to fine movements and nonverbal to verbal activities.

Taxonomy of Technology as Media: Bertram Bruce and James Levin developed a view of the effects of technologies as operating to a large extent through the ways that they alter the environments for thinking, communicating, and acting in the world (1997).

Taxonomy of Technology SeSDL: Scottish Electronic Staff Development Library (SESDL) classification system applied from the perspective of communications and information technology and concerned with the process of classifying electronic library resources that pertained to teaching and learning.

Teacher-as-Expert: The most far-reaching stage of a lifelong career in education, the Teacher-as-Expert is the teacher in the classroom. With regards to technology, the teacher-as-expert masters the theoretical foundations and practical applications to infuse and integrate technology into the scope and sequence of their everyday instruction.

Teacher-as-Learner: The first stage of a lifelong career in education, the pre-service teacher completes an initial certification program of study. With regards to technology, the teacher-as-learner concentrates on the acquisition of technical knowledge and practical skills to enhance their own learning with technology while providing a novice degree of competent technology-based classroom instruction.

Teacher-as-Scholar: The third stage of a lifelong career in education considers the professional teacher and the demands to continuously pursue excellence in teaching through reading and writing, professional interactions with peers and others, professional study, and active participation in professional organizations. With respect to technology, the teacher-as-scholar enhances quality teaching by continuous advancement of their technical skill and ongoing investigations of and solutions to classroom challenges.

Technology Domain: The domain of teaching that addresses technology as its own viable content area and as a teaching strategy centered on established computer literacy skills to be mastered.

Tech-ology: Level 6.0 of the Taxonomy for the Technology Domain refers to the ability to judge the universal impact, shared values, and social implications of technology use and its influence on teaching and learning. Tech-ology is a contraction of "tech" (technology) and "ology" (the study of) and is therefore the study of technology.

Telecommunications: Generic term for the component elements of the Internet include electronic mail, newsgroups, list servers, file transfer protocol, telnet protocols, online chat rooms, and the World Wide Web.

U

URL: A Uniform Resource Locator (URL) is a means of identifying an exact location and target file on the Internet. Synonymous with a Web address. For example, http://www.webusiness.com/temp/home.htm identifies a Web page home.htm in the /temp directory on the webusiness.com web server. As the previous example shows, a URL is comprised of four parts: the protocol type (http), machine name (webusiness.com) directory path (/temp/), and the file name (home.htm). Every Web page on the Internet has its own unique URL.

V

Virtual Tour: An instructional web-based teaching strategy that presents multi-sensory, multimedia instruction appropriate for student exploration, enrichment resource materials, and group learning experiences. The virtual tour employs teacher-authored Web sites with links to internal (computer-based) and external (Web-based) materials important to the learner.

About the Author

Dr. Lawrence A. Tomei is the dean of academic services and associate professor of education at Robert Morris University. Born in Akron, Ohio, he earned a BSBA from the University of Akron (1972) and entered the US Air Force, serving until his retirement as a Lieutenant Colonel in 1994. Dr. Tomei completed his MPA and MEd at the University of Oklahoma (1975, 1978) and EdD from USC (1983). His articles and books on instructional technology include: *Professional Portfolios for Teachers* (1999); *Teaching Digitally: Integrating Technology Into the Classroom* (2001); *Technology Facade* (2002); *Challenges of Teaching with Technology Across the Curriculum* (2003); and *Taxonomy for the Technology Domain* (2005).

Index

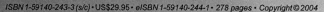